AMERICAN
HEALTH
ECONOMY
ILLUSTRATED

DISCARDED

AMERICAN
HEALTH
ECONOMY
ILLUSTRATED

Christopher J. Conover

AEI PRESS
Publisher for the American Enterprise Institute
Washington, D.C.

Distributed to the Trade by National Book Network, 15200 NBN Way, Blue Ridge Summit, PA 17214. To order call toll free 1-800-462-6420 or 1-717-794-3800. For all other inquiries please contact the AEI Press, 1150 Seventeenth Street, N.W., Washington, D.C. 20036 or call 1-800-862-5801.

Library of Congress Cataloging-in-Publication Data

Conover, Christopher J.
  American Health Economy Illustrated / Christopher J. Conover.
    p. ; cm.
  Includes bibliographical references.
  ISBN-13: 978-0-8447-7201-1 (cloth)
  ISBN-10: 0-8447-7201-1 (cloth)
  ISBN-13: 978-0-8447-7202-8 (pbk.)
  ISBN-10: 0-8447-7202-X (pbk.)
  [etc.]
  1. Medical care, Cost of—United States. 2. Health insurance—Economic aspects—United States. I. Title.
[DNLM: 1. Delivery of Health Care—economics—United States. 2. Health Services—economics—United States. 3. Insurance, Health—economics—United States. W 74 AA1]
  RA410.53.C6526 2011
  362.1068'1—dc23

Printed in China

Contents

Acknowledgments   **xv**

Foreword, *Mark V. Pauly*   **xvii**

Preface   **xxiii**

Chapter 1: Rise of a Massive Health Sector   **1**

2. Over eight decades, constant dollar health spending per person increased five times as much as real output per capita.

4. Inflation-adjusted health output per capita has increased at least eight-fold over the past 80 years.

6. The health sector absorbs an increasing share of national resources.

8. Health spending per capita is significantly more in the United States than in other large, "rich" countries—18 percent more than second-ranked Norway.

10. For 80 years, growth in real per capita health spending almost always outpaced growth in the rest of the economy by as much as 6 percentage points.

12. In the past 50 years, health spending as a share of GDP has risen in all advanced countries.

14. Most of the world's population live in countries where health spending per capita is much less than that of the United States, yet the gap has been increasing for some of the largest countries in recent years.

Chapter 2: How Is Each Health Dollar Spent?   17

18. Most health spending is for personal health services; for 40 years, such spending has exceeded 80 percent of all health expenditures.

20. From 1929 to 2009, inflation-adjusted personal health spending per capita has doubled approximately every 25 years.

22. Insurer administrative costs decline as group size increases and vary by type of coverage.

24. The combined percentage of health spending related to hospitals and nursing homes doubled from 1929 to 1989, but currently is declining.

26. More than half of health spending is for chronic diseases; chronic illness accounts for an increasing share of health spending.

28. At least half of personal health spending is for behavior, lifestyle, or other avoidable causes.

Chapter 3: Who Pays for Health Services?   31

32. Regardless of how it is measured, the public sector role in U.S. health financing has increased.

34. Private health insurance pays for a smaller share of health spending than public insurance does, even though many more Americans have private insurance.

36. For the past 70 years, virtually all growth in health spending relative to the economy has been financed by public and private health insurance.

38. Though far less visible to the average American, federal tax subsidies for health exceed federal spending on Medicaid.

40. For 80 years, the out-of-pocket share of health spending has declined while the portion paid by third parties has increased.

42. Despite a much lower publicly financed share of health spending, the U.S. out-of-pocket share of spending is among the lowest in the world.

44. The elderly and disabled constitute 25 percent of Medicaid enrollees but more than 75 percent of Medicaid spending.

46. Beneficiaries directly pay less than 15 percent of Medicare costs, but Medicare also covers less than half of all their health spending.

48. From 30 to 65 percent of all health spending by individuals who are uninsured all year is subsidized by taxpayers or private payers.

Chapter 4: The Employer Role in U.S. Health Care   51

52. A growing share of worker compensation is paid in the form of wage and salary supplements, including social insurance—such as Medicare—and private health insurance.

54. The tax subsidy for employer-provided health insurance increases with income; high-paid workers get a larger subsidy—both in dollar terms and in the fraction of premiums subsidized—than do low-paid workers.

56. For a variety of reasons, workers in small firms, health care, and retail trade are least likely to be offered health coverage at work.

58. Despite relatively stable health insurance offer rates, there has been a secular decline in employer-based health coverage across almost all firm-size categories.

Chapter 5: Government Health Expenditures, Taxes, and Deficits 61

62. Real government expenditures for health rose 30-fold during the past 50 years—or 17-fold in per capita terms. Between 1966 and 2007, the entire increase in government's share of GDP was attributable to growth in tax-financed health care.

64. Tax-financed health expenditures have risen much faster than government spending on defense, income support, and education.

66. Tax-financed health expenditures explain little of the difference between the United States and its major competitors in public sector spending as a percentage of GDP.

68. The public sector pays 80 percent of health costs for people who have poor health.

70. Taxpayers finance almost half of health spending for the highest-income families.

72. Almost all Medicare beneficiaries pay less in payroll taxes than the dollar amount of benefits they receive from the program.

74. The Medicaid share of state health spending varies by a factor of three across states.

Chapter 6: Health Services and the Family Budget 77

78. Health care is currently the second largest component of personal consumption. Since 1929, the share going to health care has risen faster than any other major category of personal consumption.

80. Because so much health spending is hidden, direct family spending on health care and health insurance premiums has accounted for only 5 percent of income for 20 years.

82. In the past 25 years, the relative burden of paying for health care has grown slightly faster among families that have the highest incomes.

84. The elderly and children rely more heavily than others do on tax-financed health coverage.

86. The risk of being uninsured is at least three times as high among young adults as among children younger than 10 or the elderly.

88. The average American's chance of being uninsured has declined substantially over the past 70 years.

90. Although per capita health costs for people uninsured all year are less than half the amount spent for those who have private coverage, more than 65 percent of their costs are subsidized.

92. In elderly households, the share of household spending for health care is more for those headed by the non-elderly and has increased faster over time.

94. Despite higher health costs, real non-health spending per person in elderly households is higher than in households headed by younger people.

Chapter 7: Who Produces Health Services? 97

98. Compared with the rest of the economy, a much larger share of health output is provided by non-profit organizations or publicly owned enterprises.

100. In most subsectors of health care, government-owned firms account for only approximately 10 percent of activity.

102. The increasing share of final demands related to health care has been a major factor in the growth of the service share of national output after World War II.

104. Over the past 80 years, the increase in health services output was almost 50 percent higher than was the increase in economy-wide output.

Chapter 8: Health Services and the Distribution of National Income 107

108. Health-related supplements accounted for almost 12 cents of every dollar of national income in 2008 compared with less than three cents four decades earlier.

110. More than 80 percent of 2009 national income for health services was for compensation of employees compared with only 50 percent in 1963. Reflecting the decline of physicians in solo practice or partnerships, the share of health-related national income accounted for by proprietors' and rental income has fallen steeply in the past 50 years.

112. The share of health-related national income accounted for by proprietors' and rental income has declined steeply in the past 50 years.

114. Corporate profits before and after taxes have now reached their highest share of health services income in the past 50 years.

116. Corporate profits before taxes in the health sector are less than that of other major sectors and private businesses overall.

118. Publicly traded health services companies generally have lower profits than do other firms listed on the stock market.

120. Pharmaceutical and medical devices have higher profits than do most industries, reflecting returns for discovery and innovation.

Chapter 9: Productivity in the Health Sector   **123**

124. Only recently has the increase in real health services output exceeded the increase in the input of labor or the combined increase in the inputs of labor and capital. Output per unit of input is called productivity.

126. Productivity growth is less in the health sector than in private business in general.

128. Productivity tends to be lower in the health sector despite more education among health workers compared with those in the rest of the economy.

130. Information capital per hour has risen far less slowly in ambulatory health services than in private business overall.

132. Expenditures for R&D have expanded our scientific and technological knowledge; this has contributed to the increase in health sector productivity.

134. Since 1982, increased personal health spending alone can explain approximately 80 percent of the decline in personal savings. Although U.S. health spending matches its gross annual savings, most of the nation's major competitors save much more than they spend on health care.

136. In many parts of the health sector, output generally has increased more slowly than the combined inputs of labor, capital, and other factors of production.

Chapter 10: The Labor Force and Employment in the Health Sector   **139**

140. Since 1930, if health services employment had increased only as fast as in the rest of the economy, the health sector would have employed nearly 11 million fewer workers in 2009. Employment has increased faster in ambulatory health services than in hospitals or nursing homes.

142. The health sector as a share of total employment is higher in the United States than in other industrialized countries. The industry's growth relative to all employment appears comparable with other G7 nations in recent years.

144. Whether the opportunity cost of health sector employment in the United States is more or less than in the rest of the G7 depends on how it is measured.

146. Females account for more than 75 percent of health sector employees but constitute fewer than half of employees in the goods-producing part of the health sector.

148. Compared with employees in general, the work-year per full-time equivalent worker is several hundred hours shorter for health services employees. Recently, annual work hours per employee generally have declined in long-term care facilities while increasing in hospitals.

150. Increased longevity and a shorter working life have lengthened the period of retirement for men but not for women.

Chapter 11: Personal Incomes and Health Care   153

154. For the average American worker, growth in real hourly earnings has in recent decades lagged behind growth in real compensation per hour, due in part to rising health costs.

156. Employee compensation in the health services industry is much more than the average for other service industries but only slightly more than the average for all workers.

158. Real compensation per hour has increased more slowly in the ambulatory health sector than in the rest of the economy.

160. Health professionals in the United States have much higher relative incomes than do their counterparts in other industrialized countries.

162. Physicians in the United States enjoyed rising rates of return for medical education for decades. Although such returns might have fallen recently, they appear to be similar for those who pursue careers in law or business.

Chapter 12: Distribution of Health Services   165

166. 1 percent of the population accounts for approximately 25 percent of health spending; 5 percent accounts for almost half.

168. After accounting for all hidden costs and subsidies, the net burden of paying for health care is 2.5 times as much for the very lowest-income families compared with the very highest-income families.

170. The net burden of paying for health care has increased. The relative burden for low- versus high-income families appears relatively stable in recent decades.

172. Per capita health spending generally increases with age; annual health costs for the elderly are at least four times as high as for children and young adults.

174. During their reproductive years, women's health costs are much higher than are men's and only slightly higher in early retirement.

176. Regional differences in both health spending per capita and income per capita have widened somewhat since 1980. Before that time, per capita income differences had been narrowing for at least 50 years.

178. Regional differences in the financial burden of health spending narrowed between 1980 and 1987 but have increased in subsequent years.

Chapter 13: Poverty and Health   181

182. Millions of people no longer would be categorized as poor if medical expenditures were handled differently when measuring poverty.

184. Approximately half of those below poverty are covered by government insurance (primarily Medicaid). Approximately 30 percent are uninsured. The chances of being uninsured decline steadily with increasing income.

186. Health status generally is worse among those who have lower incomes; poverty status explains only some of the health status differences related to race.

188. Poor children are much less likely to have private coverage than any other age group. Almost seven in 10 poor children have Medicaid/SCHIP coverage.

190. Fewer than one-third of non-elderly adults who are poor are covered through Medicaid. More than 40 percent are uninsured. Although more than 90 percent of the elderly poor have government coverage, approximately three in 10 have some sort of private insurance.

Chapter 14: The Structure of the Health Sector   **193**

194. More than half of U.S. health sector workers are employed by firms that have fewer than 500 workers. The share of employment accounted for by large firms varies significantly across health industry subsectors.

196. Seemingly high levels of concentration in the health insurance industry might not accurately depict its competitiveness. Concentration is increasing for both hospitals and health insurers.

198. The health sector is more highly regulated than almost any other segment of the U.S. economy. However, the extent of regulation varies widely across states.

200. Unionization rates in the health industry are comparable to the economy-wide rate. The unionization rate within some health occupations is much higher.

Chapter 15: Health, Wealth, and Debt   **203**

204. Since the early 1950s, real health spending per capita has grown approximately twice as fast as real per capita net worth.

206. A relatively small fraction of American households incurs annual health expenditures that exceed their net worth.

208. "Medical" bankruptcies account for 25 percent to possibly 35 percent of all bankruptcies in the United States.

Chapter 16: Economic Fluctuations and Health   **211**

212. Aggregate health spending growth appears to be largely independent of fluctuations in the business cycle.

214. Medicaid expenditures tend to be more countercyclical than are other components of NHE, generally rising faster during recessions than during recoveries.

216. Unemployment rates for workers in the health sector are lower for males but not for females, compared with workers in the rest of the economy.

Chapter 17: Health Services and Quality of Life   219

220. The value of a typical American's stock of health at birth is several multiples of his or her lifetime earnings.

222. In price measurement, the treatment of innovations or new products is perhaps the most difficult aspect of handling quality change.

224. Technology has been an important driver of health spending. However, measuring its precise role has been difficult.

226. If premature mortality and morbidity are measured in terms of lost production, the social burden of illness has increased since 1963; however, if the intangible value of human life is taken into account, the social burden of illness has declined despite the large increase in health expenditures during this period.

Chapter 18: U.S. Health Care in a Global Economy   229

230. The United States leads the world in medical innovation.

232. Among the top 10 global funders of pharmaceutical R&D, the United States accounts for more than 50 percent to 65 percent of total spending.

234. Despite its global dominance in pharmaceutical R&D, the United States accounts for a small share of pharmaceutical exports among industrialized nations. Conventional measures of U.S. trade provide an incomplete picture of the contribution of the health sector to imports, exports, or the country's overall balance of trade.

Chapter 19: Do Americans Get Good Value for Money in Health Care?   237

238. Health spending in recent decades appears to have been "worth it" on average, but this likely masks much wasted spending.

240. Geographic differences in broad health outcomes generally are associated with higher health spending both across countries and within the United States. Because higher spending also is associated with higher incomes, it is difficult to untangle the separate contribution of higher income to better health.

242. In Medicare, there are sizable geographic variations in spending and spending growth. Only a relatively small part of geographic variations in Medicare spending can be explained by differences in health status, income, or race. Most of the difference relates to "practice style."

244. Health spending per capita in the United States is not necessarily more than expected relative to the pattern seen in other industrialized countries.

246. Increased spending in the United States cannot be explained by higher use of health services, although Americans do have greater access to some expensive technologies than do those in other industrialized countries.

248. Compared with some major competitors, the United States relies more on specialists than on primary care doctors.

250. Americans pay higher prices for brand-name pharmaceuticals but lower prices for generic and over-the-counter drugs than do residents in other major industrialized countries.

252. The American system of medical malpractice likely accounts for some, but assuredly not all, of the difference in health expenditures between the United States and its competitors.

254. Excluding deaths due to violence, the United States generally leads the world in life expectancy at birth.

256. Few countries match the performance of the United States in saving the lives of pre-term infants. The higher rate of pre-term births in the United States is an important contributor to its low international ranking for infant mortality overall.

258. On average, Americans who have various types of cancer have markedly better chances of surviving five years compared with cancer patients in other industrialized nations. For several reasons, survival rates for blacks trail these averages.

260. Despite its superiority in many health outcomes related to medical care, the United States has relatively more avoidable deaths amenable to health care than do many other industrialized countries.

262. Most "avoidable" deaths are related to lifestyle or behavior.

264. The nation's obesity rate is the highest in the world, but smoking is somewhat less common among adults in the United States compared with most other industrialized countries. There are big differences in obesity and smoking rates across states.

266. Comparing health system performance across U.S. states poses many of the same challenges as do comparisons across countries.

Chapter 20: Are Health Spending Trends Sustainable?   269

270. Over the next 75 years, health benefits as a share of worker compensation could more than quadruple. Despite this, real cash wages per worker will be 7.5 times as much as the amount in 2008.

272. Technology has been a far more important driver of health spending growth during the past 60 years than has population growth or aging.

274. The excess cost ratio measures how much faster per capita health spending—adjusted for changes in age and gender—increased relative to growth in per capita GDP. Historical variations in the excess cost ratio make predicting future health spending difficult, especially over a long time.

276. Over the next 50 years, the country can "afford" growth in health spending that exceeds growth in the general economy only if the difference is not too much. Continuing historical rates of excess growth in health spending could result in a decline in real GDP per capita within 30 years.

278. Much uncertainty exists in 75-year forecasts of health spending; yet if even 1 percent excess cost growth persists, almost 90 percent of annual GDP growth will be devoted to health care by 2085.

280. In today's dollars, the long-term unfunded liabilities associated with health entitlements exceed $66 trillion—approximately four times as much as the unfunded liabilities related to Social Security.

282. The projected 75-year increase in mandatory federal health spending exceeds current revenues from the three largest sources of federal tax revenue.

284. U.S. competitors have already had to confront the challenge of an increasing number of dependents—both children and elderly—per working adult. For the United States, much of this challenge still lies in the future.

286. Projected increases in government-related health spending could, within 50 years, eradicate the margin of advantage that the United States currently has over its major European competitors in terms of the burden of government.

Glossary   **289**

References   **295**

Sources   **305**

Index   **311**

About the Author   **325**

Acknowledgments

I am indebted to Herbert Stein and Murray Foss, whose book, *The Illustrated Guide to the American Economy*, served as an inspiration and template for this book. Likewise, I am deeply grateful for the myriad ways in which David Gerson assisted in bringing this book into fruition. His patient persistence helped see this project through completion.

I could not have undertaken the research and writing for this compilation without generous support for my time and travel from the American Enterprise Institute's National Research Initiative. My thanks go to Henry Olsen for taking a gamble on this somewhat unconventional style of scholarship.

I benefited from excellent research assistance from two Duke University undergraduates, Erica Jain and Jesse Tang. Lisa Copeland, in the Center for Health Policy, skillfully assembled the various U.S. maps used throughout the book. Kristy Marynak, a public policy graduate student, provided extraordinary research support, keeping track of many moving parts even as she completed her MPP, graduated and moved to Atlanta, all without dropping a ball in the process. I also am grateful to the Sanford School of Public Policy for their loan of office space at a critical juncture during the writing process.

I very much appreciate the valuable input of AEI scholars in health care policy who reviewed chapters of the book as I completed them, through a series of meetings that lasted many months. These include Joe Antos, Jack Calfee (who died earlier this year), Bob Helms, and Tom Miller. Thanks also go to Jim Blumstein, who sat in on one of these sessions. Tom Miller and Rohit Parulkar were especially helpful in arranging logistics for these various gatherings. Although I never got to see him face-to-face even once during the long process of assembling this book, AEI adjunct scholar Ted Frech provided extraordinarily helpful fine-grained comments on each chapter. I also benefited from some useful discussions with Mark Pauly regarding cross-national comparisons and feel deeply honored by his willingness to contribute the book's foreword. I also welcomed many productive discussions with AEI visiting scholar Mark Perry, whose keen eye for graphics helped sharpen the quality of many of the book's figures.

I also thank David Cutler, Craig Eyermann, John Graham, Laurence Kotlikoff, Thomas Selden, and Douglas Sherlock for their generosity in sharing data for use in the book, as well as various organizations, including the Dartmouth Atlas of Health Care, the *New England Journal of Medicine,* the Organisation for Economic Co-operation and Development, and the World Health Organization for their copyright permissions.

The final draft was improved immensely by editing suggestions from Judy Fox Eddy that were as thorough as any author could wish. Her conscientiousness and efficiency were a marvel to behold and it was most gratifying to see the much tighter and more eloquent draft that emerged from her capable hands. Likewise, Laura Harbold at AEI Press was most patient with both of us as we labored to make this the best it could be over a six-month stretch.

None of the people listed should be held responsible for any residual errors the book might contain.

Christopher J. Conover
July 1, 2011

Foreword

Mark V. Pauly

Compared to other industries, medical care is awash in data. Both common industry practice and regulation require the collection and storage of large volumes of quantitative information. We have much more information on transactions, inputs, prices, and even outcomes for health care than we do for industries such as beer brewing, ladies' ready-to-wear, or cosmetology. Every encounter is tabulated and recorded by the provider, by the insurer, and sometimes by the consumer. And yet, this plentitude of data is often insufficient to satisfy managers, policy analysts, or external critics.

Perhaps part of the frustration has to do with high expectations. We complain that often we do not have enough data to determine whether health care produces health, but we do not seek data on whether beauty shops produce beauty, or whether beer really does make us happier. But health care is often (though not always) more consequential for human well being than any other consumer resource. This importance leads to a demand to assemble health care data in ways that suggest alternative policies that would produce better outcomes, supply them more efficiently, and distribute them more fairly. The abundance of data makes it hard for the numbers to speak for themselves, and easy for people to comb selectively for statistics that support a predetermined point of view.

This book by Chris Conover is an attempt to cut through the clutter and confusion and assemble and explain the data that bear on the most important health policy issues in the United States. It differs from other sources for health data in two ways.

First, it is organized around key health policy questions, rather than being purely descriptive, as are many government data compendia. Second, it is intended to confront complex and controversial issues by trying as much as possible to show "both sides" where there is competing evidence. The book also confronts imprecision and ambiguity head on—whether in data definition, measurement, or our ability to determine causation. Paradoxically, the data shown here are often more eloquent about what we *don't* know than what we do know.

Why don't the numbers speak for themselves? Let's consider one of the most commonly cited numbers in health economics: medical spending relative to gross domestic product (GDP). This ratio of two numbers is usually used in international comparisons to judge the relative efficiency of medical care systems. The data show that the United States spends more on health care but gets worse outcomes than other developed countries. This is unequivocally true, but what does it mean? To be useful, numbers must point to some judgments about possibilities for improvements.

An economist would think of such data as providing information about a "production function": the process that links inputs into medical care (measured by spending) with the outcomes (health) generated. On this score, the evidence seems to support the view that the United States does not have a very efficient production function, in the sense that it gets less health out of its spending than other developed countries do. Maybe the production processes, the management, or the motivational skills of health workers are better in these other countries—maybe not. Even if we think our health outcomes are as good as those in other countries (after we adjust for differences in measurement and prior risk), it still looks like we spend too much.

But Conover's data show why this interpretation is misleading. Differences in spending must be considered alongside variations in the prices of health services. After all, if you buy the same resources but pay twice as high a price, your spending will be twice as high—but the level of resources will be the same. The data shown here tell us that prices do vary; as everyone surely knows, the bad news is that prices for health care are higher in the United States than in other countries. But the good news is that, after we adjust spending levels for international price differences, much of the apparent inefficiencies in the U.S. system go away. We do not produce medical care more inefficiently than other countries—rather, we compensate health workers more generously than other countries. That may not make you happy, but it should definitely give you a new direction for your worries or your outrage. Not all of this relative overpayment goes to doctors and drug company stockholders; most goes to other health workers, and it should be up to the reader to decide what to think about that.

Here are some additional examples of where I found Conover's data both fresh and illuminating. Let's go back to those high physician incomes, higher than in other developed countries. For an economist, the right measurement for income is not the average annual net gain, but rather the return on investment. Given medical tuition costs (which are higher in the United States than anywhere else in the world) and, even more important, given the lost income if a medical student pursues additional schooling or further residency training (compared to income lost to get graduate degrees in business, law, or engineering), do doctors make enough money to cover the costs of their education? The somewhat surprising answer is that, at least in recent years and taking the average over all medical specialties, the return on medical education is not out of line with the return on education in many other professions.

This may be of interest to general readers; it may also startle economists who are trained to think of medicine as a guild charging cartel prices. Apparently, with the advent of advertising, aggressive managed care, and pressure from large and poorly funded government programs, the cartel-style market power of medicine appears to have eroded. Of course, annual income across medical specialties varies widely, while time spent in training is relatively constant. Therefore, the surprisingly moderate average return on education for medical professionals masks the fact that there are much higher returns for some specialties (orthopedics, for example) than for others (like family practice).

But consider, also, the return on investment for physicians in the United States relative to the return on investment for other well educated Americans—the latter is also higher than anywhere else in the world. So, our doctors' incomes can be simultaneously higher than they are for equally well trained doctors in other countries and still not out of line relative to other high-skilled American workers. This still leaves us with the puzzle of why so many promising undergraduates try to get into medical school, but not every phenomenon can be explained by data.

Here is another surprise. Poll after poll shows that Americans enrolled in traditional government-run Medicare like the Medicare program. One might think, then, that beneficiaries are responding with gratitude to good coverage. In fact, the Medicare population, even after many of its members add private Medigap coverage, still pays a larger share of its medical spending out-of-pocket than any other age group. Of course, part of the reason for this is that the Medicare population uses more medical care in total than any other group—so that public and private insurances also pay more benefits per capita than to any other group. But still, as insurance coverage, Medicare benefits leave a lot to be desired. One suspects that the reason for Medicare's popularity is not the quality of the product but its price for the buyer. Conover's data show that Medicare beneficiaries pay directly only about one-eighth of the total cost of their benefits. We can be happy with almost anything if it is enough of a bargain.

Even given Medicare's imperfections, and the relatively high proportion of uninsured Americans (not discussed at length in this book), we still direct our public subsidies for insurance in generally the right direction. Conover shows that 80 percent of Americans identified as being in poor health already (before health reform) have public insurance, through Medicare for the elderly or Medicaid for the poor and sick. There is still a gap to be closed here, but it is not nearly as enormous as many think.

Having given public policy a compliment, however, I also need to point out a serious criticism made apparent in Conover's data: The second-largest source of public subsidies to health insurance in the form of tax breaks for employment-based coverage is not directed to the poor and needy. Instead, because it gives people a pass on the taxes they would otherwise have paid on compensation from work, it gives much more to higher-income workers who would otherwise have paid higher taxes.

Conover's data also provide surprising reassurance about private insurance. The proportion of medical spending Americans risk having to pay out-of-pocket is falling continuously, and has reached a level which is, on average, below that of many other countries, so much so that the amount paid out-of-pocket for health care in the United States is among the lowest in the world. This is a far cry from the typical view of critics at home and abroad that the American health care system is a Darwinian horror of high bills that people cannot pay. Notably, this low rate of risk has been achieved by a system with nearly the world's highest share of private insurance. Of course, here again the average masks substantial variation; the elderly and, to a lesser extent, the uninsured do pay a lot out-of-pocket—but the generosity of coverage for the average insured American (especially the average upper-middle-class American) is actually quite lavish. People do complain about rising deductibles, but do not complain as their insurance covers more prescription drugs, preventive care, and home health care than ever before.

But what about the health economics bottom line? Does all of this spending make us healthier? Here Conover gives a perhaps less surprising but still appropriately nuanced answer. If we had stopped increasing our health spending earlier—say, when President Nixon declared that medical costs were disastrously out of control—we would not be nearly so healthy, especially in terms of cardiovascular disease and stroke. This is because much, if not most, of spending growth goes to the development of new medical technology, which is highly beneficial, if costly. So, some of the spending has undoubtedly made us healthier but, as Conover points out, probably not all of it, and perhaps some was not effective enough to justify its cost.

Unfortunately, Conover does not have good data—nor does anyone else—on what kinds of spending are least effective at boosting health. There are many strong opinions on what kinds of medical spending are wasteful, but there are few examples of instances where spending was cut and did no harm. This is because the uncertainty of health and illness makes it hard to predict what will or will not work. Consequently, proposals for aggressive cost containment always raise concerns; our evidence base is not precise enough to tell what works, and personal variations in what we want and need from health care make us suitably apprehensive about anyone—whether in government or in private insurance—making those decisions for us.

How to manage health spending is still a major frontier for public and private policy, where judgments about the value of health, the value of dignified care, and the appropriate degree of risk-taking make it impossible to please everyone. This book may lack information on variations in what people value, what they want, and what they are willing to pay for health care—but that is because this information does not exist.

This sampling of findings from *American Health Economy Illustrated* may not help us reach a conclusion about the best health policy, but it surely proves the provocative and practical value of the information compiled here. At a minimum, this book tells us what we believe that isn't so, helps to pinpoint gaps in public information, and prevents sweeping conclusions in support of talking points that would be persuasive if only we could believe they were true. Finally, and most important, it stimulates demand for that missing link in the data chain that will allow us to assemble the facts to reach a conclusion.

I am not sure that one can characterize a compilation of data as a "page-turner," but I found myself doing just that here, and to considerable fun and intellectual profit.

Mark V. Pauly
Bendheim Professor and Professor of Health Care Management
The Wharton School at the University of Pennsylvania

Preface

I wrote *American Health Economy Illustrated* in the belief that despite more than a year-long debate about health care reform in 2009–2010, much of the debate suffered from a plethora of myths about the U.S. health system. An attempt to present some basic facts might help as the debate rages, almost certainly through the election of 2012. The debate has generated great interest in statistics related to the health economy—not only its size, scope, and evolution but also solid comparative statistics about its performance relative to the health systems of other major industrialized countries. Many resources address these issues. The challenge in crafting this volume lay in deciding what to leave out rather than in finding data to make a particular point or paint a general picture.

A long list of questions whose answers are relevant to any serious discussion about how to reform the current health system, but whose answers too often appeared unknown, ignored, or misunderstood, motivated the content. Examples include:

- How large is the American health economy, compared with other important aggregates, other times, and other countries?
- How much do Americans really spend on health administration, chronic conditions, or conditions related to behavior, lifestyle, or other "avoidable" causes?

- Who actually pays for health services underneath the Byzantine system of cross-subsidies that has shielded most Americans from even realizing how much health care really costs?
- Do Americans get good value for money in health care in either absolute terms or in comparison with other countries?
- Are current health spending trends sustainable through the twenty-first century?

I wrote this book with the belief that a certain number of basic facts about the health economy, important to the continuing debate, could be identified and presented in a readily understandable way. "Basic" facts are those that refer to the condition of the health system as a whole, that affect or interest large numbers of people, and throw some light on subjects of greatest concern.

A "fact" in this book refers to something that can be measured, expressed in numbers, and presented in charts. Much about the American health economy cannot be described with facts. The facts herein are the consequence of behavior by millions of individuals. This book will not explain the behavior of such individuals or the interactions among them. Likewise, other important aspects of the health economy—freedom of choice, quality of care, and distributive justice—are addressed only marginally, if at all.

The facts I include are important because they say much about the current state of our health system.

Measurement of the health economy, changes over time, and comparisons across states and nations are inherently difficult. We are interested in conditions and changes that affect real people, but in a free society we cannot acquire all the information we want about all the people in it, nor do we have a satisfactory way of combining it even if we could get a full census of information.

Because different consumers spend different amounts on different health services, analysts must rely on averages that might not fit any one person very well. Medical services change in quality over time and it is challenging to distinguish how much of the increase in health spending over time is due to changes in "pure" prices as opposed to changes in quality.

The selection and presentation of data are as objective as I can make them. I have tried not to make a book of Republican or Democratic, conservative or liberal, optimistic or pessimistic data. I believe most would agree that any reasonable description of the U.S. health economy would have to include much of the information presented here. The goal was not to find things that would surprise the reader, although I was surprised by some of what I learned in the 18 months spent assembling this book. In the acknowledgments, I codify the numerous individuals to whom I am indebted. None of the many people who helped me is responsible for any residual errors the book might contain.

CHAPTER 1

Rise of a Massive Health Sector

Over eight decades, constant dollar health spending per person increased five times as much as real output per capita.

Spending on health care in the United States has increased more than 60-fold since 1929. This remarkable growth is measured in constant dollars that equalize general purchasing power across decades. In contrast, the U.S. economy grew only 12-fold over the same period (figure 1.1a).

National health expenditures (NHE) and NHE per capita are the best available single measures of the size of the health sector. NHE reflects the total amount of spending on health care, including goods and services having to do with personal health care, public health activities, public and private health insurance, related investments in research, and capital investment. Both gross domestic product (GDP) and NHE measure output only within the borders of the United States.

The U.S. population is approximately 2.5 times as large as it was in 1929. Even when considering spending growth in per capita terms, inflation-adjusted health spending was 25 times as large at the end of these 80 years as at the start. GDP per capita quintupled (figure 1.1b). Does this mean that today's average Americans receive 25 times as much medical care as their counterparts did in 1929? It does not. Figures 1.1a and 1.1b show how the total dollars spent on health care changed over time, but the estimates shown are adjusted only for changes in *general* purchasing power rather than purchasing power within the health sector. Devoting 25 times as much real economic output to purchasing medical care is *not* equivalent to saying that U.S. residents receive 25 times as much medical services (for example, physician visits, hospital days) as they did in 1929.

The GDP implicit price deflator is the most comprehensive measure of pure price inflation for the economy as a whole. The Consumer Price Index (CPI) is better known but covers only approximately 60 percent of the economy, omitting rural areas, government purchases, and investment goods. Because half of health spending currently is publicly funded, it is more accurate to use a price index, such as the GDP deflator, that broadly reflects the entire economy. Adjusting NHE by the GDP deflator reflects the opportunity cost of health care, which measures how the total value of other goods and services that society could have purchased instead of health care has changed over time, while excluding a cause of growth—economy-wide inflation—largely beyond the control of the health sector.

1.1a In constant dollars, national health spending increased more than 60-fold over the past eight decades; real GDP grew far less in this period

Index of real spending using GDP price deflator: 1929=100

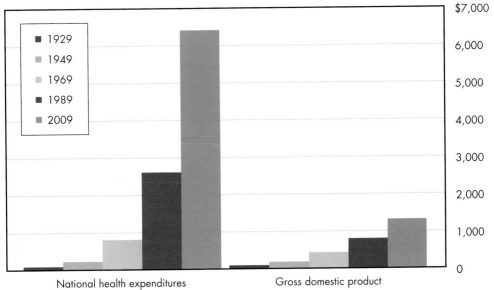

1.1b Even in per capita terms, real health spending increased approximately 25-fold in just 80 years while GDP per capita quintupled

Index of real spending using GDP price deflator: 1929=100

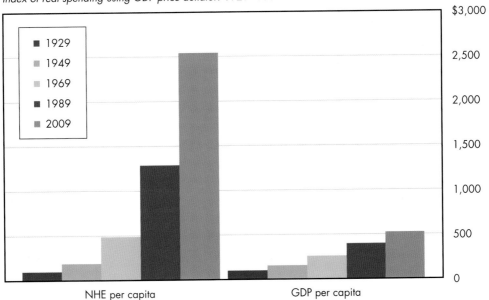

Inflation-adjusted health output per capita has increased at least eight-fold over the past 80 years.

Adjusting medical care prices in several ways, inflation-adjusted health care output rose at least 20-fold over the past 80 years. Estimates of NHE output cannot be precise; thus, estimates of changes over decades are unavoidable approximations. NHE includes many different goods and services. No adequate way exists to convert them to a common unit of output to measure a combined total. Therefore, adding all health care goods and services in proportion to their relative prices is customary.

For decades, medical price inflation usually has outpaced general inflation. To gauge how much the quantity of NHE has grown exclusive of *medical* price changes, NHE must be deflated by a measure of price inflation specific to medical care. Because relative prices change over time (for example, the hourly rate of physician pay versus that of licensed practical nurses [LPNs]), the measured size of the health sector depends on the year of the prices used.

Both the health care deflator for personal consumption expenditures (PCE) and the CPI for medical care have limitations. The PCE health care deflator counts all household medical care use regardless of how it is financed. Therefore, it is a more complete measure of price changes across the entire medical market. The medical CPI is intended to reflect household out-of-pocket prices. Consequently, it places a smaller weight on expensive services disproportionately paid by insurance, such as hospital care. Either index shows that real health output is at least 20 times as large as it was in 1929 (figure 1.2a).

NHE generally includes only output that is bought or sold in markets (including hospital and doctor care, even if these are provided "free" to the patient). It understates total output by excluding informal care provided by family or friends despite its importance for long-term care patients. Good data do not exist for every item included in the NHE.

Real health output per person rose at least eight-fold in this period (figure 1.2b)— an amount much more comparable to the quintupling of real economic output per resident shown in figure 1.1b. There is little question that this increase in health output per capita has contributed to better health and longevity. However, which of these health gains has been worth its cost is a matter of considerable debate.

1.2a No matter what price index is used to standardize health purchasing power, real health output increased approximately 20-fold since 1929

Quantity index of real health output: 1929=100

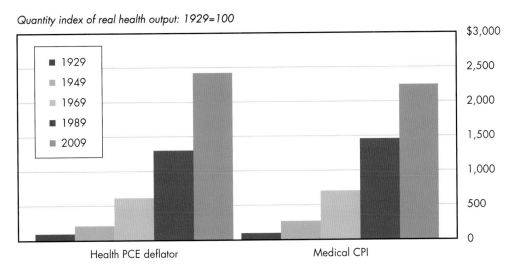

Note: Price index used to estimate real (inflation-adjusted) output of health care goods and services.

1.2b Real health output per capita increased approximately eight-fold over 80 years, an increase well ahead of growth in total national output

Index: 1929=100

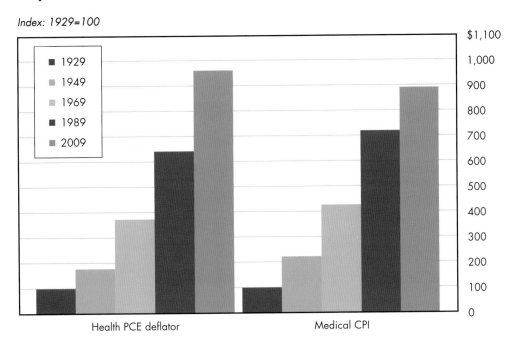

Note: Price index used to estimate real (inflation-adjusted) output of health goods and services.

The health sector absorbs an increasing share of national resources.

The percentage of GDP devoted to health care has more than quadrupled during the past 80 years to more than one-sixth of the entire economy. Indeed, health spending has grown faster than almost all other major components of the economy. Thus, an alternative way of assessing long-term trends in the size of the health sector is by examining how the health care share of national output and some of its largest basic parts have grown over time.

PCE accounts for approximately 70 percent of GDP. Thus, changes in the fraction of PCE devoted to health care (including spending for health insurance) mirror the general pattern observed for GDP. However, the health share of PCE is consistently larger than the fraction of GDP attributable to health care: It now exceeds 20 percent (figure 1.3a).

Moreover, a growing share of health care is financed by government at all levels. Consequently, the percentage of public sector spending having to do with health care has risen even faster than in the general economy or in total consumption (figure 1.3b). However, viewing aggregate health spending across all levels of government masks a sizable difference in trends at the federal government level compared with state and local governments—especially since the introduction of Medicare and Medicaid in 1966. Health spending now makes up 25 percent of all federal spending compared with only one-sixth of total spending by state and local governments. As of 1969, the health share of non-federal government spending still slightly exceeded the share of government spending at the federal level. These initial comparisons provide a broad view of the size and direction of expenditure trends (chapter 3 provides detailed public spending).

Before 1969, there was not a big difference between health care's share of public spending or public revenue. However, because deficit financing has become an enduring feature of the federal budget in recent decades, measuring health spending against government revenues shows an even more dramatic rate of growth in the past 40 years. Health care now absorbs almost one in three tax dollars—a share that is more than eight times as large as it was in 1929. Considering only federal revenues, this share would be even more.

1.3a Health spending absorbs an ever-growing fraction of the economy and personal consumption

Percentage of total expenditures

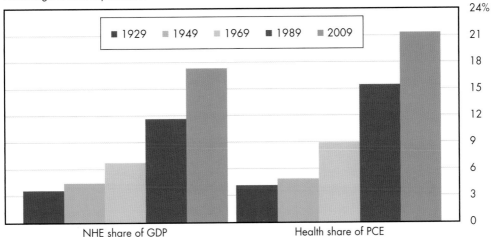

NHE share of GDP   Health share of PCE

1.3b The share of government spending or revenues accounted for by health has increased even faster than the health share of GDP

Percentage of total spending or revenue

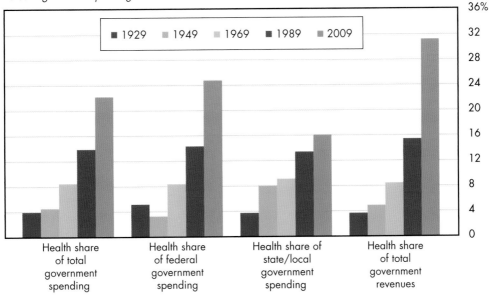

Health share   Health share   Health share of   Health share
of total   of federal   state/local   of total
government   government   government   government
spending   spending   spending   revenues

Note: In this NHE Accounts framework, federal government health spending includes all of Medicare (including components financed privately, such as Parts B and D premiums), the federal share of Medicaid spending, and other public health-related programs such as Department of Defense (DOD) and Veterans Administration (VA) health. State/local government health spending includes the non-federal share of Medicaid, workers' compensation, hospital subsidies, and the non-federal share of categorical or block grant programs such as maternal and child health.

Health spending per capita is significantly more in the United States than in other large, "rich" countries— 18 percent more than second-ranked Norway.

A precise comparison across countries of total output (or consumption) having to do with health care is as difficult as a precise comparison of health care output across widely separated years in the same country. Even when accurately valuing the output of each country in its own currency, no precise, accurate way exists to convert these values into a common currency. In 2007, NHE per capita in Canada was $4,713 Canadian, whereas U.S. NHE per capita was $7,290. How many Canadian dollars equal a U.S. dollar in terms of the amount of health services they represent? Both the mixture of health services and relative health prices differ in the two countries; this fact negates any possibility of a certain answer.

The best, though imperfect, way to arrive at an answer involves three steps. The mathematics are too complicated to explain here. Conceptually, purchasing power parity (PPP) essentially represents how many Canadian dollars would match the U.S. dollar in terms of purchasing the identical "market basket" of goods.

This computing method provides a PPP exchange rate for the entire economy (termed GDP PPP here) or for a single sector such as health care. Using GDP PPPs to adjust health spending provides a measure of how the opportunity cost of health spending varies across countries. As shown in figure 1.4a, to purchase its health care, the United States foregoes 50 percent more output in absolute terms than second-place Norway. However, because U.S. health prices are 25 percent higher than in the Organisation for Economic Co-operation and Development (OECD)—although its economy-wide prices are 5 percent lower—the GDP PPP exchange rate overstates the amount of health output a U.S. dollar could buy. The health PPP exchange rate provides a more accurate comparison of actual health resource use across countries: U.S. output of health resources is only 18 percent higher than in Norway, rather than the 50 percent previously stated.

Health PPP in U.S. dollars is lower than GDP PPP for all OECD members (figure 1.4b); thus, the widely reported cross-national health spending dollars (calculated using GDP PPP) greatly exaggerate the true differences in health resource use between the United States and other nations.

1.4a The difference in per capita health spending between the United States and its OECD competitors is much less when adjusted for U.S. health prices

Per capita health spending as a percentage of U.S. per capita NHE (2007)

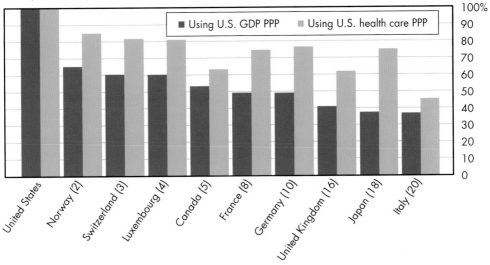

Note: Numbers in parentheses show OECD country ranking on health spending per capita using GDP PPP index. The GDP purchasing power index (PPP) standardizes health spending in terms of its general purchasing power in the U.S. economy. The health care PPP standardizes spending in terms of its power to purchase a standardized bundle of health care goods and services in the U.S.

1.4b Failure to account for higher U.S. health prices greatly exaggerates per capita health cost differences between OECD nations and the United States

Ratio: health purchasing power parity/GDP PPP in 2007 (both PPPs indexed to U.S. prices)

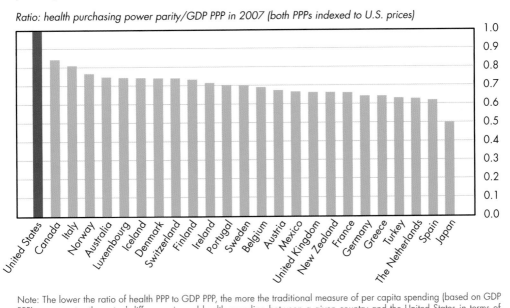

Note: The lower the ratio of health PPP to GDP PPP, the more the traditional measure of per capita spending (based on GDP PPP) exaggerates the actual difference in real health spending between a given country and the United States in terms of constant health purchasing power.

For 80 years, growth in real per capita health spending almost always outpaced growth in the rest of the economy by as much as 6 percentage points.

For 80 years, per capita health spending has grown persistently each year from one to six percentage points faster than the non-health portion of the economy. Since 1929, annual growth in per capita NHE (4.1 percent) was slightly more than double the rate experienced in the rest of the economy.

However, the size of the disparity has changed dramatically over this period (figure 1.5a). Health spending growth has outpaced general economic growth by the largest margins during periods of significant expansions of public health insurance coverage (the introduction of Medicare and Medicaid in the 1960s, Medicaid expansion in the 1980s), and years marked by poor economic performance (for example, stagflation during the 1970s).

The more fine-grained data shown (figure 1.5b) are for a shorter time but demonstrate how infrequently annual growth in per capita non-health sector GDP has outpaced the rate of increase in NHE per capita since 1960. Rather than exhibiting a common pattern, the few cases in which this has occurred have unique explanations.

It is worth emphasizing from the previous discussion what these trends do (and do not) imply. Both sets of growth rates have been calculated from "real" (inflation-adjusted) per capita estimates of NHE and non-health sector GDP (that is, GDP minus NHE), using the GDP deflator to remove the effects of general economy-wide inflation. (Using chained dollars is a more precise way of measuring inflation than using the standard CPI.) Including the effects of health-specific inflation, the higher observed growth in real per capita NHE does *not* imply that growth in per capita health *output* has been double that of the rest of the economy. As well, components of both NHE and GDP reflect investments in capital or research and development (R&D) that might not pay off until future years. Thus, the growth rate differential is not a precise comparison of how Americans have consumed health care relative to everything else.

Our apparent willingness to increase expenditures on health care even during periods that the real economy is shrinking is suggestive of the relative priority of health care over everything else. Conversely, to date Americans have been able to enjoy a rising standard of living notwithstanding their high level of spending on health.

1.5a After adjusting for inflation, increased health spending per person has outstripped the increase in non-health GDP per capita for many decades

Compound annual growth rate in inflation-adjusted spending over period shown

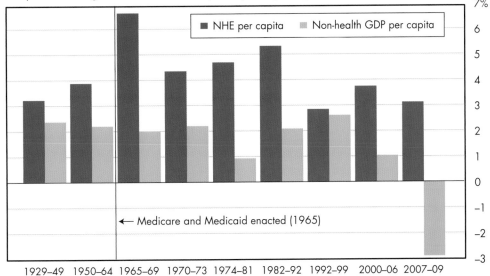

← Medicare and Medicaid enacted (1965)

1929–49 1950–64 1965–69 1970–73 1974–81 1982–92 1992–99 2000–06 2007–09

Note: Non-health GDP = GDP minus NHE. Growth rates calculated from real GDP per capita (chained 2005 dollars) and real NHE per capita (calculated in 2005 dollars from GDP price deflator).

1.5b Since 1960, annual growth in inflation-adjusted health costs per U.S. resident fell below the rise in non-health costs per capita only seven times

Annual percentage change

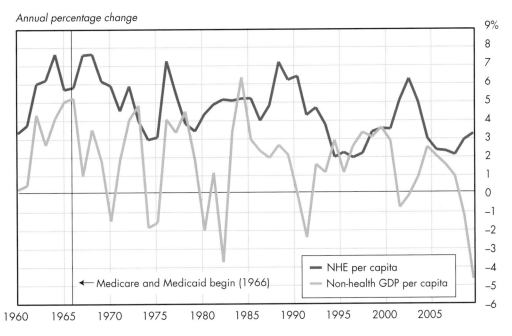

← Medicare and Medicaid begin (1966)

In the past 50 years, health spending as a share of GDP has risen in all advanced countries.

Without exception, in all so-called advanced countries, NHE accounts for a larger share of GDP today than it did 50 years ago. Each 1 percent increase in GDP has been associated with approximately a 1.3 percent increase in health spending. This proclivity to devote a bigger share of rising GDP to gains in health status might make the growing share of GDP allocated to health care appear "inexorable"; however, it is not inevitable. In some countries, the health share of GDP has declined or remained relatively flat for periods of years.

In the early 1960s, the health sector share of U.S. GDP was much more similar to that of its major competitors than it is today (figure 1.6a). Inferring from these changes that the United States spends "too much" or that other G7 nations spend "too little" on health care is inappropriate. In 1980, real GDP per capita (using 2005 dollars and purchasing power) was lower in every other G7 nation than in the United States—a difference ranging from 11 percent (Canada) to 25 percent (Italy). From 1980 to 2007, real GDP per capita grew *faster* in the United States than in all G7 countries except the United Kingdom. This combination—a higher base level of per capita GDP and faster growth—permitted the United States to afford a much higher increase in health spending.

What does this mean? In 1980, real non-health GDP per capita in all other G7 countries was lower than in the United States Yet with the exception of the United Kingdom (where such spending grew from 71 percent of the U.S. average in 1980 to 82 percent by 2007), the U.S. margin of advantage in non-health spending had *increased* in 2007 relative to 1980.

Moreover, growth in real NHE per capita has *not* been persistently higher in the United States relative to its major economic competitors (figure 1.6b). That is, even though health spending growth outpaced GDP growth by a greater extent in the United States than in other G7 nations, it did not become relatively less affordable in terms of GDP purchasing power. This fact illustrates the importance of making apples-to-apples comparisons when assessing the relative performance of different health sectors. Chapter 19 explores how well the American health system performs in obtaining value for money in health care.

1.6a The difference between the United States and other G7 nations in the health spending share of GDP has increased since 1980

NHE as a percentage of GDP

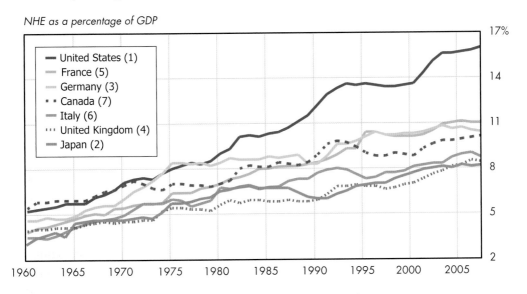

Note: Numbers in parentheses show country ranking within G7 based on size of GDP in 2007.

1.6b For 50 years, growth in real health spending per capita has not been noticeably higher in the United States relative to other G7 countries

Compound annual growth rate in inflation-adjusted health spending per capita

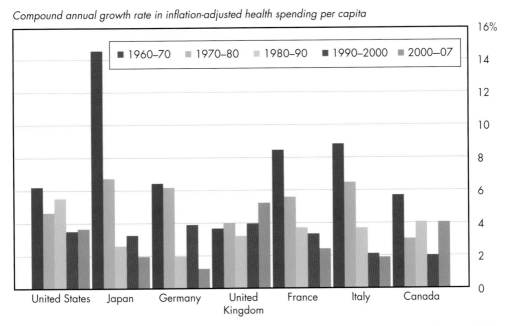

Note: Countries listed (left to right) in order of the size of their GDP in 2007. Growth rates estimated from real NHE per capita (calculated in chained 2005 U.S. dollars using a GDP price deflator).

Most of the world's population live in countries where health spending per capita is much less than that of the United States, yet the gap has been increasing for some of the largest countries in recent years.

Even from a world perspective, the American health system is massive, accounting for approximately 40 percent of an estimated $5.2 trillion in health expenditures across the globe (figure 1.7a). This share is far higher than the U.S. share of worldwide gross national income (GNI)—a sharp contrast to the rest of the G7, where the shares are almost equal. These calculations are based on estimates by the World Health Organization (WHO). In most countries, GNI is approximately equivalent to GDP so it is a reasonable approximation of national output. However, to equalize purchasing power, WHO estimates health spending using the rough equivalent of GDP PPP. As noted previously, this approach tends to overstate relative U.S. health spending. The difficulties noted about making international comparisons of output in general (or health sector output in particular) are even more severe when countries as different as the United States and Ethiopia are involved. Despite such measurement problems, there is no doubt that differences in per capita income and health spending are extremely large.

The concentration of world population in the group with fewer than 10 percent of U.S. per capita income and health spending is magnified by the inclusion of China and India, where almost 40 percent of the world's population reside (figure 1.7b). This group also includes four of the world's most populated countries (Indonesia, Bangladesh, Pakistan, and Nigeria).

Among the world's 10 most populated countries, recent growth in per capita income has exceeded that in the United States, implying a shrinking income gap. In contrast, with the exception of Indonesia, China, and the Russian Federation, NHE per person has grown *less* rapidly in all of these nations compared with the United States (figure 1.7c). These three nations increased health spending relative to the United States while the others fell further behind. However, except for Indonesia, health spending growth has been slower than growth in income.

The OECD has compiled reasonably good data over decades; however, health spending data in some of these developing countries is much more uneven in quality and spans a much shorter timeframe. Reaching strong conclusions from growth differentials observed over only five years would be wrong.

1.7a The U.S. share of world health expenditures is substantially larger than its share of either world population or GDP

Percentage of world total (2006)

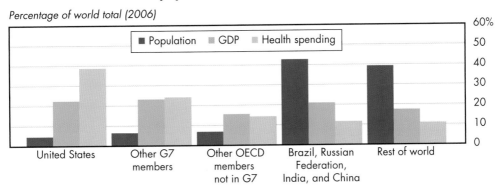

1.7b More than 70 percent of the world's population live in nations with health spending per capita below 10 percent of U.S. levels

Percentage of world population living at the level of per capita GNI or NHE (2006)

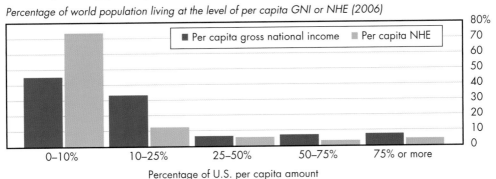

Percentage of U.S. per capita amount

1.7c In the 10 most populous countries, increased per capita income has outpaced the increase in NHE per person, but not in the United States or Indonesia

Compound annual growth rate from 2002–2006

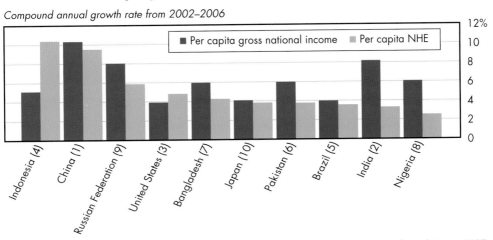

Note: Countries ranked by NHE per capita. Numbers in parentheses show ranking by size of population in 2007. Growth rates estimated from real NHE per capita (calculated in chained 2005 U.S. dollars using a GDP price deflator).

CHAPTER 2

How Is Each Health Dollar Spent?

Most health spending is for personal health services; for 40 years, such spending has exceeded 80 percent of all health expenditures.

Different methods exist to measure spending for health care. One measure—the NHE—encompasses all private and public spending having to do with health care. However, 1 in 15 dollars of NHE includes what might be regarded as investment, including expenditures for medical research, construction of new facilities, and purchases of new major equipment (figure 2.1a).

Administrative costs associated with public programs such as Medicare and Medicaid, and private health insurance plans, amount to only 1/16 of NHE. This might seem low in light of the purportedly high administrative costs associated with U.S. health care. A main reason is that it excludes large provider-related administrative costs embedded in various health services that make up personal health care expenditures (PHCE).

Government public health activity includes spending for surveillance, inoculations, immunizations and vaccinations, disease prevention activities, and public health laboratories. Currently, fewer than three cents of every health dollar goes to public health. This total should *not* be interpreted as a measure of all preventive health spending. As with administrative costs, the providers of various health services included under PHCE also engage in clinical preventive services. Public health spending does not capture these costs.

The remainder, PHCE, constitutes 5/6 of all health spending. This includes the full continuum of health care services ranging from primary care through long-term care (for example, nursing homes and home health care). PHCE includes inpatient care (for example, in hospitals, nursing homes, and intermediate-care facilities), and all services by medical professionals (for example, doctors, mid-level practitioners, allied health personnel). Finally, it includes ancillary services such as medical and dental laboratories, medications (prescription and non-prescription), durable medical equipment (for example, wheelchairs), non-durable medical products (for example, bandages), and even medical care provided at worksite clinics. The PHCE share of health spending has exceeded 80 percent of NHE for more than 40 years (figure 2.1b).

2.1a Five-sixths of NHE is devoted to PHCE

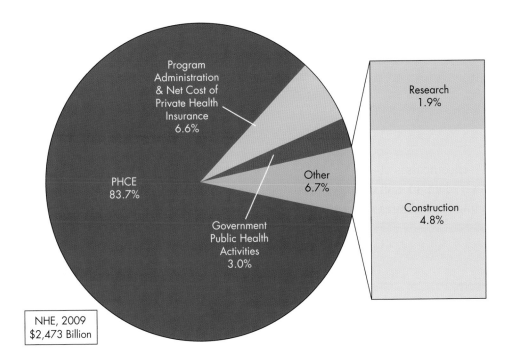

Program Administration & Net Cost of Private Health Insurance 6.6%

PHCE 83.7%

Government Public Health Activities 3.0%

Other 6.7%

Research 1.9%

Construction 4.8%

NHE, 2009
$2,473 Billion

2.1b For 40 years, spending on personal health care has exceeded 80 percent of national health outlays

Percentage of NHE

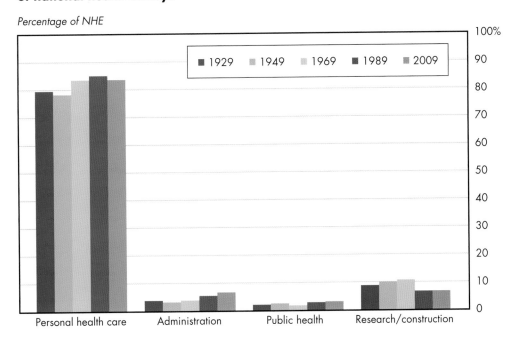

■ 1929 ■ 1949 ■ 1969 ■ 1989 ■ 2009

Personal health care   Administration   Public health   Research/construction

From 1929 to 2009, inflation-adjusted personal health spending per capita has doubled approximately every 25 years.

In terms of the constant purchasing power of health care, today's per capita spending on personal health care is 9.2 times as large as in 1929—an annual increase of 2.8 percent. Although the PCE denotes spending by individuals and households excluding goods and services used by government and business, PHCE reflects *all* spending on health services, including those paid by government and business.

Recall that PHCE excludes current investment in research, new construction, and equipment because their payoffs occur in the future and last more than one year. Realistically, some of the annualized costs of *past* investments *are* embedded in the prices paid to medical providers—reflecting funds borrowed to make such investments or funding of depreciation to finance replacement of aging plants and equipment. However, even these costs are understated if they were publicly subsidized.

That said, the measured total of PHCE is the best indication of the extent to which the output of the health sector contributes to the satisfaction of the wants of millions of individuals for medical services. However, PHCE surely is a lower bound on annual expenditures whose motivation is to improve health. For many other purchases (for example, food or even automobiles), health and safety considerations can play an important role. In contrast, PHCE-related purchases typically are motivated solely by considerations of health: Patients do not rely on ambulances to commute to work, nor do they seek a doctor's care to satisfy an empty stomach.

On a per capita basis, real PHCE (that is, inflation-adjusted using the GDP price deflator) has grown over the last 80 years at an annualized rate of 4.1 percent. This implies a doubling of real PHCE every 18 years. Whereas real GDP per capita was approximately 5.3 times as large in 2009 as in 1929, real PHCE per capita grew 24-fold during the same period (figure 2.2). Thus, in terms of what can be purchased in the rest of the economy, PHCE grew more than four times as fast as output. Because health prices have gone up much faster than general prices, this is *not* the same as saying that real resources devoted to PHCE have grown at that rate. Using the PCE deflator for health care to adjust for prices, today's real per capita PHCE is "only" 9.2 times as large as in 1929.

2.2 The rate of growth in PHCE per capita is much slower when adjusted for the effect of increasing health prices or general inflation

PHCE per capita

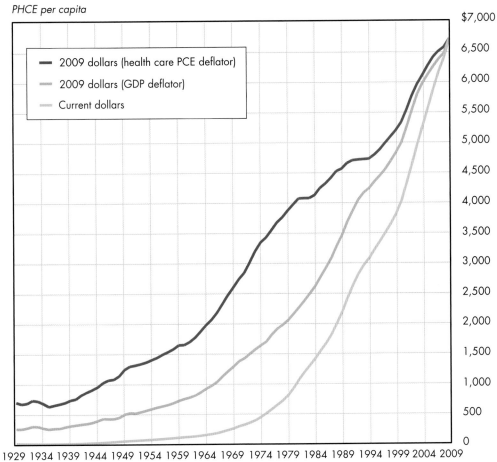

Legend:
— 2009 dollars (health care PCE deflator)
— 2009 dollars (GDP deflator)
— Current dollars

Insurer administrative costs decline as group size increases and vary by type of coverage.

Many misconceptions about insurer administrative expenses are grounded in some kernels of truth. For example, there certainly are economies of scale in the administration of health benefits, although their extent is often exaggerated. Although the unit costs of administering claims varies little across different size groups, the administrative loading factor is much higher for individual (non-group) policies compared with large group policies. For example, an insurance agent might have to spend somewhat more time to market a plan to a large group compared with marketing to an individual. But because this cost can be spread over so many lives, the unit costs of marketing are much lower for the group policy.

The administrative costs for small groups (2–50 employees in figure 2.3a) therefore fall in between those for individuals and large groups. The weighted average—accounting for the far larger number of individuals covered by large groups relative to small groups or non-group policies—is slightly more than nine cents of every premium dollar.

This amount is much higher than the administrative share of costs ascribed to traditional Medicare (where services are paid on a fee-for-service basis). However, that is an apples-to-oranges comparison for two reasons. First, administrators of Medicare's private health plans do not have to perform as many functions as do their private counterparts (for example, marketing and provider rate negotiations). When only Medicare administrative services are taken into account, the administrative costs for private plans are cut approximately in half (figure 2.3b). The second reason is that the average dollar amount per Medicare claim is much higher than for private insurance because the elderly and disabled use hospital and nursing home services far more than do children or non-elderly adults.

Thus, an alternative way of assessing administrative costs compares administrative costs per member per month. On average, private commercial health plans spend a little less than $25 monthly—approximately twice the amount for traditional Medicare (figure 2.3c). However, when only Medicare-comparable administrative costs are taken into account, the private plans have administrative costs per member per month almost indistinguishable from those experienced by Medicare carriers.

2.3a Because of economies of scale, administrative costs in the individual insurance market are at least twice as much as in the large group market

Administrative costs as a percentage of health insurance premiums

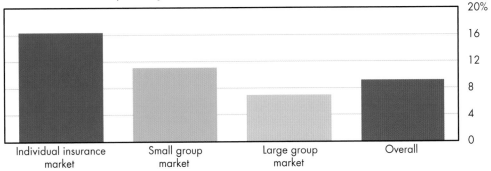

2.3b If private health insurance covered a similar mix of services as Medicare does, this alone would cut average administrative costs by half

Administrative costs as a percentage of health insurance premiums/health spending (2009)

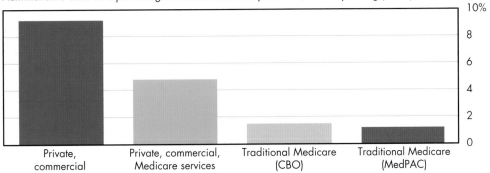

2.3c On a per-member per-month basis, Medicare's purported cost advantage over private plans is small or non-existent

Administrative costs per member per month (2009)

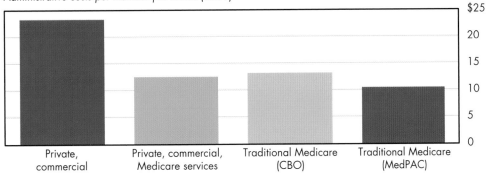

Note: Both the Congressional Budget Office (CBO) and the Medicare Payment Advisory Commission (MedPAC) have done analyses of Medicare administrative costs that are reflected in the figures above.

The combined percentage of health spending related to hospitals and nursing homes doubled from 1929 to 1989, but currently is declining.

The dominance of health facilities during the 1960s through 1980s has given way to a shift toward outpatient care in recent decades. Hospital care accounted for just slightly more than 20 percent of PHCE in 1929, but this share peaked at 48 percent in 1982 and has declined to less than 40 percent today (figure 2.4a). Nursing home care accounted for only slightly more than a penny per PHCE dollar in 1929, but this amount peaked in 1998 at 8.9 cents, after which it now has declined to seven cents. Combined "institutional" spending on hospitals and nursing homes was less than 25 percent of spending in 1929, but it too peaked at 56 cents per dollar of PHCE in 1982, declining to approximately 44 cents today.

The services of health professionals, in contrast, declined from almost half of all spending in 1929 to a low of 31 cents per PHCE dollar in 1982, followed by a subsequent rise to 38 percent. Medicare began paying a flat rate per hospital stay that varied based on a patient's diagnosis in 1983. This so-called prospective payment system (PPS) provided a strong incentive to discharge patients early, resulting in a sizable decline in hospital use among the elderly in the years that followed.

Sales of non-durable medical products such as band-aids declined steadily from almost 25 percent of PHCE in 1929 to slightly more than 10 percent by 1989, but then rose to 15 percent by the year 2009. In contrast to the other medical services shown, where pricing often is far from transparent and health insurance coverage far more common, these medical products generally are sold in retail outlets such as drugstores or grocery stores, where pricing is transparent and competition fierce.

Although physician and clinical services hovered for decades at approximately 25 percent of PHCE, the dental services share of spending declined steadily (figure 2.4b). Although dental insurance coverage has expanded gradually, the out-of-pocket share of dental care is more than four times the corresponding share (less than 10 percent) of physician and clinical services that is not financed through third-party payers. Similarly, 60 percent of pharmaceuticals were paid for out-of-pocket as of 1988, compared with 20 percent by 2009. This helps explain the patterns shown.

2.4a **Professional services, once accounting for almost half of all health costs, currently account for the largest single share of spending**

Percentage of PHCE

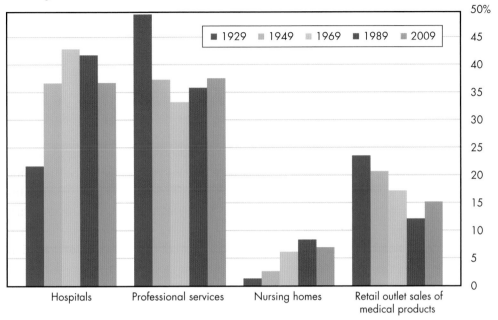

2.4b **Although the share of PHCE accounted for by dental services has declined steadily, trends for other components are mixed**

Percentage of PHCE

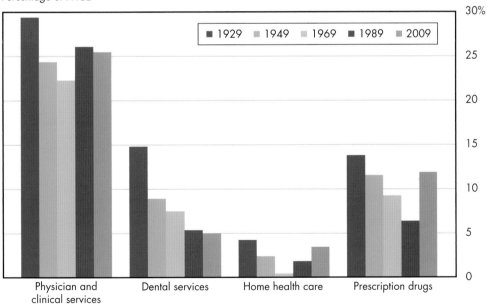

More than half of health spending is for chronic diseases; chronic illness accounts for an increasing share of health spending.

Just over half of adult health spending pays for chronic conditions. However, this average masks a lot of variation across age groups. For adults younger than age 35, just less than 30 percent of spending is specifically attributable to treating chronic conditions. In contrast, among the elderly, the share of PHCE having to do with chronic conditions is approximately double this level (figure 2.5a).

Approximately 60 percent of civilian adults not living in institutions have at least one chronic condition. Again, this ranges from a low of 36 percent of young adults to approximately 92 percent of the elderly. Consequently, those with at least one chronic condition account for more than 60 percent of total PHCE among young adults and 99 percent among the elderly.

Chronic conditions are one reason that health expenditures increase so dramatically by age—something that will be examined in more detail (refer to figure 12.4a). Among adults having no chronic conditions, annual health expenses in 2005 averaged less than $1,000 per person, with elderly individuals experiencing only slightly higher spending than their adult counterparts in the lowest age category.

Average spending for those who had one or more chronic conditions was approximately 2.5 times as high as for those who had no such conditions—ranging from approximately 1.5 for young adults to almost 3.5 for the elderly (figure 2.5b). This rising differential with age reflects two mutually reinforcing effects. First, average spending per person for a given number of conditions rises with age. Thus, among adults with just one chronic condition, per capita spending for elderly adults is more than triple the annual spending incurred by their counterparts in the young adult age group. Some of this difference reflects the high cost of dying.

Second, the average number of chronic conditions per person also rises with age. The prevalence of two or more chronic conditions is more than five times as large for elderly adults compared with young adults (hence the reason for pre-existing conditions to matter so much in accurately pricing health insurance coverage). Setting prices based solely on age captures some of the variation that arises because of age-related differences in the rate and cost of chronic conditions. However, even within a fixed age group, the number and nature of chronic conditions results in large cost differences.

2.5a Approximately half of adult health spending is for chronic conditions; 90 percent of spending is for adults who have at least one such condition

■ All adults ▪ Age 18–34 ▪ Age 35–54 ■ Age 55–64 ▪ 65 and older

Percentage of total health expenditures

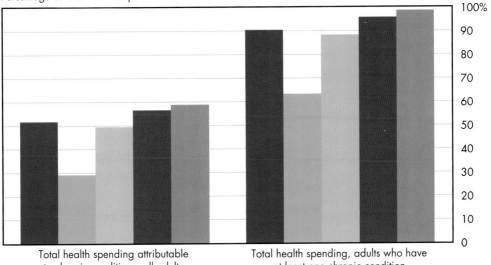

| Total health spending attributable to chronic conditions, all adults | Total health spending, adults who have at least one chronic condition |

2.5b Compared with those who have no chronic illness, annual health costs are two to three times as much for adults who do have one or more chronic conditions

Annual medical expenses per person (dollars)

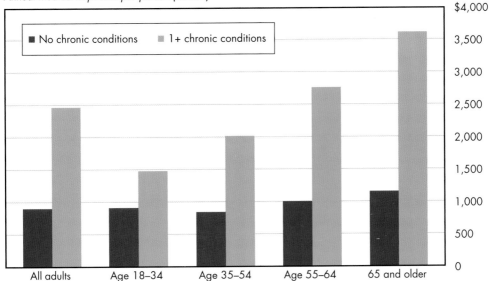

■ No chronic conditions ▪ 1+ chronic conditions

All adults   Age 18–34   Age 35–54   Age 55–64   65 and older

Note: Estimates exclude expenses for dental care, or other medical equipment and services.

At least half of personal health spending is for behavior, lifestyle, or other avoidable causes.

Accounting for expenditures based on disease classification clouds the extent to which much health spending is avoidable. Consider the underlying causes of diseases that give rise to health spending. Figure 2.6 lists 15 such causes, together with estimates of the share of 2009 PHCE attributable to these causes. These are approximate estimates calculated by estimating the fraction of PHCE devoted to underlying causes in a reference year (usually 2000 or later, but in some cases as early as 1992). This fraction was assumed to be identical in 2009.

Another caveat is that there might be some overlap between categories. Although every effort was made to create categories that were mutually exclusive, limitations in how data were reported sometimes precluded doing this in every case where it was needed. Taken at face value, these 15 categories collectively account for just over half of PHCE. In light of the minimal duplication that remains, it appears almost certain that these categories collectively account for a minimum of 40 percent of PHCE.

Figure 2.6 defines behavior broadly, including efforts by individual people to live healthier lives. It also can include actions taken to improve health system performance (shown in green, for example, reducing medical errors), other worksite activities to improve worker safety, transportation safety efforts to improve the quality of roads and/or automobiles, or even efforts to improve nutrition for schoolchildren.

Note that the data represent the *gross* amount of health spending that hypothetically could be avoided in a perfect world. Because we do not live in a perfect world, it is not possible to eradicate every dollar of avoidable spending. Although individual efforts to "try harder" can yield fruitful results virtually without costs, any serious effort to influence spending of this magnitude would require an investment of resources to alter systems (for example, electronic medical records to reduce medication errors) or behaviors (for example, smoking cessation aids). Although it never would make sense to spend a dollar to save less than a dollar, some of these initiatives might well use a sizable fraction of the potential savings. Thus, it would be imprudent to spend hundreds of billions in potential savings before ascertaining the actual net savings attainable.

2.6 Probably half or more of health spending has to do with behavior, lifestyle, or other avoidable causes

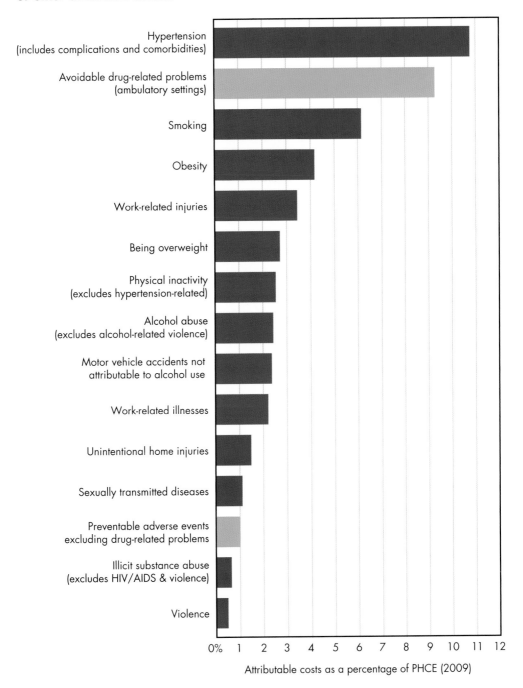

Attributable costs as a percentage of PHCE (2009)

Note: Every effort has been made to create mutually exclusive categories, but in some cases, some duplication across categories is unavoidable.

CHAPTER 3

Who Pays for Health Services?

Regardless of how it is measured, the public sector role in U.S. health financing has increased.

Examining health financing from the standpoint of who literally pays the final bills, a rather steady expansion in the public-sector share of NHE that goes back at least 80 years becomes obvious (figure 3.1a). Starting in the 1960s, when both Medicare and Medicaid first began, the public share of financing increased much more sharply than it had previously.

From this standpoint of government as payer, Medicare is a federal responsibility because all funds flow through the general treasury before distribution to private administrators who pay claims from providers. This includes all the payroll taxes used to support Part A (inpatient hospital and nursing home services), together with the voluntary premiums for Part B (physician and other outpatient services) and Part D (prescription drugs). Medicaid—jointly financed by the federal and state governments—nominally increased state and local responsibility for care. In reality, the greatly expanded federal role in health care financing in 1965 displaced much of the traditional state and local government role in paying for care of the poor, disabled, and elderly. Consequently, the state and local share of health spending declined steadily since the 1960s as the federal share expanded. The federal displacement of private insurance and family out-of-pocket payments in this period was even greater.

An alternative way to view health spending is in terms of sources of revenue. Even though households ultimately incur the burden of all health spending, it is possible to differentiate revenues flowing from households, businesses, and various levels of government. In this so-called *sponsor* view, half of Medicare payroll taxes are assumed to be paid by employers and half paid by employees (households) rather than by the federal government. Conversely, the cost of the Federal Employee Health Benefits Plan (FEHBP) is shifted from private insurers (under the payer view) to the federal government (employer contributions) and households of covered members (premiums paid by federal employees/retirees).

From this sponsor view of health financing, the relative shares of spending paid by business, households, the federal government, and state and local governments have been remarkably stable over the past 20 years (figure 3.1b). Nevertheless, the public role in financing has grown slightly over this period.

3.1a Since 1965, the increasing federal share of PHCE has displaced much private and state health spending

Percentage of PHCE

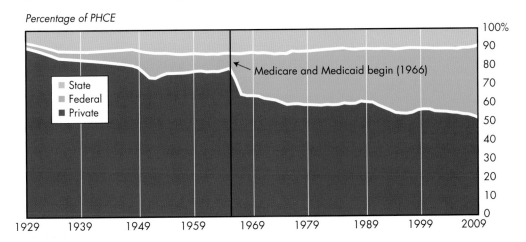

Note: In the NHE Accounts framework, federal government health spending includes all of Medicare (including components financed privately, such as Parts B and D premiums), the federal share of Medicaid spending, and other public health-related programs such as DOD and VA health. State/local government health spending includes the non-federal share of Medicaid, workers' compensation, hospital subsidies, and the non-federal share of categorical or block grant programs such as maternal and child health.

3.1b Accounting for each sponsor's share of health revenues results in a much more stable federal share of spending over 20 years

■ State and local governments   ■ Federal government   ■ Private business   ■ Households

Percentage of health services and supplies expenditures

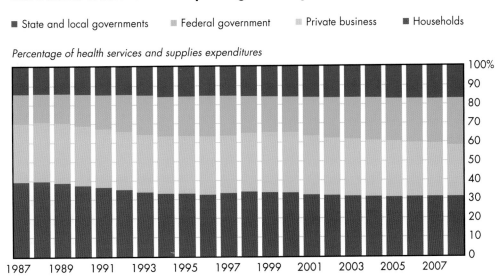

Note: In the framework of "health sponsors," household health spending includes only components that are directly paid, including the employee share of group health insurance premiums, the employee share of Medicare Part A payroll taxes, voluntary premiums paid for Medicare Parts B or D and non-group health insurance, and any out-of-pocket spending not covered by public or private insurance. Business health expenditures include only the private employer share of health insurance premiums for workers and dependents, Medicare Part A and workers' compensation, and industrial in-plant health services.

Private health insurance pays for a smaller share of health spending than public insurance does, even though many more Americans have private insurance.

Under the payer view, private health insurance pays for a somewhat smaller share of health spending than do Medicare and Medicaid combined (figure 3.2a). As noted earlier, the Medicare share includes all components paid by Medicare, regardless of source. These include Medicare payroll taxes from all employers (including state and local governments), all premium payments (including premiums paid by state governments under Medicaid for individuals dual-eligible for both programs), and all federal general funds used to finance Parts B, C (managed care plans), and D (prescription drugs).

The federal government also covers approximately two-thirds of Medicaid benefits costs, with state and local governments picking up the balance. When all other federal and state programs for direct health services, such as community health centers, local health departments, and maternal and child health are taken into account, government currently finances slightly less than half of all PHCE.

Private health insurance includes all directly purchased health insurance (non-group plans) and all group plans such as employer-sponsored plans, including plans for public employees and self-insured plans typically offered by large employers. In the latter plans, the employer is at risk for most or all of the costs of health services for plan members. However, health claims under such plans usually are processed by private health insurers or third-party administrators.

Out-of-pocket spending (which includes only payments made at the time of service, but *not* premium payments for either private or public health insurance) accounts for only 14 percent of spending.

Although Medicare covers more than 90 percent of the elderly, public health plans cover fewer than half of children and younger adults (figure 3.2b). Employer-sponsored insurance covers a majority of both groups. Public insurance—notably Medicaid—is more common for children than for younger adults. In the entire population, Medicare and Medicaid constitute less than 30 percent of coverage (this will increase if health reform is implemented). The large mismatch between shares of spending and population illustrate that public plans already cover many of those who are most sick.

3.2a Private health insurance pays slightly less for personal health care than do Medicare and Medicaid combined

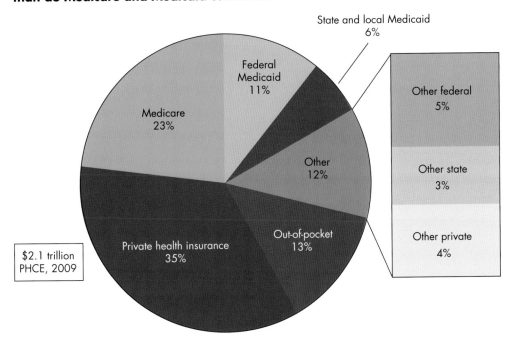

State and local Medicaid
6%

Federal
Medicaid
11%

Medicare
23%

Other
12%

Other federal
5%

Other state
3%

Out-of-pocket
13%

Private health insurance
35%

Other private
4%

$2.1 trillion
PHCE, 2009

3.2b Children and the elderly rely much more on public health insurance than adults younger than age 65 do

Percentage of population who have coverage (March 2009)

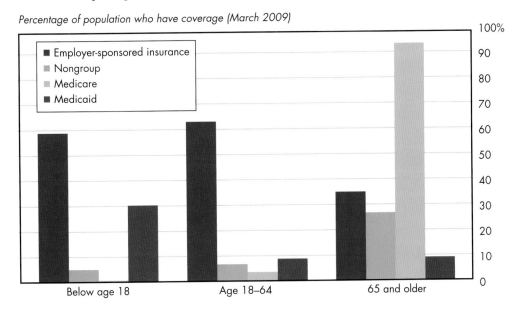

- ■ Employer-sponsored insurance
- Nongroup
- Medicare
- ■ Medicaid

Below age 18   Age 18–64   65 and older

Note: Figures add to more than 100% for each age category because of individuals with more than one form of health insurance coverage.

For the past 70 years, virtually all growth in health spending relative to the economy has been financed by public and private health insurance.

Health spending as a percentage of GDP has more than tripled since 1949 (figure 3.3a). The share of GDP paid through out-of-pocket health spending has declined steadily during this same period (except in a handful of years). The growing share of expenditures paid by private insurance and public insurance has bankrolled the entire increase in the health sector share of the economy during this time.

There was little private insurance in 1929, but it grew rapidly after World War II. This was fueled by an IRS decision (later codified into law) that employer-provided fringe benefits (including health insurance) would not be taxable. Thus, a dollar of employer-paid health insurance was more valuable to the employee than a dollar of wages from which taxes were deducted. In 1965, Medicare and Medicaid displaced what might have been continued growth in private insurance, as shown in figure 3.3a. In fact, for several years in the late 1960s, the private insurance share of GDP *declined* slightly. Even so, this share more than tripled between 1969 and 2009.

Spending on other government programs also declined slightly with the introduction of public health insurance coverage. This makes sense insofar as Medicaid in particular replaced many state and local programs that had provided direct medical services to indigent individuals. Even so, such other government spending subsequently grew for a period before declining rather steadily until today.

At a more fine-grained level, Medicare grew in size somewhat more rapidly than did Medicaid, while growth in Medicaid slightly outpaced the rate of growth in private insurance.

An alternative view of the same data shows more clearly how public spending grew as a share of personal health spending after World War II, but subsequently was eclipsed in importance by the rapid rise of private health insurance (figure 3.3b). However, this explosion in private health insurance also halted temporarily, starting in 1966 when both Medicaid and Medicare began. Even so, within a few years, although the Medicaid and Medicare shares of spending continued to grow, the role of private health insurance also began to increase.

3.3a Since 1949, all the growth in the personal health spending share of GDP has come from increased payments by third parties

PHCE as percentage of GDP

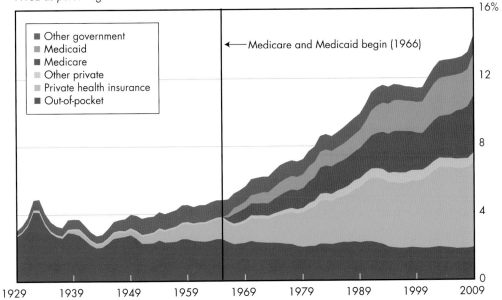

Legend:
- Other government
- Medicaid
- Medicare
- Other private
- Private health insurance
- Out-of-pocket

←— Medicare and Medicaid begin (1966)

16%

12

8

4

0

1929 1939 1949 1959 1969 1979 1989 1999 2009

3.3b Tax-financed health spending expanded more rapidly than private health insurance did after 1965

Percentage of PHCE

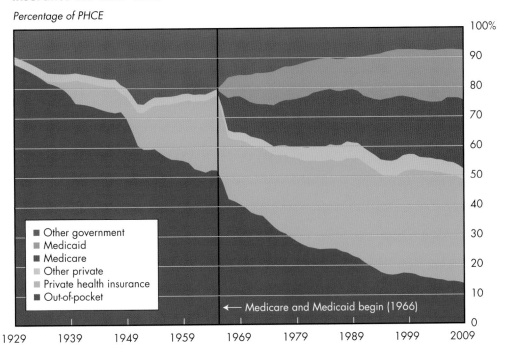

Legend:
- Other government
- Medicaid
- Medicare
- Other private
- Private health insurance
- Out-of-pocket

←— Medicare and Medicaid begin (1966)

100%
90
80
70
60
50
40
30
20
10
0

1929 1939 1949 1959 1969 1979 1989 1999 2009

Though far less visible to the average American, federal tax subsidies for health exceed federal spending on Medicaid.

Tax subsidies having to do with health care now amount to approximately $300 billion a year. The federal share of this total is more than the federal government now pays for its share of Medicaid. Thus, ironically, the federal government in 2009 paid more to encourage employer-based health insurance than it spent on public health insurance for those who have low incomes, although this no longer will be true whether or not health reform is implemented.

Tax expenditures represent the lost tax revenue associated with giving more favorable treatment to particular actions or activities. Unlike Medicare and Medicaid, such subsidies do not show up as a line item in the federal budget either as expenditures or as deductions from expected revenue. For this reason, tax expenditures are far less visible to most Americans than are the direct expenditures financed by the national treasury.

Health-related tax expenditures take many forms, but more than 90 percent of costs attributable to them relate to the previously mentioned tax exclusion. This tax exclusion results in income tax losses at the federal and state levels, but also payroll taxes for Medicare and Social Security. By comparison, other tax expenditures (such as the Schedule B deduction for households that have large health expenses relative to income) are minuscule. The large expense threshold currently is 7.5 percent of adjusted gross income (AGI) but will increase to 10 percent in 2013 under the new health reform bill. Other miscellaneous health-related tax benefits received by individuals or corporations account for even smaller amounts of tax expenditures.

The magnitude of tax expenditures changes the picture of who is actually paying for health care. In the traditional payer view of financing, business accounts for more than 40 percent of spending, while the federal government accounts for just over 30 percent. With tax expenditures factored into NHE, the federal government by far becomes the largest payer, accounting for 45 percent of spending (figure 3.4b, left columns). All levels of government account for almost 60 percent of NHE compared with less than half this amount when tax expenditures are ignored. Even under the sponsor view of health spending described previously, government accounts for more than half of all health spending when tax expenditures are made visible.

3.4a More than 90 percent of tax expenditures used to subsidize health care is from the tax exclusion for employee health benefits

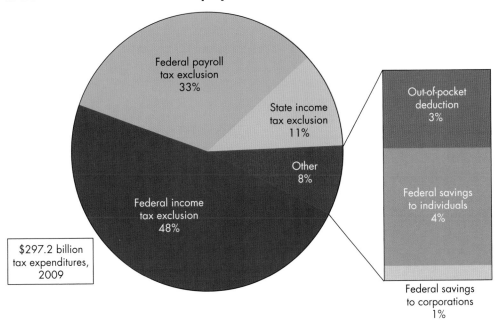

$297.2 billion tax expenditures, 2009

3.4b Failure to account for health-related tax subsidies substantially understates the government share of NHE

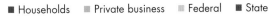

Households   Private business   Federal   State

Percentage of NHE (2008)

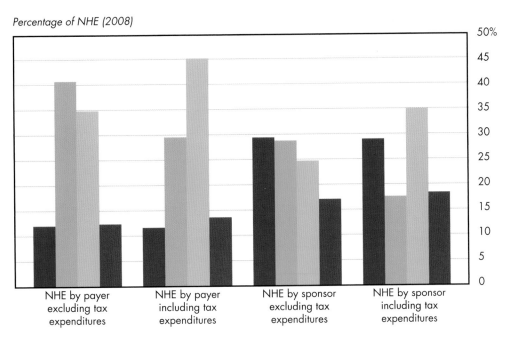

For 80 years, the out-of-pocket share of health spending has declined while the portion paid by third parties has increased.

One in seven dollars of personal health care spending now is paid for out-of-pocket compared with seven in eight dollars 80 years ago (figure 3.5a). This by far is the most significant change in health care financing over the past 80 years. Combining all other spending into a single amount, figure 3.5a illustrates quite clearly that the "wedge" of health insurance payments displaced both out-of-pocket and other health spending. This wedge has grown steadily larger each decade.

It is also easy to see that although public insurance and private insurance were approximately equal in amounts as late as 1979, public insurance today accounts for more than 40 percent of spending while private insurance accounts for less than 35 percent. If the recent health plan is implemented, the projected increase in Medicaid enrollees would exceed 30 percent, in which case this differential would grow faster in future years.

Fig. 3.5b shows how the out-of-pocket share of spending varies by type of service. In 2009, it was highest for durable medical equipment (exceeding 50 percent) and lowest for hospital services (under 5 percent). Even for physician and clinical services, out-of-pocket spending is less than one-tenth of the total. In contrast, more than one-fourth of spending on pharmaceuticals and non-durable medical supplies (e.g., band-aids) and more than one-fifth of nursing home spending is financed out of pocket. Since 1949, the out-of-pocket share of spending has declined much more rapidly for hospital and physician care than for other health services.

The out-of-pocket share of spending might be leveling out. Absent health reform, this share might have begun to increase over time as more employers and individuals switched to high-deductible health plans as a way of lowering premium costs. Health reform is projected to expand coverage to tens of millions of uninsured. Although common sense would require that out-of-pocket expenditures for the newly covered would decline, this is not necessarily the case. On average, per capita out-of-pocket spending for privately insured individuals is approximately 15 percent higher than it is for people who are uninsured all year. Counterbalancing this, however, are provisions in the new law that will set an income-related ceiling on out-of-pocket spending and various expansions in coverage such as prohibiting cost-sharing for preventive services and eliminating lifetime limits on coverage.

3.5a One in seven dollars of personal health care spending currently is paid for out-of-pocket compared with seven in eight dollars out-of-pocket 80 years ago

■ Out-of-pocket   ■ Private third party   ■ Public third party   ■ All other

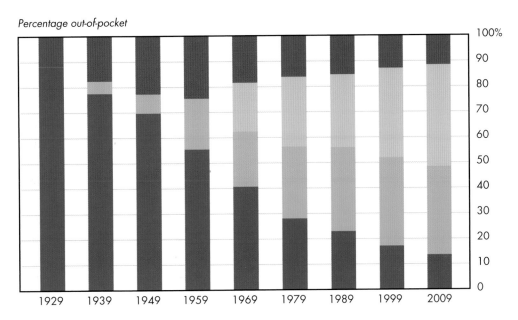

Percentage out-of-pocket

3.5b The out-of-pocket share of spending has declined much more rapidly for hospital and physician care than for other health services

■ 1929   ■ 1949   ■ 1969   ■ 1989   ■ 2009

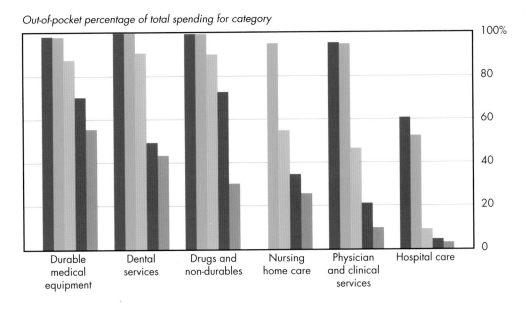

Out-of-pocket percentage of total spending for category

Despite a much lower publicly financed share of health spending, the U.S. out-of-pocket share of spending is among the lowest in the world.

Among the 20 largest countries in the OECD, the United States has the fourth lowest share of health spending paid through out-of-pocket payments (figure 3.6a). This might seem surprising because the tax-financed share of spending in the United States is the lowest among these countries. Private health insurance more than makes up for the fact that government is responsible for a smaller fraction of health spending. Compared with its largest OECD competitors, the United States by far relies much more heavily on private health insurance.

Even citizens of countries such as Canada—who pride themselves for having tax-financed universal coverage—pay a higher share of health spending out-of-pocket than do Americans. Switzerland, which relies on an individual mandate analogous to the one recently included in the U.S. health reform plan, has more than 30 percent of its health spending financed through out-of-pocket payments. To be fair, another country with an individual mandate, the Netherlands, is one of only three countries to have a lower out-of-pocket share than does the United States. Even in countries that have universal or near-universal coverage, there is quite a bit of diversity in terms of how much out-of-pocket burden citizens are left to experience.

The current U.S. rank is a sharp change from 1960, when almost half of American health spending was out-of-pocket (figure 3.6b). Unfortunately, there are gaps in the historical data on this measure for the other countries, but at that time, a 20-percentage-point difference existed between France and the United States in terms of the out-of-pocket share of health expenditures. Today that differential is less than five percentage points. Moreover, the U.S. out-of-pocket share now is much more comparable to the other members of the G7, with Japan, Germany, Italy, and Canada all having *higher* out-of-pocket shares than does the United States.

3.6a Among the 20 largest economies in the OECD, the United States has the fourth lowest percentage of health costs paid for out-of-pocket

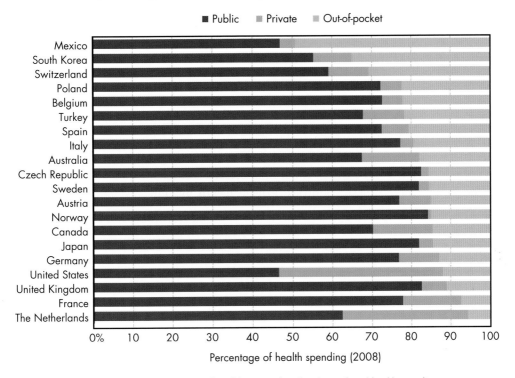

Percentage of health spending (2008)

Note: Countries are listed (top to bottom) in order of their out-of-pocket share of total health spending.

3.6b The United States in the past relied far more on out-of-pocket spending compared with its competitors, but that is less true currently

Out-of-pocket spending as a percentage of NHE

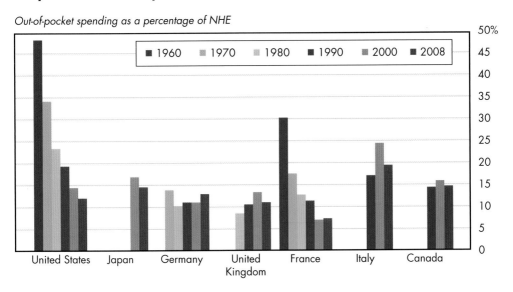

The elderly and disabled constitute 25 percent of Medicaid enrollees but more than 75 percent of Medicaid spending.

The average Medicaid beneficiary is much younger than those who are covered by Medicare. Children account for almost half of Medicaid enrollees, with non-elderly, non-disabled adults (predominantly young parents) accounting for an additional 25 percent (figure 3.7a).

Although the elderly and disabled make up approximately 25 percent of beneficiaries, they account for more than 75 percent of all expenditures for medical services. In contrast with Medicare, which was designed to be an acute-care insurance program, Medicaid spending is far more heavily tilted toward long-term care, particularly nursing home care. Approximately 30 percent of Medicaid spending is for long-term care services.

Medicaid accounts for more than 40 percent of all nursing home spending in the United States, and almost 40 percent of home health services (figure 3.7b). Other personal health care includes spending for Medicaid home- and community-based waivers, care provided in residential care facilities, ambulance services, school health, and worksite health care, so it too predominantly consists of long-term care services.

Medicaid enrollees account for fewer than 20 percent of the population, which is similar to the share of hospital spending financed by Medicaid. However, Medicaid covers fewer than 10 percent of all spending on care provided by physicians, dentists, and other health professionals, and prescription drugs.

This largely is a reflection of low Medicaid fees. For example, on average, physician fees under Medicaid are 28 percent lower than Medicare fees, but this varies enormously by state. Some states have physician fees that are 63 percent below Medicare on average, whereas in other states, average Medicaid fees exceed Medicare's by more than 40 percent. In addition, by federal law, state Medicaid programs are given a sizable discount on prescription drug prices in the form of mandatory rebates that must be paid to states by pharmaceutical manufacturers.

Under health reform, this is supposed to change. The new law requires states to raise Medicaid provider payment rates to Medicare levels in 2013 and 2014 for primary care services of pediatricians, internists and general and family practitioners. States subsequently can roll back these fee increases, but this might be politically difficult. Medicare fees for primary care also will be increased 10 percent between 2011 and 2015.

3.7a The elderly and disabled constitute 25 percent of Medicaid enrollees but more than 75 percent of Medicaid spending

Percentage of total (2007)

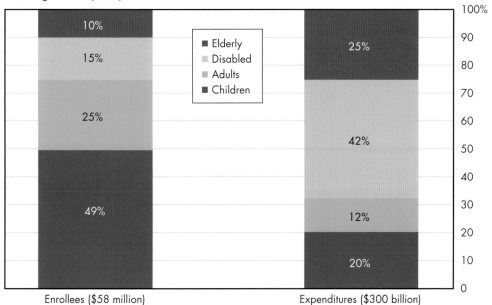

Enrollees ($58 million)   Expenditures ($300 billion)

3.7b Medicaid covers approximately 40 percent of the nation's long-term care spending but a much smaller share of acute-care spending

Percentage of PHCE paid by Medicaid (2010)

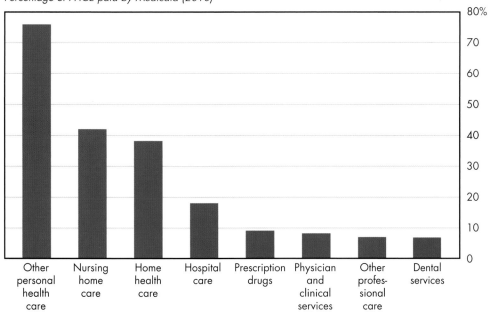

Beneficiaries directly pay less than 15 percent of Medicare costs, but Medicare also covers less than half of all their health spending.

Recall that Medicare is the nation's single largest program financing medical care in the United States, with more than one-half trillion dollars in spending in 2009 (figure 3.8a). Most people think of Medicare as being supported primarily through payroll taxes (1.45 percent each, for employers and employees). Currently, however, *a larger share of Medicare is paid with federal general revenues than from payroll contributions.* The payroll taxes are used exclusively to finance Medicare Part A, which covers inpatient hospital stays, limited skilled nursing facility care, home health, and hospice.

By law, beneficiary premiums cover 25 percent of the costs of Part B, which covers physician care, hospital outpatient services, home health care, durable medical equipment, laboratory, ambulance and related services. The lion's share of remaining expenses is covered from general fund revenue. Part D covers prescription drugs. Beneficiary premiums cover only 10 percent of its costs, with more than 75 percent paid by the federal general fund (the remainder is from state government transfers). Thus, for the Medicare program as a whole, less than one dollar in eight is financed from premium payments made by beneficiaries. The remainder is tax-financed.

Despite its size, Medicare covers less than half of annual medical and long-term care costs for the average beneficiary (figure 3.8b, left bar). However, from a beneficiary perspective, some of those Medicare payments are financed by beneficiary-paid premiums; the same is true for private third-party coverage. Yet even from this perspective, beneficiaries pay only approximately 25 percent of annual costs, including amounts paid out-of-pocket for medical services and the amounts that beneficiaries pay in voluntary premiums for Parts B and D and supplemental insurance ("Medigap" policies and employer-sponsored health plans).

The remaining expenses are covered by third-party payers. These expenses include Medicaid coverage for so-called "dual eligibles" (whose spending is more than double that of other beneficiaries), private supplemental Medigap policies (held by 25 percent of enrollees), and group health coverage for retirees (held by almost 30 percent of beneficiaries).

3.8a Less than 12 percent of Medicare spending is financed through beneficiary premiums, but this varies greatly by component

Percentage of Medicare income (2009)

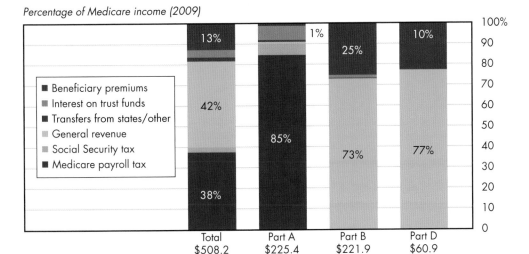

Legend:
- Beneficiary premiums
- Interest on trust funds
- Transfers from states/other
- General revenue
- Social Security tax
- Medicare payroll tax

	Total $508.2	Part A $225.4	Part B $221.9	Part D $60.9

Note: Part A covers inpatient hospital stays, limited skilled nursing facility care, home health, and hospice. Part B covers physician care, hospital outpatient services, home health care, durable medical equipment, laboratory, ambulance, and related services. Part D covers prescription drugs.

3.8b Medicare pays for less than half of health spending by Medicare beneficiaries; approximately 25 percent is paid for by beneficiaries

Percentage of total medical and long-term costs (2005)

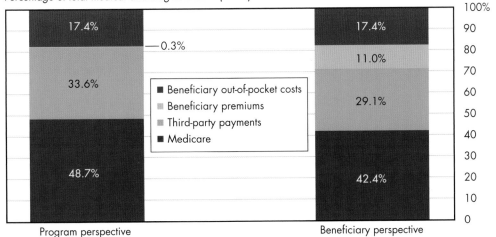

Legend:
- Beneficiary out-of-pocket costs
- Beneficiary premiums
- Third-party payments
- Medicare

Program perspective — Beneficiary perspective

Note: The program perspective counts all Medicare spending under Medicare and all bills paid through public and private third-party payers under third-party payments. Administrative costs related to Medicare and other third-party payers are included as part of beneficiary premiums. The beneficiary perspective includes the full amount of premiums paid to Medicare and third parties under beneficiary premiums and deducts these amounts from Medicare and third party payers. Beneficiary premiums do not appear in the program perspective because they are included as part of third-party and Medicare payments (spending).

From 30 to 65 percent of all health spending by individuals who are uninsured all year is subsidized by taxpayers or private payers.

In absolute dollars, per capita out-of-pocket health spending is similar among those uninsured all year, those uninsured part-year, and those with year-round private health insurance coverage (figure 3.9a). This might seem counterintuitive, but it reflects the fact that the typical individual with private coverage has a higher income and hence willingness-to-pay for medical goods and services. Among children (where the age distribution is quite similar), total spending is approximately 80 percent higher among those with private coverage compared with individuals uninsured the entire year.

In figures 3.9a and 3.9b, *implicitly subsidized* care represents the cost of care indirectly subsidized by hospitals, physicians, and other providers. *Other public care* includes payments by the Veterans Health Administration (VHA), CHAMPUS-TRICARE (for civilian dependents of military personnel), workers' compensation, and other federal, state, and local public programs that pay directly for care (for example, maternal and child health). Thus, it combines subsidized care to individuals lacking the means to pay, with care to which one might be entitled (for example, work injury). Likewise, *other private* includes unsubsidized care (for example, payments from accident, automobile, and indemnity policies), and care that likely is subsidized, such as private philanthropy and cash payments by non-family members.

The per capita amount of non-Medicaid subsidized care is highest among those uninsured all year, followed by the part-year uninsured and the privately insured. Because the part-year uninsured lack coverage for approximately six months, their annual spending includes some care paid through public and private health plans. If Medicaid is included as a form of subsidized care, those who are uninsured part of a year actually receive more subsidized services than do those without coverage the entire year.

Viewing the same data in terms of shares of spending provides a different result. For the all-year uninsured, at least 30 percent but no more than 65 percent of spending is subsidized (figure 3.9b). In contrast, such sources pay for only approximately 10 to 13 percent of annual spending for the part-year uninsured. However, if Medicaid were counted as subsidized care, this would add almost 30 percentage points to the total for this group.

3.9a Out-of-pocket spending is similar among the uninsured and privately insured, but the former receive much more subsidized care

Estimated per capita PHCE (2008)

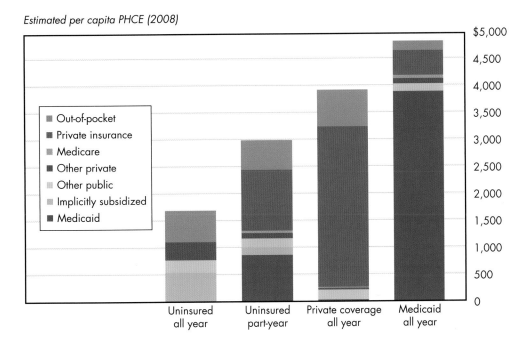

3.9b Almost 65 percent of health expenditures for people uninsured all year is subsidized through taxes or private charity

Estimated per capita PHCE (2008)

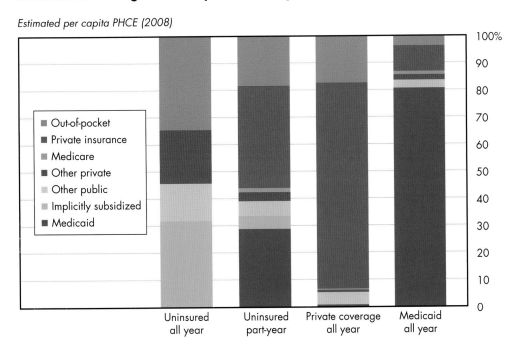

CHAPTER 4

The Employer Role in U.S. Health Care

A growing share of worker compensation is paid in the form of wage and salary supplements, including social insurance—such as Medicare—and private health insurance.

Over the past 60 years, the amount of employee compensation for wage and salary supplements has more than quadrupled (figure 4.1a). The average worker now receives approximately 23 cents in such employer-paid supplements for every dollar of wages and salaries. This growth has been variable, including brief periods in which wages and salaries grew faster than supplements. A relatively small amount of this increase relates to government-required health-related supplements—including payroll taxes for Medicare and workers' compensation (which pays for job-related injuries or illness).

The employer share of employer-sponsored insurance (ESI) has been an important factor in driving growth in supplement payments. Even so, increases in non-health fringe benefits such as retirement contributions also have had an important role in this upward trend. In both cases, tax policy has encouraged such growth because fringe benefits are excludable from federal, state, and local income taxes and payroll taxes. For the highest income workers who in some states face marginal tax rates of 50 percent, the tax exclusion permits employers to provide two dollars in pre-tax fringe benefits for every dollar that otherwise would be paid as wages or salaries.

ESI includes all types of plans, including fee-for-service indemnity plans, and managed care plans such as preferred provider organizations (PPOs) and health maintenance organizations (HMOs). Managed care plans use various cost control mechanisms (for example, pre-authorization of care and financial incentives for patients to use preferred provider networks). However, indemnity plans also have begun to use some of the same tools.

In general, over these 60 years, health-related supplements have grown as a fraction of all employer-provided supplements (figure 4.1b). This implies that health-related supplements have generally grown faster than other fringe benefits. For a typical worker, employer premium payments now constitute 36 percent of all fringe benefits, with Medicare and workers' compensation absorbing another 5 and 6 percent, respectively. All other fringe benefits have declined from almost 80 percent of the total just after World War II to slightly more than half today.

4.1a Over 60 years, both health and non-health supplements to wages and salaries have grown dramatically relative to worker pay

Employer contributions per dollar of wages and salaries (cents)

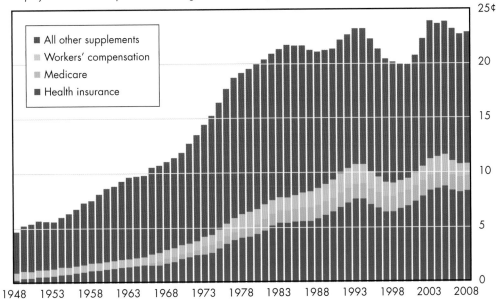

4.1b Health-related employer contributions have absorbed a growing share of supplements, currently accounting for almost half the total

Percentage of all employer-paid supplements to wages and salaries

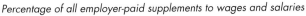

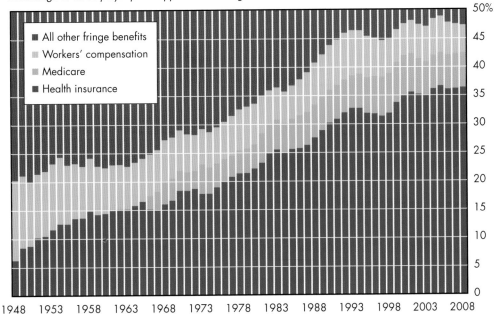

The tax subsidy for employer-provided health insurance increases with income; high-paid workers get a larger subsidy—both in dollar terms and in the fraction of premiums subsidized—than do low-paid workers.

The employer tax exclusion for health benefits has been characterized as an upside-down subsidy. Our generally progressive tax system results in higher marginal tax rates for high-income workers compared with rates for low-income workers. Consequently, both the dollar value of the tax subsidy and the percentage of the premium that is implicitly subsidized by the federal government are larger for higher-paid workers compared with that for lower-paid workers (figure 4.2a).

For example, a company CEO earning $300,000 would receive a subsidy of approximately $4,800, which amounts to a discount of 37 percent on the premiums required for health insurance. A janitor earning the minimum wage in that same company would get a subsidy equal to less than $500—enough to cover only 7 percent of health plan premiums.

Even though the employer appears to be paying most or all of the premiums for employer-provided health benefits, empirical studies have demonstrated that the cost of such benefits actually is paid by workers in the form of lower wages or salaries. Thus, another way to view the subsidy is to consider it relative to the overall share of family income required to pay for health insurance coverage (inclusive of the employer share).

When calculated as a share of family income, the subsidy generally declines with income (figure 4.2b). This makes it appear less regressive. However, the share of family income required for health insurance rises sharply for workers at the lowest end of the income distribution. The tax subsidy does not grow nearly as fast. Thus, even with the tax subsidy, the net share of income (that is, after deducting the subsidy) required for health insurance declines with income.

Under the newly enacted health reform plan, the share of family income required to pay the family's share of premiums will be capped at 2 to 9.5 percent of income. However, these caps apply only to the family share of premiums, *not* to the employer-paid portion. Thus, for the most part, the hidden inequities just noted will persist for those who continue to rely on employer-based coverage.

4.2a Higher-income families get a substantially higher subsidy from the employer tax exclusion compared with the subsidy for low-income families

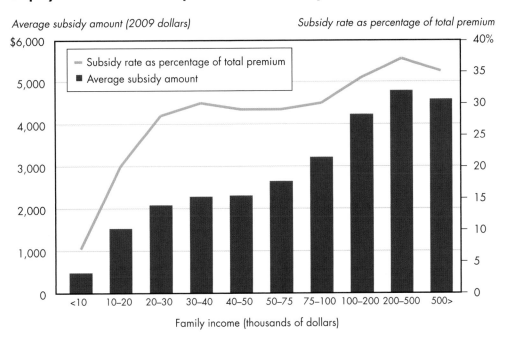

Average subsidy amount (2009 dollars)   *Subsidy rate as percentage of total premium*

4.2b The share of income needed for health insurance rises sharply as income declines; the tax exclusion mitigates this only slightly

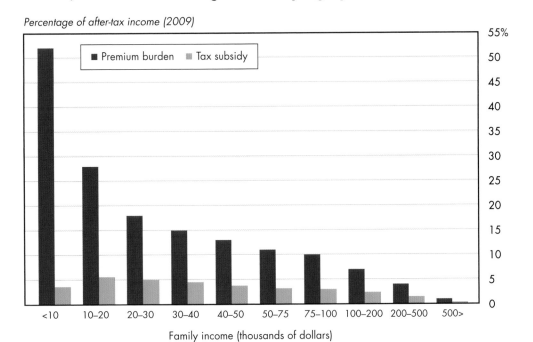

Percentage of after-tax income (2009)

For a variety of reasons, workers in small firms, health care, and retail trade are least likely to be offered health coverage at work.

Fewer than half of firms that have 25 or fewer employees even offer health insurance coverage. In contrast, virtually all firms that have 1,000 or more workers offer such benefits (figure 4.3a). Thus, if a worker gets employer-sponsored health benefits depends heavily on the number of workers at a given firm.

In general, employer-provided health benefits are not as attractive to small-firm workers compared with those who work in large firms. Premiums generally are higher for the same amount of coverage because the administrative load is higher. Some costs, such as general administration, do not vary much by firm size, resulting in economies of scale in health insurance for firms that have more workers to share the administrative cost. With fewer workers among whom such costs can be spread, the per-person cost is higher in small firms. To reflect greater volatility in expected claims for small firms relative to large firms, insurers also must include a higher risk premium.

In a voluntary market, insurers know from experience that the small firms have sicker employees than do large firms. That is, small firms will know the individual health needs of their employees much better than large firms do. Moreover, they have far fewer plan members among whom to spread the cost of someone who has a high-cost medical condition. In a market where premiums are higher for the smallest firms, the companies that have the greatest individual employee health needs will be the most motivated to search for coverage. This amplifies the tendency for insurers to charge small firms higher premiums to reflect the generally poorer health among workers in small firms seeking coverage.

However, when an employer has made the decision to offer health coverage, firm-size differences are attenuated considerably. In fact, the percentage of workers eligible for the health plan actually is slightly higher among small firms relative to larger firms, although the percentage of workers who accept whatever health coverage offered is only slightly less.

The variation in the percentage of firms offering health insurance by industry is somewhat smaller than by firm size, with health care and retail trade having the lowest offer rates, while transportation, communications, utilities, wholesale trade, and manufacturing have the highest (figure 4.3b). The higher concentration of small firms in health care and retail trade contributes to these differences.

4.3a Fewer than 65 percent of small firms offer health plans, but the share of workers eligible and participating in such plans is similar to that in large firms

■ 3–24 workers   ■ 25–49 workers   ■ 50–999 workers   ■ 1,000 or more workers

Percentage (2010)

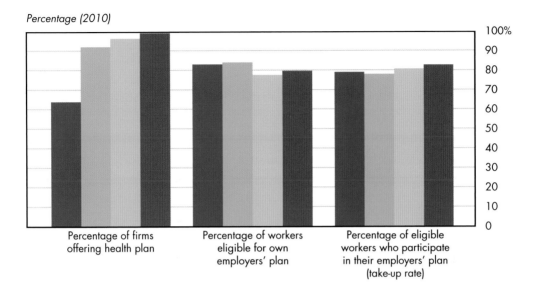

| Percentage of firms offering health plan | Percentage of workers eligible for own employers' plan | Percentage of eligible workers who participate in their employers' plan (take-up rate) |

4.3b Among all industries, health care and retail trade have the lowest rates of offering health plans, reflecting their large number of small firms

■ Transportation/communications/utilities   ■ Wholesale
■ Manufacturing   ■ Retail   ■ Health care

Percentage (2010)

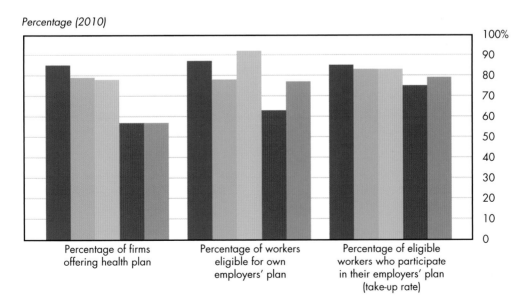

| Percentage of firms offering health plan | Percentage of workers eligible for own employers' plan | Percentage of eligible workers who participate in their employers' plan (take-up rate) |

Despite relatively stable health insurance offer rates, there has been a secular decline in employer-based health coverage across nearly all firm-size categories.

Health insurance offer rates have been remarkably stable over the past decade (figure 4.4a). Ignoring year-to-year variation, the offer rate for firms with fewer than 10 employees has consistently been less than 60 percent. It is not clear whether the recent uptick in offer rates for the smallest firms is an anomaly or a reversal of recent trends.

Even though offer rates have been relatively stable over the past decade, the percentage of workers who have employer-based coverage has been eroding rather steadily over the past two decades. Figure 4.4b provides a consistently measured picture of this decline since 1999, and other data confirm similar trends occurring throughout the 1990s. This decline reflects in part trends displayed in figure 4.1a. With health benefit costs rising much faster than wages and salaries, more employees declined offered coverage. Because employers generally contribute a higher share of the premium for an employee's own coverage than for dependent/spouse coverage, this refusal rate tends to be higher for dependent coverage. However, it also can be attributed to a rather steady expansion of public coverage since the mid-1980s—notably Medicaid and the State Children's Health Insurance Plan (SCHIP).

In recent years, this erosion in coverage has been largest among the smallest and mid-sized firms. Because small firms face higher premiums for the equivalent level of coverage, any given percentage increase in medical costs will produce a higher absolute dollar impact relative to larger firms. As well, large firms enjoy the stability that comes with sizable health plan memberships. That is, if medical trends are increasing by 10 percent, the largest firms will tend to experience rate increases in a comparable range. In contrast, small employers may face annual rate increases that are several multiples of the general trend.

In the small-group market, there also is considerably more "churning" as such employers seek a better deal on health insurance coverage. This means that firms that switch face additional costs for broker commissions and underwriting that are avoided by firms opting not to switch. The vast majority of large employers are self-insured, so generally the principal savings that can be attained by switching carriers to administer such plans relate to administrative costs that are not terribly large in the first place. Consequently, the incentive to change carriers is much lower.

4.4a **The percentage of the smallest firms offering health benefits has been less than 60 percent for more than a decade**

Percentage of employers offering health insurance benefits

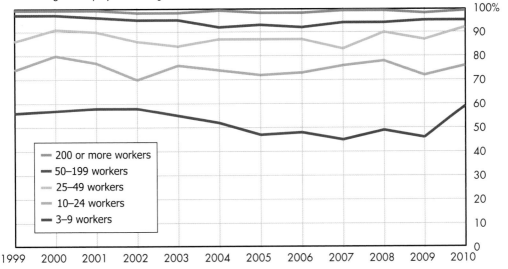

Legend:
- 200 or more workers
- 50–199 workers
- 25–49 workers
- 10–24 workers
- 3–9 workers

4.4b **Over the past decade, the percentage of employees in health benefit plans has declined in almost all firm-size categories**

Percentage of workers in own employer's health plan

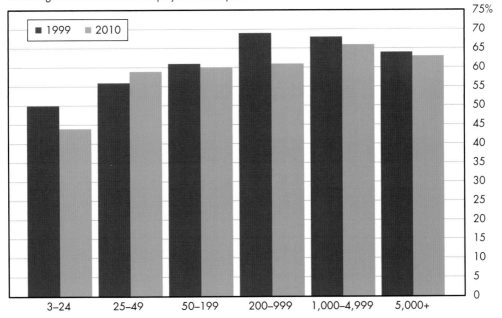

■ 1999 ■ 2010

Firm size (number of employees)

CHAPTER 5

Government Health Expenditures, Taxes, and Deficits

Real government expenditures for health rose 30-fold during the past 50 years—or 17-fold in per capita terms. Between 1966 and 2007, the entire increase in government's share of GDP was attributable to growth in tax-financed health care.

The rise in government-funded health care has been extraordinary by any measure. In terms of constant purchasing power for everyday goods, tax-financed health care has increased 30-fold just since 1960 (figure 5.1a). This includes all federal, state, and local government spending for health care, such as public health, direct delivery of health services, public health insurance, and investments in medical R&D and facilities construction. However, real federal spending on health care grew far faster than tax-paid health care overall. This reflects a substantial shift in the relative roles of federal government vis-à-vis state and local governments in financing (and regulating) health care.

In per capita terms, the overall increase was 17-fold. This does *not* mean that real health *output* funded by taxpayers rose 17-fold in 50 years. The inflation adjustment used for all series in figure 5.1a is based on the GDP price deflator rather than a medical price deflator. Thus, the increase represents how much more real output in the general economy was foregone to bankroll the tax-financed share of U.S. health spending. This rapid increase in government health spending was approximately five times as large as the increase in overall government spending during the same time.

Recall from chapter 1 that real GDP also grew enormously during this period. As a share of GDP, publicly-financed health spending in 2007 (the most recent "normal" year) was five times as large as it was in 1965 (figure 5.1b). In contrast, the share of the economy attributable to government spending on all other activities unrelated to health was almost identical in these two years. In summary, the entire amount of the increase in the size of government between those years was accounted for by rising public expenditures on health care.

Except for a brief downward turn during the latter half of the 1990s, the tax-financed health share of the economy has risen without exception each year since 1929.

5.1a Real government spending on health has increased 30-fold in the past 50 years; the increase is 17-fold in per capita terms

Indexes of real government spending on health using chained GDP deflator: 1960=100

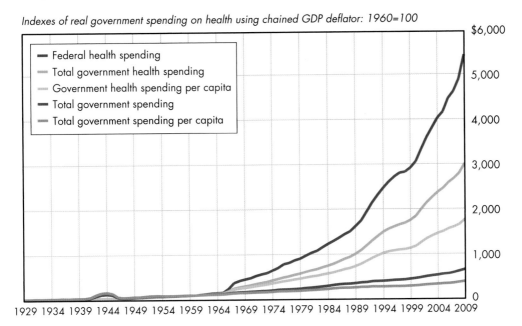

5.1b Between 1966 and 2007, all of the increase in the size of government was attributable to growth in tax-financed health care

Government spending as a percentage of GDP

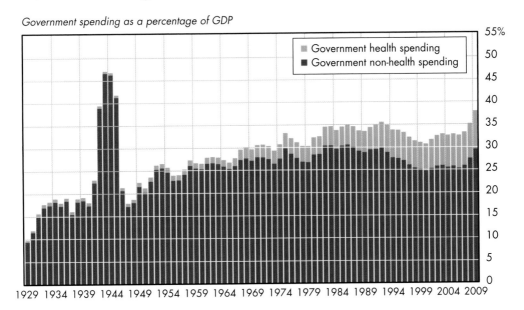

Note: Data include debt service, but the entire amount appears under non-health spending. If allocated by shares of spending, this would increase government health spending and reduce non-health spending.

Tax-financed health expenditures have risen much faster than government spending on defense, income support, and education.

Tax-financed health expenditures over the past 50 years have grown faster than any other major functional area of government spending, including defense, income support, and education. Since 1959, the increase in government health spending as a percentage of GDP more than exceeded the decline in defense spending's share of the economy through 2008 (figure 5.2a).

Along with defense, transportation funding declined as a share of GDP relative to 1959 levels. In the aftermath of the Great Society initiatives in the 1960s, it should not be too surprising that both income support and education grew as a percent of GDP between 1959 and 1989, but both also subsequently had declined by 2008. Even interest payments on the national debt followed a similar path (although this will change considerably in the decades going forward).

Of the seven largest functional areas of federal, state, and local budgets, the only one (other than health care) that grew in the 30 years from 1959 to 1989 and the almost-30 years from 1989 to 2008 was spending for public order and safety. However, the increase in GDP share attributable to government-paid health care during this period was almost five times as large as the increase for public order and safety.

This highlights the reason why health care has become such an intense focus of attention at all levels of government in recent years. In almost every state, health care has become either the largest or the fastest-growing component of public spending, making it increasingly difficult to finance other priorities such as education or criminal justice.

The federal share of government-paid health spending has generally risen during this period, as has the role played by intergovernmental transfers (IGTs) of funds from the federal government to state and local governments (figure 5.2b). These include federal matching funds provided under Medicaid (ranging from a minimum of 50 percent in the wealthiest states such as New York and Massachusetts to more than 80 percent in Mississippi), federal categorical grants for health care, and federal block grants for health care, such as maternal and child health services. If IGTs are counted on the federal side of the ledger, the federal share of health spending is now approaching 75 percent.

5.2a Government health spending has been the fastest growing major component of government budgets for the past 50 years

Percentage of GDP

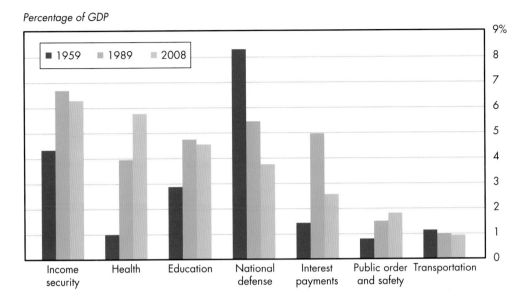

Note: This chart shows the seven largest functional areas of federal, state, and local budgets in 2008, displayed (left to right) by percent of GDP in 2008.

5.2b Taking into account federal transfers to states for health, the federal share of government health spending exceeds 70 percent

Federal percentage of total government health expenditures

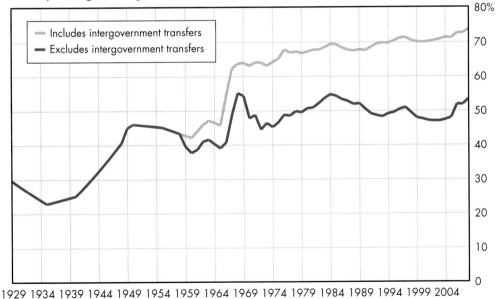

Tax-financed health expenditures explain little of the difference between the United States and its major competitors in public sector spending as a percentage of GDP.

The government share of GDP is lower in the United States than in any other country in the G7 except Japan (figure 5.3a). However, the share of GDP attributable to tax-financed health care is higher in the United States than in all other G7 nations except Germany and France. Currently, the difference is not large but is likely to grow because of the new U.S. health reform law. Even for Germany and France, the lion's share of the large difference in government spending relative to GDP relative to the United States is accounted for by factors unrelated to public spending on health care.

Figure 5.3b compares in a different way the public role in health spending between countries. The United States outpaces all of its G7 competitors in terms of the fraction of total government spending that is devoted to health care (this would be true even if the pool of major competitors is extended to include China and Russia). Again, this relatively small difference is likely to increase if the health reform law is implemented over several years.

Despite this, the overall fraction of total health spending that is financed by government is far lower in the United States—by 25 to 35 percentage points—than in any of the other G7 nations. Recall from figure 3.6a that except for a handful of countries, private health insurance in the United States more than fills this "gap" in spending, resulting in out-of-pocket spending as a lower share of U.S. health spending than in almost any other OECD country. Thus, the main difference between the United States and its competitors is not in terms of the fraction of spending that is financed through third parties, but simply the extent to which the United States relies on public insurance rather than private insurance.

5.3a The U.S. share of GDP devoted to tax-financed health spending is comparable to that of its G7 competitors.

Percentage of GDP (2007)

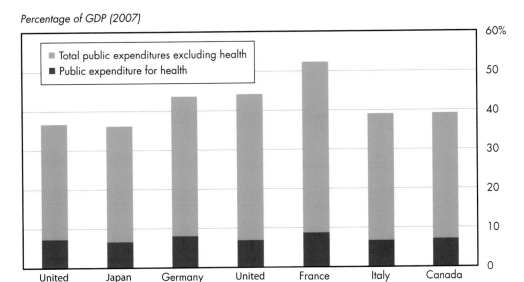

- Total public expenditures excluding health
- Public expenditure for health

G7 countries listed (left to right) by GDP in 2007

5.3b In the G7, the United States has the highest share of government spending devoted to health but the lowest public share of total health spending

Percentage (2007)

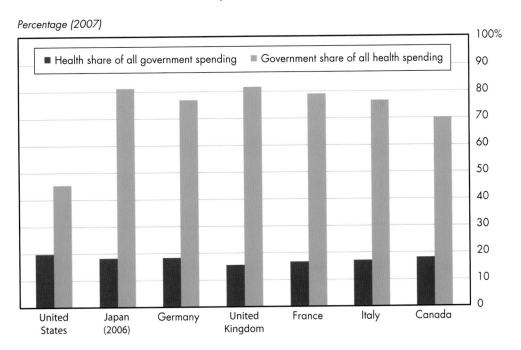

- Health share of all government spending
- Government share of all health spending

The public sector pays 80 percent of health costs for people who have poor health.

Approximately 80 percent of health spending by people who have the worst health is tax-financed. This is true whether health status is measured in terms of physical health or mental health. The numbers shown in figure 5.4 are based on self-reported health status, in which individuals categorize their health as *Excellent, Very Good, Good, Fair,* or *Poor.* Self-reported health status has been shown to be a good proxy for mental and physical health, using "objective" measures such as the ability to perform activities of daily living (eating, bathing, and so forth).

As shown in figure 5.4, the share of health spending paid by the government rises steadily as health status worsens. This suggests at least some degree of "target efficiency" in terms of focusing public spending on those most in need of medical care. Yet even among those in excellent health, more than 40 percent of health spending is publicly financed. This happens for two reasons. First, Medicare provides near-universal coverage for the elderly, some of whom report excellent health. Although Medicare covers less than half the health spending for a typical person age 65 or older, an important reason for this low percentage is that Medicare was not designed to cover long-term nursing care costs. Among the elderly who have excellent health, nursing home expenses would be minimal; hence, Medicare would finance a higher share of their total annual spending. The second important contributor to this result is that the public spending amounts include tax expenditures such as the subsidy for employer-based health benefits. Given the large fraction of the population who have employer-provided health insurance, this particular subsidy is largely independent of health status. It should not be surprising that many in excellent health benefit from it.

Those who live in families below the poverty level tend to have worse health than those with higher incomes. Nevertheless, many such individuals are in excellent health. However, to the degree that the tax exclusion subsidizes both a higher dollar amount and share of health spending for those who have high incomes and who are in excellent health, the targeting efficiency of taxpayer-financed health spending might be questioned.

5.4 The share of health spending covered by government increases as physical or mental health status declines

Percentage of personal health spending paid by government (2007)

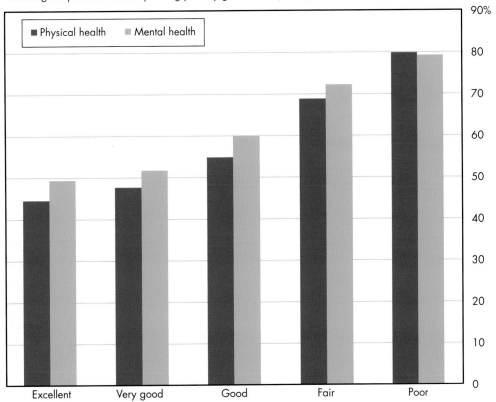

Self-reported health status, 2002

Taxpayers finance almost half of health spending for the highest-income families.

Although more than 80 percent of health spending among those with incomes below poverty is tax-financed, so too is almost half of the spending for families with incomes at four or more times the poverty level (figure 5.5a). As with health status, there is some evidence of target efficiency in terms of greater reliance on public financing for health expenses as family income declines.

Despite major expansions of Medicaid in recent decades, fewer than half of those with incomes below poverty are enrolled in Medicaid or the State Children's Health Insurance Program (SCHIP). Medicaid covers much more than half of health spending for the poor. Many states have "spend-down" programs that permit those with high medical expenses to deduct those from family income for purposes of determining Medicaid eligibility. Consequently, Medicaid covers nearly two-thirds of nursing home patients. Almost 10 percent of the poor are covered by Medicare, which further boosts the share of spending covered by taxpayers. Finally, it was shown previously that a high fraction of health spending among those uninsured all year is uncompensated care—much of which is indirectly paid through taxpayers.

As for the tax exclusion, in a technical sense, individuals at the highest income level pay for themselves. That is, assuming that every dollar of tax expenditures must be offset by a dollar of tax revenue obtained elsewhere, the gross amount of taxes paid by the highest income households to make up this revenue difference will exceed the value of the tax benefit provided by the exclusion. However, especially in the light of the deadweight losses imposed by various forms of taxation, it would be far more efficient to simply let such households pay for their own health benefits directly rather than subsidize these through the tax system. The Office of Management and Budget (OMB) estimates the amount to be at least 25 cents per dollar of taxes collected, but it could be anywhere from 30 cents to more than one dollar, according to other estimates.

The formula used to determine the federal funding share of Medicaid and the Children's Health Insurance Program (CHIP) takes into account per capita income. Even so, there are wide state-level disparities in Medicaid/CHIP funding per poor person, partly due to higher federal spending per poor person in some of the wealthiest states (figure 5.5b).

5.5a Although the public share of health expenses increases as income declines, almost half of spending for families above 400 percent of poverty is tax-financed

Percentage of personal health spending paid by the government (2002)

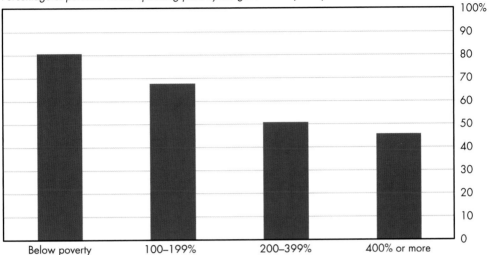

Family income as a percentage of federal poverty level

5.5b Federal Medicaid and CHIP spending per poor person varies widely by state; the amount does not decline as state income rises

Medicaid and CHIP spending per poor person (2008)

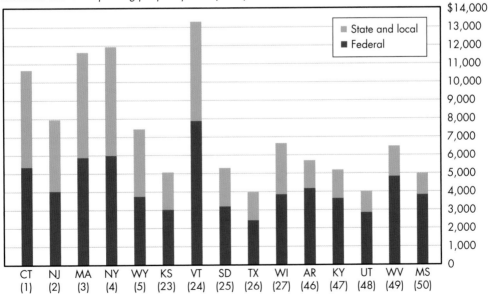

States ranked by size of 2008 per capita income

Almost all Medicare beneficiaries pay less in payroll taxes than the dollar amount of benefits they receive from the program.

Most Medicare beneficiaries—even those who have high incomes—do not pay for themselves. The difference between the dollar value of lifetime benefits paid and the dollar amount of lifetime payroll taxes is generally measured in tens of thousands of dollars per Medicare beneficiary, as shown in figure 5.6. These calculations use inflation-adjusted dollars and a reasonable discount rate to equalize future dollars with today's dollars.

For most income groups, the net lifetime benefits of Medicare have increased over time. This reflects that growth in per capita medical spending has outpaced the rate of increases in wages and salaries over time. It also is a function of increases in life expectancy, which have had a far larger impact on lifetime medical expenses financed by Medicare than on the amount of lifetime payroll taxes paid into Medicare. In figure 5.6, low-income individuals are represented by those whose average lifetime earnings are $5,000 annually, while high-income individuals are assumed to have average annual lifetime earnings of $140,000; these individuals comprise a small fraction of Medicare beneficiaries.

For this highest-income group, net lifetime benefits no longer kept increasing for those who became eligible for Medicare in 1995. This reflects the elimination of the cap on earnings to which the 2.9 percent Medicare payroll tax originally applied. Clearly, for those who have extremely high incomes, for example, averaging $300,000 per year, lifetime Medicare benefits might well be negative, but this situation affects a minuscule fraction of current eligible individuals. This number surely would grow under the new taxes included under health reform. These are restricted to high-income households and include increasing the payroll tax deduction by 0.9 percentage points and imposing, for the first time, a 3.8 percent tax on investment income.

Regardless of whether their net Medicare benefits are positive or negative, it would be far more efficient, as noted for the tax exclusion, for high-income individuals to finance their own Medicare benefits directly than to provide benefits because they already had paid for them through various taxes.

5.6 Lifetime Medicare benefits grew fastest for low-income workers; even for high-income workers, net lifetime benefits exceed $30,000

Net lifetime Medicare benefits (own benefits minus own taxes paid), 2010 dollars in thousands

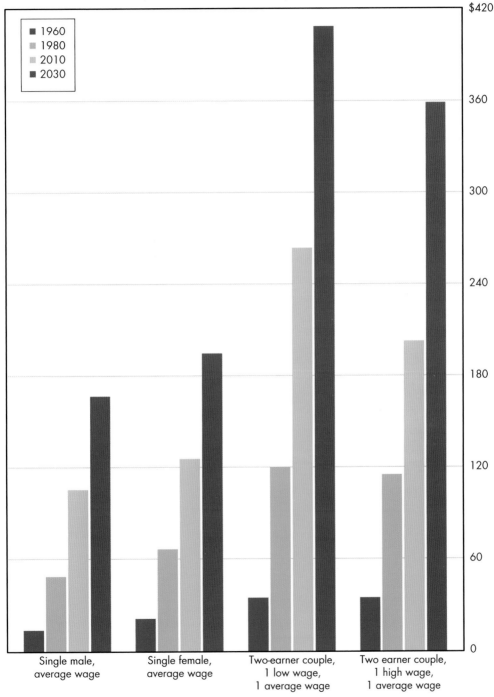

The Medicaid share of state health spending varies by a factor of three across states.

Medicaid spending now is the largest single component of state government expenditures. With the exception of Arizona, states that have the largest Medicaid programs relative to all other spending are concentrated in the eastern half of the United States, predominantly in the northeastern region (figure 5.7a).

These numbers are for 2007 because it might be more representative of relative differences across states than data from more recent years. The federal government now finances almost 60 percent of Medicaid and SCHIP costs. The federal share of overall spending for these programs ranges from a high of 76.3 percent in Mississippi to 50 percent in 12 states whose high per capita income precludes their qualifying for a higher federal matching rate. The numbers on the map are derived by counting all Medicaid/SCHIP spending (including federal funds), and dividing this amount by the total amount of consolidated state expenditures (which also include federal funds). Using this measure, the Medicaid share of total spending averages approximately 21 percent nationally but varies by a factor of three across states (figure 5.7b). In the five states that have the largest shares, Medicaid spending represents approximately 30 cents of every dollar spent. Conversely, in states with the lowest shares, Medicaid spending is only approximately 10 cents on the dollar.

When federal Medicaid spending is excluded, a somewhat different view emerges. The national Medicaid share of state spending is approximately 13 percent, but by this metric, there is a four-fold difference across the states (figure 5.7c). However, although the rankings change a bit, the states included in the top and bottom five are identical to the states facing the highest and lowest burdens when federal funds are included.

5.7a FY2007 Medicaid expenditures as a percentage of total state government expenditures are highest in the Northeast

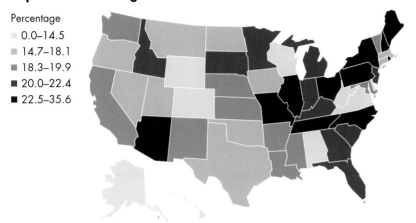

Percentage
- 0.0–14.5
- 14.7–18.1
- 18.3–19.9
- 20.0–22.4
- 22.5–35.6

5.7b The Medicaid share of state spending varies by a factor of three across states

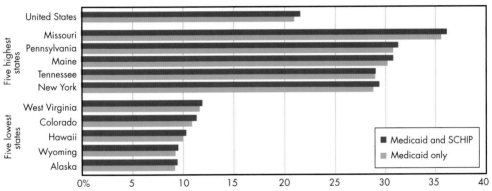

Five highest states: Missouri, Pennsylvania, Maine, Tennessee, New York

Five lowest states: West Virginia, Colorado, Hawaii, Wyoming, Alaska

■ Medicaid and SCHIP
■ Medicaid only

Medicaid percentage of total state/local government expenditures, including federal funds (2007)

5.7c If federal funds are excluded, the Medicaid share of state expenditures is much smaller, but this share varies by a factor of four

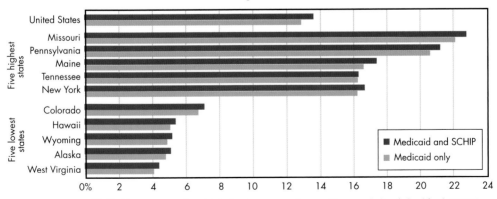

Five highest states: Missouri, Pennsylvania, Maine, Tennessee, New York

Five lowest states: Colorado, Hawaii, Wyoming, Alaska, West Virginia

■ Medicaid and SCHIP
■ Medicaid only

Medicaid percentage of total state/local government expenditures, excluding federal funds (2007)

CHAPTER 6

Health Services and the Family Budget

Health care is currently the second largest component of personal consumption. Since 1929, the share going to health care has risen faster than any other major category of personal consumption.

Health care now ranks second in importance in the share of personal consumption spending devoted to it (figure 6.1a). At current rates of change in these shares, health care will overtake housing within five years to become the single largest category of consumption.

Hospitals and nursing homes account for 40 percent of this health care total, but health consumption also includes payments for medical services and products (for example, pharmaceuticals) and the cost of insurance administration (right side of figure 6.1a). Because this category is intended to measure total consumption of health care goods and services, the total includes both out-of-pocket spending and expenditures covered through public or private health insurance.

The extraordinary productivity of the American economy over the past 80 years has made the necessities of life far more affordable for the typical family. Before the Great Depression, Americans devoted approximately 65 percent of personal consumption spending solely to food, clothing, and shelter (figure 6.1b). By 2008, such necessities constituted only 40 percent of all household consumption. During the same period, health care's share almost quintupled to 20 percent of all personal consumption.

Briefly, the declining share of family spending on necessities over this period more than made up for the rising share of consumption devoted to health care. Health care is not unique in absorbing an ever-rising share of family spending since 1929, but the aggregate increase in its share is by far the largest. Just in the past 40 years, the health share has more than doubled. No other category of consumption exhibits a relative rise of comparable magnitude.

The rising share of consumption devoted to health care reflects higher incomes, more new and costly medical procedures and drugs, an aging population, and the increasing prevalence of public and private health insurance that weakens most incentives to economize on medical care.

6.1a Health care is the second largest component of personal consumption spending by families

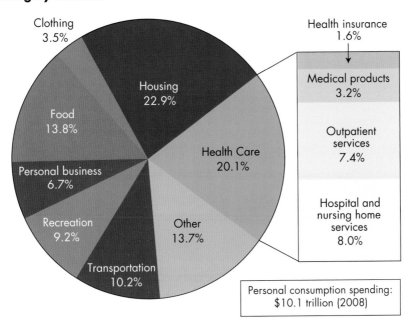

Clothing 3.5%

Housing 22.9%

Food 13.8%

Personal business 6.7%

Recreation 9.2%

Health Care 20.1%

Other 13.7%

Transportation 10.2%

Health insurance 1.6%

Medical products 3.2%

Outpatient services 7.4%

Hospital and nursing home services 8.0%

Personal consumption spending: $10.1 trillion (2008)

6.1b The health share of family spending has grown as the portion for food, clothing, and shelter has declined

Percentage of PCE

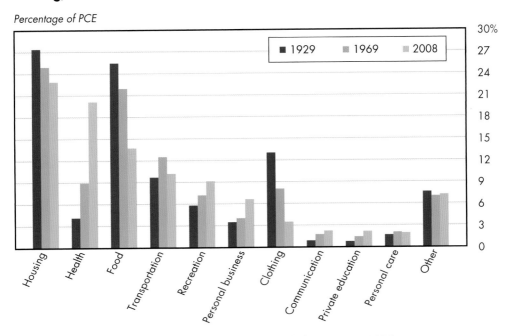

■ 1929   ■ 1969   ■ 2008

Housing, Health, Food, Transportation, Recreation, Personal business, Clothing, Communication, Private education, Personal care, Other

Major components of PCE (listed [left to right] by amount in 2008)

Because so much health spending
is hidden, direct family spending on health care
and health insurance premiums has accounted for
only 5 percent of income for 20 years.

Only 5 percent of family income pays *directly* for health care in the form of the worker share of group health premiums and Medicare Part A payroll taxes, voluntary premiums paid for non-group health insurance, Medicare Parts B and D, and out-of-pocket medical expenses not covered by insurance. Thus, even though health care now accounts for more than 20 percent of personal consumption spending, this greatly exaggerates the visibility of health expenditures in a typical family's budget.

Careful studies have demonstrated that most or all of the cost of employer-paid health premiums actually is borne by workers in the form of lower wages or other forms of fringe benefits. The same logic applies to the 1.45 percent payroll tax paid directly by employers for Medicare Part A (separate from the matching "employee share" that workers see deducted from paychecks). Many (possibly most) workers might not realize this insofar as employer-paid health costs—including workers' compensation or employer-funded on-site health clinics—generally are invisible to them.

Relative to payroll, these directly paid private employer-paid health expenses have risen steadily for decades; even so, such costs are less than $10 for every $100 of private wages and salaries (figure 6.2a). In contrast, when compared with pre-tax profits, the ratio of health spending to profits is lowest when the economy is growing and highest during economic recoveries such as in 1992. This pattern is less pronounced in the ratio of business-paid health costs to after-tax profits, which at times has been as high as $60 to $70 per $100 of profits. Yet by 2007, this ratio had declined sharply to less than $40 per $100 of profits after taxes.

6.2a In terms of direct spending on health care, households largely have been insulated from increasing health costs; businesses have not

Direct household health spending per $100 of personal income

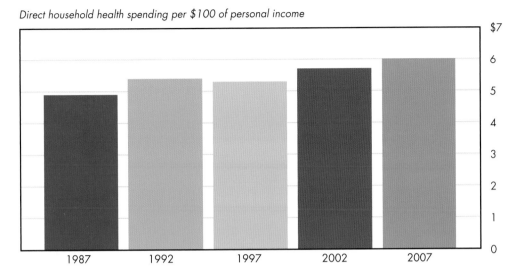

Note: In the framework of "health sponsors," household health spending includes only components that are directly paid, including the employee share of group health insurance premiums, the employee share of Medicare Part A payroll taxes, voluntary premiums paid for Medicare Parts B or D and non-group health insurance, and any out-of-pocket spending not covered by public or private insurance.

6.2b Business-paid health spending has increased modestly relative to wages and salaries

Ratio: sponsor-paid health spending to totals (dollars)

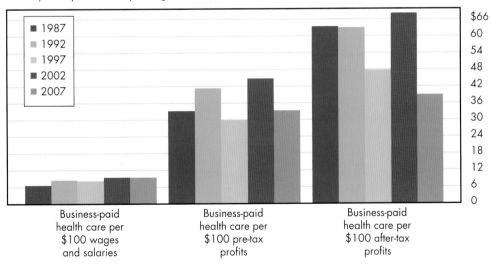

Note: In the framework of "health sponsors," business health expenditures include the private employer share of health insurance premiums for workers and dependents, Medicare Part A and workers' compensation, and industrial in-plant health services.

In the past 25 years, the relative burden of paying
for health care has grown slightly faster
among families that have the highest incomes.

Direct purchases of health care comprise only one in 16 dollars of annual household spending in families in the bottom fifth of families ranked by income (figure 6.3a). How can health care comprise 20 percent of household consumption yet only five to seven cents per dollar of spending? The explanation is simple. A huge fraction of family health consumption is financed outside the family (or at least appears to be). For example, the numbers shown in figure 6.3a exclude all tax-financed health care financed by third parties. Although households ultimately pay for such care through their own taxes, the amount of tax-financed care for any given family will almost never match that family's implicit contribution in health-related taxes. Likewise, the numbers also exclude employer-paid premiums for health insurance even though such costs generally are borne by covered workers in the form of lower wages.

Viewed from this more limited perspective, the health-spending share of family budgets is only slightly higher among the lowest-income families compared with the highest-income families (figure 6.3b). This occurs because so much health care for those at the bottom of the income distribution is financed through taxes. The hidden costs of employer-provided coverage represent a much higher share of income for low-wage workers compared with those who have high salaries or wages. Visible and hidden premium expenses amounted to almost half of family income for those who had the lowest incomes (chapter 4).

Even though other components of spending also are subsidized (for example, food assistance, housing programs), the lowest-income families devote almost half of their spending to food, clothing, and shelter. Worth noting also is that in such families, the share of annual spending for alcohol, tobacco, and recreation is only slightly smaller than the health share.

The relative financial burden of health care rose approximately 25 percent between 1984 and 2008. Growth in this burden was slightly faster among the highest-income households relative to those in the lowest-income group. A different result emerges when the hidden costs of health care are allocated to the households that actually incur them.

6.3a Direct health care expenditures constitute only one in 16 dollars spent by the lowest-income families

Percentage of total annual expenditures, families in lowest 20% income before taxes

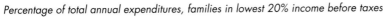

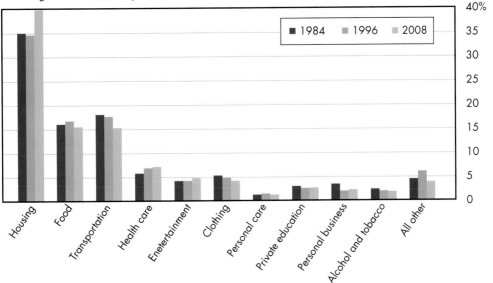

Major components of household expenditures (ranked by size in 2008)

6.3b Direct health care expenditures constitute less than one in 20 dollars spent by the highest-income families

Percentage of total annual expenditures, families in highest 20% income bracket before taxes

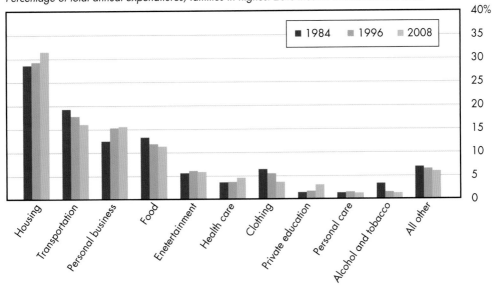

Major components of household expenditures (ranked by size in 2008)

The elderly and children rely more heavily than others do on tax-financed health coverage.

Approximately 60 percent of non-elderly adults and children rely principally on employer-provided coverage (figure 6.4a). In contrast, those 65 and older rely extensively on Medicare, although many also have supplemental private insurance through an employer or a policy that is directly purchased.

Medicaid covers much of the residual gap in coverage for children, but plays a much smaller corresponding role for non-elderly adults. Adults are twice as likely to be uninsured, even though they have somewhat higher rates of coverage for non-group, military, and Medicare compared with coverage for children.

More than nine of every 10 elderly are covered by Medicare. Medicare Part A (predominantly hospital and nursing home care) is provided at no cost to those qualifying for Social Security. Medicare Part B (predominantly physician and home health care) and Medicare Part D (prescription drugs) require the payment of premiums. These premiums amount to approximately one-fourth of the cost of Parts B and D benefits. All components also have patient cost-sharing in the form of deductibles and copayments. The percentage covered by Medicaid is almost identical for non-elderly and elderly adults, but almost all of the latter group are so-called "dual eligible." This means that they also qualify for Medicare; thus, Medicaid covers all or some of their premium payments and cost-sharing obligations. Fewer than 2 percent of the elderly are uninsured.

Public programs finance 65 percent of health spending by the elderly and 40 percent of expenditures for children (figure 6.4b). In contrast, the public program share of health spending for adults younger than age 65 is less than half that of the aged. Data for all the years shown are not available, but in 2007, Medicaid covered 75 percent of the tax-financed amount of medical care provided to children. In contrast, for the elderly, Medicare financed 75 percent of the public spending for health care.

Taking into account the hidden tax expenditures discussed previously, public programs finance more than half of health spending for both children and non-elderly adults—considerably narrowing the gap between these two groups and the elderly.

6.4a Most non-elderly rely on private health insurance coverage, typically through an employer health plan

Percentage with coverage (March 2009)

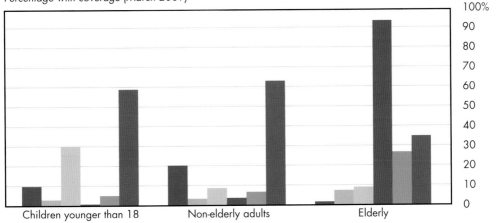

Note: HI = health insurance.

6.4b The elderly depend most heavily on publicly provided health care, which covers approximately two-thirds of their medical costs

■ Younger than 19 ■ 19–64 ■ 65 and older

Percentage of PHCE paid by public insurance or public programs

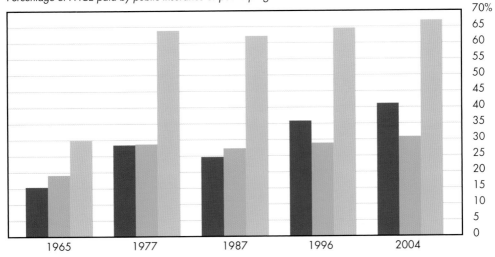

Note: Public insurance includes Medicare. Because a portion of Medicare spending is paid through voluntary premium payments, the entire amount should not be viewed as taxpayer-financed spending even though Medicare is categorized as "federal" spending in the standard National Health Expenditure Accounts framework.

The risk of being uninsured is at least three times as high among young adults as among children younger than 10 or the elderly.

A more detailed view of the uninsured makes obvious that lack of coverage rises during teenage years and peaks in the early 20s. As indicated in figure 6.5, in subsequent years, the rate of being uninsured declines rather steadily until a sharp drop-off among those age 65 and older.

Over the past 25 years, a series of Medicaid expansions (starting in the mid-1980s) and SCHIP contributed to reducing the uninsured risk, especially among infants and children younger than age six. Young adults face a higher risk of being uninsured not only because many entry-level jobs do not offer coverage but also because they generally have lower incomes than established workers do, and their perceived need for coverage also is lower than that of older workers. Even though age-related premiums are legally permissible, employer coverage usually is community-rated, so the employee share of the premium is typically the same for all workers even though the youngest workers are less likely to use the plan. Thus, even when the employer pays 80 percent of the premium, such coverage is less of a deal for younger workers than for older workers. For all these reasons, young workers are less likely to be willing to pay the costs of offered coverage or to obtain non-group coverage when their employer elects not to offer a plan.

More generally, both the need for coverage and earnings typically increase with age, contributing to an increase in the demand for health coverage that levels off for those in their early 50s. Because a large number of retirees automatically qualify for Medicare coverage, the residual number without any coverage at all is quite small. Such uninsured elderly might not have a long enough earnings history to qualify for Medicare, or they might have been in a category of worker not covered by Medicare (for example, government workers were not required to be covered until the 1980s).

If health reform is fully implemented, the absolute number of uninsured will decline, but this age profile is likely to persist. Because the new health law moves the system further in the direction of community rating, many young people are likely to find it is less expensive to pay the penalty for not having coverage than to purchase it.

6.5 The probability of being uninsured is much higher among young adults

Percent uninsured (March 2009)

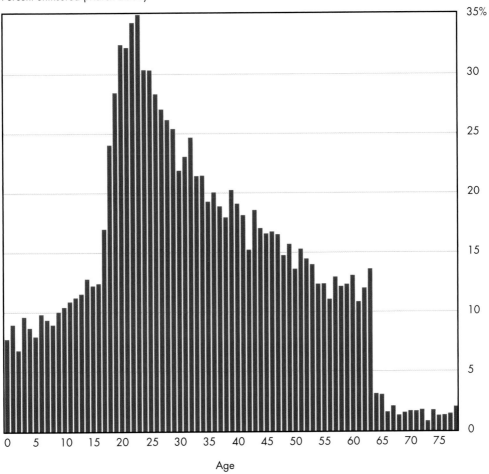

Age

The average American's chance of being uninsured has declined substantially over the past 70 years.

Over 70 years, the uninsured rate has declined by more than 80 percent (figure 6.6). It is noteworthy to see how much of this decline occurred before the arrival of Medicare and Medicaid. In 1940, approximately nine of 10 Americans lacked health insurance coverage. By 1960, this had fallen to 25 percent. This dramatic decline reflected the enormous expansion of employer-based health coverage fueled by the tax subsidy that began in 1943.

These numbers are approximations for the earliest decades. The nation did not start to seriously measure the extent of lack of coverage until the mid-1970s. Before that time, only insurance industry surveys of members who might have duplicate coverage across various types of policies exist (for example, hospital insurance). Thus, using assumptions about the fraction of the population without any coverage and how much overlap there was between policies of various types and then subtracting this insured number from the total population provides a count of the uninsured. Today, the most widely quoted current numbers about the uninsured come from the Current Population Survey (CPS), which did not start collecting a consistent measure of coverage until 1988. Now there are multiple surveys, each with various shortcomings. The point is that the numbers for 1990 forward are a better approximation of the truth than the numbers that precede it.

By 1970, the uninsured rate had fallen to less than 15 percent, reflecting continued expansion of employer-provided coverage and the introduction of Medicare and Medicaid. As will be shown, there is substantial evidence of "crowd-out" of private health coverage by both programs, so the entire decline cannot be attributed to public coverage. After 1970, the uninsured rate remained quite stable for decades. The slight increase between 1990 and 2010 is barely a blip from this much longer-term view.

Official government projections of what is supposed to happen to the uninsured rate if health reform is fully implemented are included. If this will happen remains to be seen, but the 2019 number is simply a reminder that the health reform plan did not intend, nor will it possibly achieve, universal coverage. Some 20 million uninsured Americans would still be uninsured that year, according to official forecasts.

6.6 The risk of being uninsured has decreased by more than 80 percent between 1940 and 2010

Percent uninsured

Number of uninsured (millions)

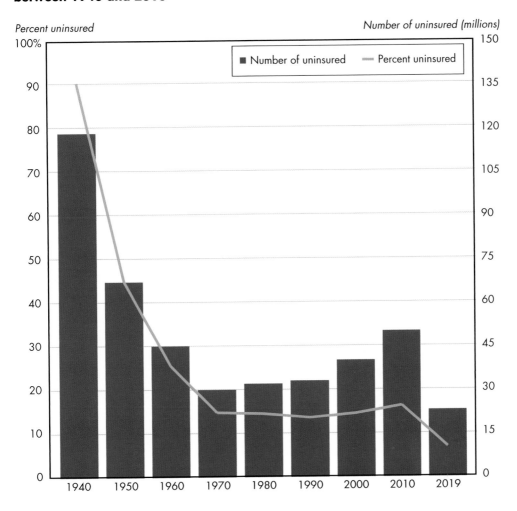

Note: Data simulate the gross number of uninsured as if measured by today's Current Population Survey. No adjustments have been made for the 10% to 20% over-counting of uninsured by the CPS.

Although per capita health costs for people uninsured all year are less than half the amount spent for those who have private coverage, more than 65 percent of their costs are subsidized.

Per capita health costs for non-elderly individuals who are uninsured for the entire year are less than half the medical spending for their counterparts who have private insurance coverage (figure 6.7a). Slightly more than half of those who are uninsured at least some portion of the year are without coverage the entire year. In any given year, the part-year uninsured lack coverage for approximately six months. Therefore, individuals uninsured the entire year constitute approximately 70 percent of the number of uninsured on any given day.

Although they are uninsured half the year, seven-eighths of spending for the part-year uninsured occurs during the portion of the year they are insured. This reflects the higher propensity of insured people to get care, but it also reflects strategic behavior by those drifting in and out of coverage. By deferring care when uninsured and using care as much as feasible if they know they are likely to lose coverage, they minimize the out-of-pocket burden associated with being without coverage.

Per capita spending on those privately insured all year is lower than for those on Medicaid the entire year. This disparity would be even larger if Medicaid payments to hospitals and doctors matched the levels paid by private health plans. Much of the difference reflects Medicaid coverage of expensive services not covered by standard private health plans (for example, long-term care costs such as extended nursing-home stays or home health for those whose condition is not likely to improve). The average non-elderly person covered by Medicare (that is, work-disabled) or Medicaid is in worse health than those who have private coverage.

Access to care appears to be somewhat better for uninsured children relative to uninsured adults. Spending for full-year uninsured children is approximately 60 percent of the level of statistically equivalent individuals having coverage the entire year; for their counterparts who are adults, spending is less than half that for equivalent adults having full-year coverage (figure 6.7b). Publicly subsidized care might be more accessible to children (for example, free clinics); likewise, the propensity for care-seeking among uninsured adults—some who have chosen to be uninsured—might be lower.

6.7a Annual health spending for a non-elderly person uninsured all year is less than half the amount for those privately insured all year

Annual health spending per capita index: 100=full year privately insured (2008)

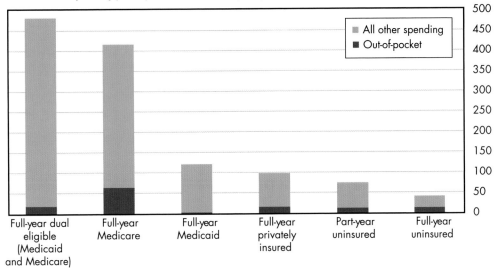

Type of insurance coverage (non-elderly Americans)

Note: Estimated spending for full year privately insured individuals younger than age 65 was $3,914 in 2008.

6.7b Relative to their adult counterparts, uninsured children have annual spending that is closer to the levels of those covered all year

Annual health spending per capita index: 100=full year insured (2008)

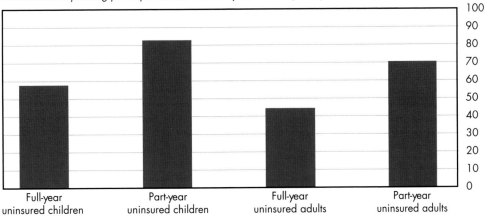

Type of insurance coverage (non-elderly Americans)

Note: All data compare estimated spending for the uninsured in each category to simulated spending if the individuals in each category were fully insured, taking into account differences in health status, demographic, and socioeconomic characteristics.

In elderly households, the share of household spending for health care is more for those headed by the non-elderly and has increased faster over time.

Despite the near-universal coverage of the elderly through Medicare, households headed by those 65 and older devote a considerably higher fraction of household spending for health care compared with households headed by younger adults. Moreover, over the past 25 years, the health care share has grown faster in elderly households compared with non-elderly households (figure 6.8a).

The relative difference in shares would be much smaller if the hidden costs of health coverage were taken into account. The amounts shown for health insurance include only the employee share of premiums. Because the average employer contributes approximately 80 percent of premiums for coverage provided through work, the amounts shown for health insurance premiums would have to be almost quadrupled were this cost made visible.

The large increase in the health insurance premium share of family spending for elderly households between 1996 and 2008 reflects the introduction of Medicare Part D drug coverage. Except for low-income households eligible for subsidies, Part D requires the payment of a premium covering approximately 25 percent of the costs covered by the benefit. It is interesting to note that little of this increase in premiums was offset by a corresponding decline in the share of household spending for out-of-pocket pharmaceutical payments.

Real health spending also has increased far more rapidly for elderly households than for non-elderly households, increasing by more than $1,000 in the past 25 years (figure 6.8b). Remember that this includes only direct spending by households and excludes the significant share of spending financed by taxes.

Among non-elderly households, the health spending share has grown slowly but steadily over 25 years in households headed by 35–44 year olds, whereas the health spending share of household consumption spending for households headed by those younger than age 25 is currently somewhat less than it was 25 years earlier.

6.8a **The share of consumption spending devoted to health has grown faster in elderly households than in non-elderly households**

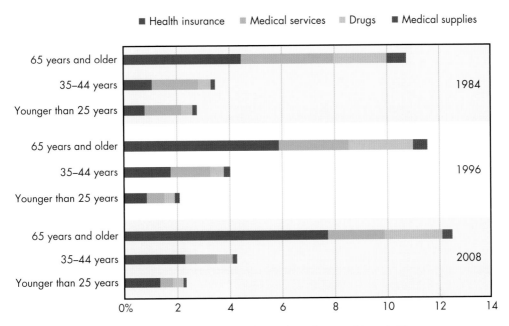

Percentage of annual PCE by age of householder

6.8b **Real household spending on health has increased much more rapidly in elderly households than in non-elderly households**

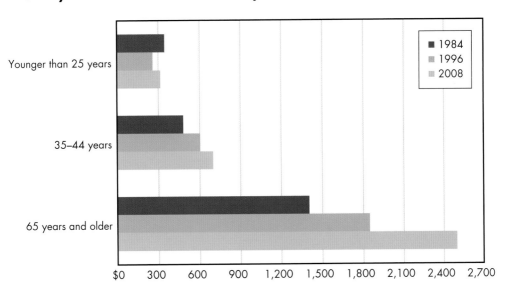

Real per capita health expenditures (2005 dollars using GDP price deflator)

Despite higher health costs, real non-health spending per person in elderly households is higher than in households headed by younger people.

Although households headed by those 65 and older spend a higher fraction of their income on health care, the per capita resources left over to spend on everything else are higher than in households headed by the non-elderly (figure 6.9a). This might seem counterintuitive, but it has occurred because growth in real total spending in elderly households has outpaced that of younger households over the past 25 years. Note that these numbers are based on household surveys of consumer expenditures that reflect actual spending on health care (out-of-pocket costs and premium spending by each family).

In terms of constant purchasing power, elderly households 25 years ago lagged behind households headed by younger adults in terms of the amount available per capita for all other consumption except health. By 1996, per capita non-health consumption for the elderly outpaced that of the youngest households by more than $2,000—a gap that grew to $4,000 by 2008. This demonstrates the importance of comparing health spending burdens across households both in relative terms (percent of income or expenditures) and as absolute dollar amounts (both health and non-health spending).

To summarize, this increase in consumption by the elderly resulted in higher health spending (shown previously) and higher spending in almost all categories of non-health spending.

Unfortunately, comparative data on elderly health spending relative to non-elderly spending is sparse. In the United States, this ratio is approximately the same as that in other European countries, but markedly lower than in Canada (figure 6.9b). Taken at face value, it appears that this ratio is declining in the United States while increasing in Canada. Such sparse data do not allow strong conclusions about any trends. The recently enacted health reform law likely would reduce this ratio further because, on balance, it increases spending mostly for non-elderly uninsured while reducing expenditures for Medicare. Thus, why the ratios would be so divergent in countries having near-universal coverage is somewhat puzzling.

6.9a Real per capita non-health spending currently is higher in households headed by elderly people; this was not true in 1984

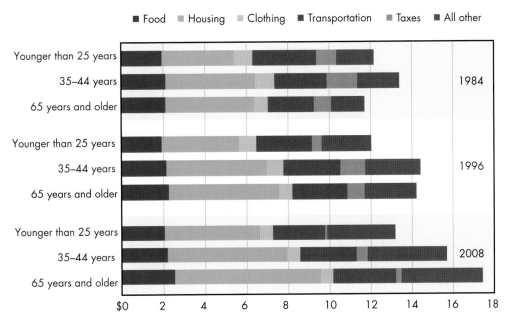

■ Food ■ Housing ■ Clothing ■ Transportation ■ Taxes ■ All other

Real per capita non-health spending (thousands of 2005 dollars using GDP price deflator)

6.9b The ratio of annual health spending for the elderly relative to the non-elderly is similar in the United States and in other countries

Ratio of annual health spending for the elderly relative to non-elderly

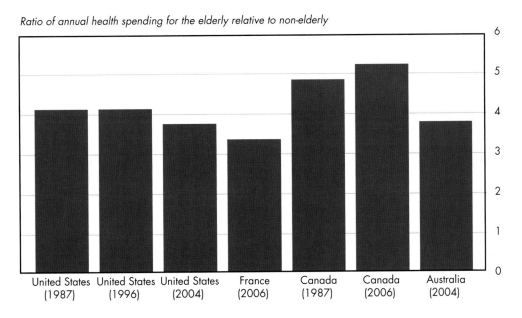

CHAPTER 7

Who Produces Health Services?

Compared with the rest of the economy, a much larger share of health output is provided by non-profit organizations or publicly owned enterprises.

Almost half of all revenues in the health system are generated by tax-exempt organizations, including both those that are publicly owned or are organized as non-profit firms. The share of revenues flowing through such enterprises is far larger in the hospital sector than in any other area of health care delivery. The relative importance of government-owned firms varies by subsector.

On average, 40 percent of nursing home care is provided through tax-exempt firms, but this is a blend of nursing homes—where for-profit firms account for 75 percent of revenues—and various types of residential care facilities for the elderly, along with those requiring care for mental health, mental retardation, or substance abuse. The tax-exempt share among such facilities is approximately 65 percent. Among home health agencies, the tax-exempt share is less than 30 percent (figure 7.1).

It has been postulated that non-profit or public enterprises might be attractive in sectors such as health care in which consumer trust is an important factor. Many studies compare the performance of non-profit firms relative to for-profit firms in terms of various measures of efficiency, profitability, access to care, and similar metrics. Although the evidence is mixed, with neither form having a clear advantage, the performance has been sufficiently similar that it has prompted IRS scrutiny of whether tax exemption is warranted for hospitals. Current federal tax rules require hospitals to demonstrate that the dollar value of the community benefits they provide equal or exceed the amount of tax savings resulting from exemption. A far smaller literature compares the relative performance of government-owned firms with either for-profit or non-profit health care organizations.

7.1 Public and non-profit owners dominate the hospital sector and provide a large fraction of nursing home and home health care

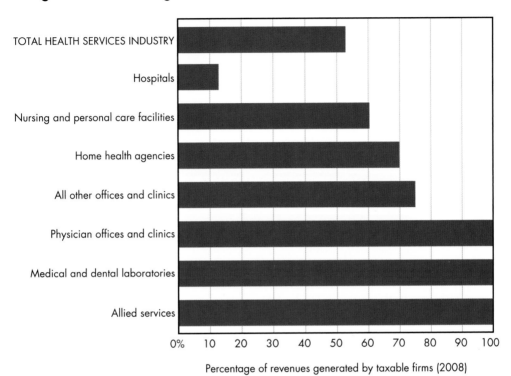

Percentage of revenues generated by taxable firms (2008)

Note: "Health services" includes ambulatory health care services and hospitals, nursing, and residential care facilities. It does not include pharmaceuticals, medical devices, non-durable medical products, or the health insurance industry.

In most subsectors of health care, government-owned firms account for only approximately 10 percent of activity.

Government's role in the production of health services is far smaller than its role in health care financing. In most subsectors, government-owned firms account for approximately 10 percent of overall activity, the chief exception being the health insurance industry. These observations require several important caveats.

First, there is no standardized way to measure the relative importance of government-owned firms in health care. The previously cited numbers on revenues by ownership permit only a clear division between firms subject to federal taxes and those that are not. To understand the relative importance of government-owned firms compared with non-profit firms requires data on activity that differ by industry. As shown in figure 7.2, the available measures of "activity" range from firms, to beds, to enrollment, none of which is entirely satisfactory.

Second, ownership is not equivalent to management. Many county- or city-owned hospitals, for example, have their day-to-day operations managed by either for-profit or non-profit firms. More than 20 percent of all hospitals, including federal, state, and local (city or county) facilities, are publicly owned. However, this includes military and specialty hospitals (for example, psychiatric, tuberculosis). Among so-called community hospitals, only approximately one in six beds is publicly owned—almost identical to the share owned by for-profit facilities (figure 7.2).

In the health insurance industry, the public sector role is defined in terms of enrollment in public health plans such as Medicare and Medicaid. However, government does not "own" any Medicare plans. All claims processing for those using fee-for-service Medicare is handled by private-sector intermediaries such as Aetna or Blue Cross and Blue Shield. Either many states permit those eligible for Medicaid or SCHIP to enroll in private health plans such as HMOs or they contract out their claims-processing to private insurance companies or third-party administrators. Based on membership, approximately half of the insurance business is handled by non-profit firms such as Blue Cross and Blue Shield plans, Kaiser Permanente, and HIP Health Plan of New York. Non-profit Blue Cross and Blue Shield plans alone cover more than 30 percent of the private health insurance market.

7.2 Most tax-exempt firms are voluntary non-profit agencies; government accounts for only approximately 10 percent in most subsectors

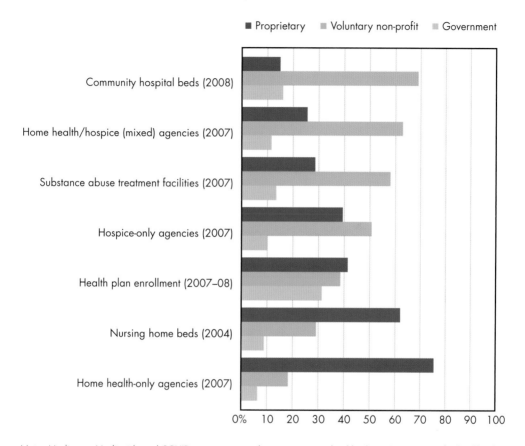

Note: Medicare, Medicaid, and SCHIP are categorized as government health plans. Percentages for health plan enrollment add to more than 100 percent because of duplicate coverage.

The increasing share of final demands related to health care has been a major factor in the growth of the service share of national output after World War II.

Since 1948, more than 40 percent of the growth in the services share of the economy can be attributed to the rapid growth in health services (figure 7.3a). America has become a service economy, with an expanding health sector an important driver of that trend. Some components of personal health care are counted as goods (pharmaceuticals, non-durable medical products, and durable medical equipment) and other components of national health spending fall under construction. The rest is labeled health services in figure 7.3a.

Final demands take into account personal consumption by households, government purchases, and private and public investments. From 1948 to 2009, all services excluding health grew from just over 30 percent of the economy to more than 50 percent. Thus, the shift to services would have happened—albeit less rapidly—even had health services remained at its 1948 level of 3 percent of GDP. Services now constitute almost 65 percent of final purchases, but an ever-increasing share of that is accounted for by health care. Currently, that share is more than 20 percent of all services, compared with only 6 percent in 1929.

Another way to decompose total output (GDP) is in terms of the industries that produce it. The consumer who purchases health care—a final demand—might rely on the output of many other industries such as transportation, real estate, finance, and manufacturing. Value added is simply an industry's gross output minus all the resources produced by other industries that were used to create it. In this view, the share of output attributable to *goods* equals the value added from the industries that supply the goods. These include agriculture, forestry and fisheries, mining, construction, and manufacturing. In this alternative way of breaking down output, all other industries are classified as services.

Unfortunately, detailed value-added data are available only for private output, so the scenario is incomplete. Services overall account for almost 80 percent of private business output (figure 7.3b). The health services contribution is much more modest and growing much less rapidly from this producer view (i.e., "supply-side" view) than the demand-side perspective described previously.

7.3a Since 1948, rapid growth in the health sector has been a major factor in the increasing share of total national output purchased for services

Percentage of GDP

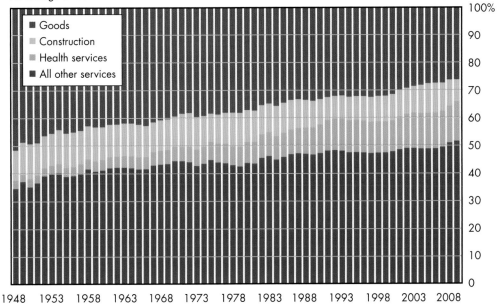

7.3b As a producing industry, the value added by health services has grown more rapidly than for goods or non-health services

Value added as percentage of private industry output (based on current dollars)

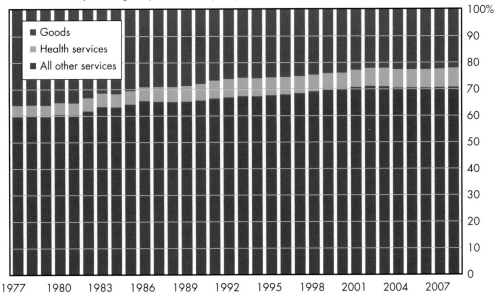

Over the past 80 years, the increase in health services output was almost 50 percent higher than was the increase in economy-wide output.

Overall output for health services has increased 19-fold since 1929. In contrast, GDP rose only 13-fold. The numbers shown in figure 7.4 remove the effects of inflation and are intended to measure the net increase in quantity of goods and services produced relative to the base year. As with the numbers for workers' compensation, these estimates exclude some important components of health sector output, including pharmaceuticals, medical devices, non-durable medical products, and output for government-run enterprises such as publicly owned hospitals.

Until the early 1960s, the rate of increase in health sector output did not diverge substantially from growth in economy-wide output (that is, GDP). The introduction of Medicare and Medicaid substantially expanded the number of individuals who have health insurance coverage, producing a surge in added demand for health services. With the exception of a brief period in the mid- to late-1990s, health services output almost invariably has grown faster than real GDP. In contrast, the real quantity of all services (inclusive of health services) rose almost in lockstep with GDP, while output in goods-producing industries lagged behind GDP growth. This might seem inconsistent with the previous data that America has increasingly become a service economy. The numbers shown in figure 7.4 isolate the quantity of output from the cost of providing it. It is possible to infer from the difference that prices in the service sector (including health) have increased much more rapidly than in the economy overall.

It is noteworthy that although GDP and output in goods-producing industries declined during the most recent recession (and real output in the service sector remained flat), health care output continued to rise. While past recessions have tended to slow the rate of growth in real health output, they rarely have resulted in an actual downturn. This is discussed further in chapter 16.

Even under the most ambitious versions of health reform, long-term trends in health spending are likely to absorb a growing share of GDP (chapter 20). Thus, the divergence in growth rates between health care and the rest of the economy is extremely likely to grow larger, certainly within the next decade or two.

7.4 Output in the health sector has increased much more rapidly than in goods-producing industries, the service sector or the GDP

Chained quantity index (1929=100)

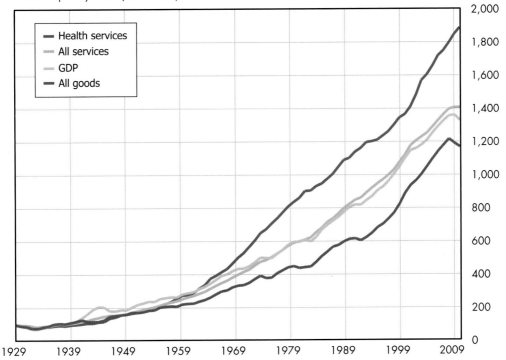

CHAPTER 8

Health Services and the Distribution of National Income

Health-related supplements accounted for almost 12 cents of every dollar of national income in 2008 compared with less than three cents four decades earlier.

Health-related fringe benefits have grown far more rapidly than has national income over the past 60 years. Yet the share of national income accounted for by employee compensation—wages, salaries, and supplements—has declined somewhat since its 1980 peak (figure 8.1a). This again shows that in the end, fringe benefits come out of worker pay, not corporate profits.

National income can be viewed as an alternative way of measuring the net value of annual output, by adding all the costs of producing it. GDP measures gross output, but to arrive at a net national product (NNP), capital consumption (for example, depreciation of machinery) is not included. In the Bureau of Economic Analysis (BEA) National Income and Product Accounts (NIPA), national income measures the earnings of all factors of production used to produce NNP. These factors include wages, salaries, supplements, rents, interest, and profits and losses. In principle, this should equal the same sum measured in terms of final products (consumption + investment + government purchases + imports). However, because NNP and national income are measured using completely different methods, a small statistical adjustment is needed to reconcile the two totals.

Health-related supplements include not only employer-provided health coverage, but also legally required payroll deductions made by employers for Medicare and workers' compensation. Other fringe benefits, such as pensions or employer-paid retirement contributions, also grew much more rapidly than wages and salaries during this period, although not as rapidly as health-related supplements.

Examined in more detail, mandatory health-related payroll deductions for workers' compensation and Medicare peaked at 1.7 percent of national income in the early 1990s and have declined subsequently (figure 8.1b). Employee health benefits reached 4.1 percent of national income by 1993, declined during the boom years of the 1990s, peaked again at 4.4 percent in 2003 to 2005, slightly declining again thereafter. Non-health supplements peaked at 7.4 percent in the early 1980s and steadily declined thereafter until 2002, when they began increasing again. If health reform is implemented, the combination of employer penalties and mandatory increases in generosity of coverage make it possible that the employee health-benefits share will increase in future years.

8.1a Despite rapid growth in health-related supplements, employee compensation as a share of national income has declined since 1980

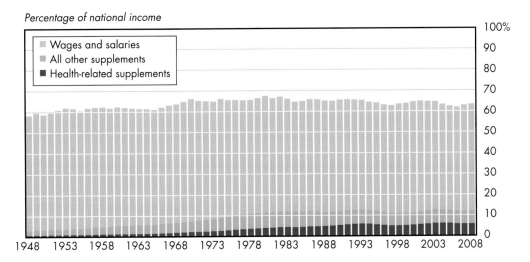

Percentage of national income

Note: Health-related supplements include employer contributions to health-related social insurance (Medicare Part A, workers' compensation, temporary disability insurance) and private group health insurance.

8.1b Over 60 years, health-related supplements have increased steadily as a share of national income except in the 1990s and recent years

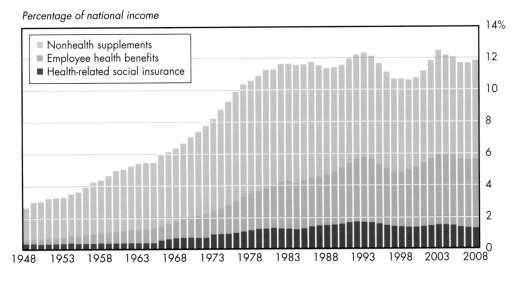

Percentage of national income

Note: Health-related social insurance includes mandatory employer payroll taxes for Medicare Part A (hospital insurance), military medical insurance (CHAMPUS/VA), state/local temporary disability insurance, and mandatory and voluntary employer contributions toward workers' compensation. Depending on jurisdiction, workers' compensation can serve as wage replacement (disability insurance), compensation for past or future economic loss, or payment of work injury-related medical expenses. Temporary disability insurance is for wage replacement but is counted as health insurance in the National Income and Product Accounts; the minuscule amounts for such insurance therefore are included in the data.

More than 80 percent of 2009 national income for health services was for compensation of employees compared with only 50 percent in 1963. Reflecting the decline of physicians in solo practice or partnerships, the share of health-related national income accounted for by proprietors' and rental income has fallen steeply in the past 50 years.

A much higher share of national income for the health services sector flows to employee compensation than in the economy in general (figure 8.2a). The share allocated to wages and salaries, and fringe benefits, is higher than in the economy overall or in the services sector. The combined total exceeds 80 percent of health services-related national income. In the breakdown in figure 8.2a, health services include ambulatory care, hospitals, nursing homes, and residential care facilities. The category excludes the pharmaceutical industry, medical devices, and non-durable medical products sold in retail outlets such as pharmacies. More than 90 percent of national income from health facilities goes to employee compensation, compared with approximately 75 percent of national income having to do with ambulatory health services.

The share accounted for by proprietors' and rental income is more in the health services industry than in the general economy, albeit less than that in the services industry overall. Conversely, the share flowing into pre-tax corporate profits is twice as much in the general economy as in the health services industry, reflecting the dominance of non-profit and public service providers in health care described in chapter 7.

The employee compensation share of national income in the health services sector has grown dramatically in less than 50 years (figure 8.2b). Just before the introduction of Medicare and Medicaid (which began in 1966), employee compensation accounted for less than half of the national income generated by health services. But in less than 20 years after the massive infusion of public dollars into these new entitlement programs, the employee compensation share had climbed to more than 80 percent (where it has stayed ever since).

Unionization has helped spur this growth, but another factor has been the declining share of health services national income that went to proprietors' and rental income. Physicians who own their own practices get proprietors' income rather than wages. However, an increasing number of physicians are salaried, thereby elevating the relative importance of wages as a form of health sector compensation.

8.2a In health services, the share of income for wages and salaries as well as for fringe benefits are higher than in the service sector or general economy

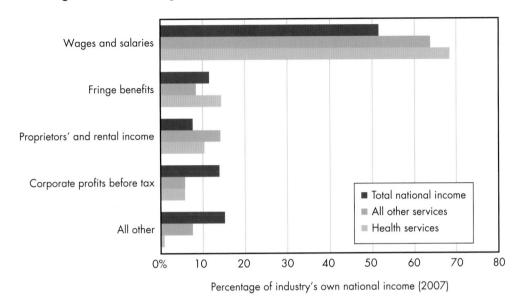

Percentage of industry's own national income (2007)

Note: "Health services" includes ambulatory health care services and hospitals, nursing, and residential care facilities. It does not include pharmaceuticals, medical devices, non-durable medical products, or the health insurance industry.

8.2b In the health services sector, both wages and salaries, and fringe benefits are substantially higher than they were 50 years ago

Percentage of national income related to health services

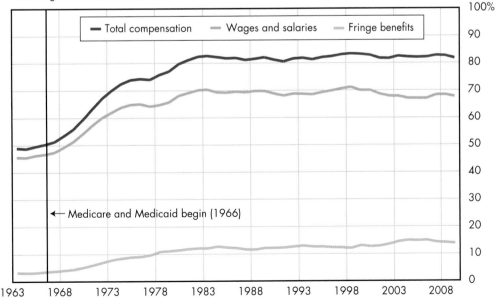

The share of health-related national income accounted for by proprietors' and rental income has declined steeply in the past 50 years.

Before Medicare and Medicaid, approximately half of national income for health services went to proprietors' and rental income. Not even 20 years later, this amount was less than 15 percent. It has steadily declined further to approximately 10 percent today (figure 8.3a). During this period, the rest of the services sector also saw a declining share of its national income going to proprietors' and rental income, but this occurred much less rapidly than in health services.

The current level in health care (just over 10 percent) is below the share seen in the rest of the services sector and is only slightly more than the percentage in the economy overall. In contrast, the share is less than 3 percent in manufacturing.

A growing number of physicians have abandoned their own practices in favor of a buy-out by hospitals or managed care plans. There now are thousands of retail clinics run by major chains such as CVS, Walgreen's, and Wal-Mart. With health reform, pressures to adopt electronic medical records are likely to fuel a continuation of this trend away from solo practices and partnerships into corporate medicine.

In principle, owner income reflects both what unincorporated health professionals earn as labor (wages, salaries, fringe benefits) and some hard-to-measure remainder (if anything) that represents profits. If a solo practitioner with a net income of $200,000 became a hospital employee whose total compensation was $200,000, total spending would remain unchanged. However, the employee compensation share of national income would rise by the identical amount that proprietors' income fell.

Another way to look at these trends is to consider what share of total proprietors' and rental income is accounted for by the health sector. Today, health services account for approximately one in eight dollars of such income (figure 8.3b), contributing more than $100 billion to the national total. In absolute dollar terms, this is the highest it has ever been. One-eighth also is the highest share since 1994 and is almost identical to the share observed in 1929. Even so, over 80 years, the health sector share has never exceeded 20 percent except in 1932.

8.3a The share of health-related national income accounted for by proprietors' and rental income has declined dramatically over 50 years

Percentage of sector-specific national income attributable to proprietors' and rental income

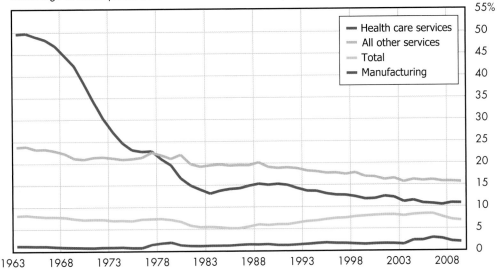

Note: Health services includes 1) ambulatory health care services, and 2) hospitals and nursing and residential care facilities. It does not include pharmaceuticals, medical devices, non-durable medical products, or the health insurance industry.

8.3b The health services share of owner income is almost as high today as it was in 1929; the share for all other services has increased

Percentage of total proprietors' and rental income

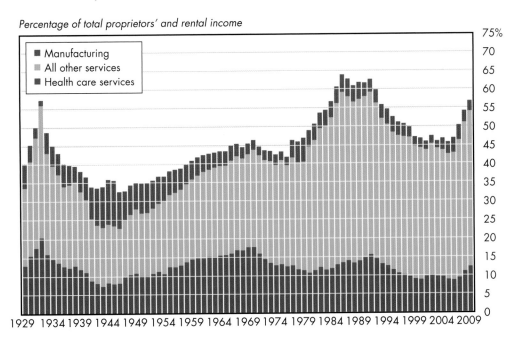

Corporate profits before and after taxes have now reached their highest share of health services income in the past 50 years.

After-tax corporate profits for health services now exceed $58 billion. This is a large number in absolute terms but accounts for only 6.1 percent of health services–related national income. The share of such income accounted for by profits has grown considerably since 1963, when both pre-tax and after-tax profits were less than 0.5 percent of health care's national income (figure 8.4a).

These numbers reflect the growing share of health services provided by for-profit organizations and the declining share of health-related national income accounted for by proprietors' and rental income. These numbers do not include profits in pharmaceuticals or medical devices, or they assuredly would be higher.

Corporate profits in most of the rest of the economy tend to be highly sensitive to changing business conditions. Little evidence of parallel fluctuations in health services profits exists. The decline in profits starting in 1983, for example, occurred after the deep recession of 1981-1982 had ended. It can be attributed to the introduction of the Medicare PPS for hospitals, which limited payments to a fixed amount that varied by diagnosis. In contrast to the earlier cost-based reimbursement system, PPS forced hospitals to economize by limiting lengths of stay and reducing the intensity of care per admission.

Likewise, much of the downturn in profits starting in 1997 is likely caused by the Balanced Budget Act of 1997 (BBA97), which included the largest cuts in Medicare's history. BBA97 included payment cuts for hospitals and home health agencies that sharply crimped their profitability. In late 1999, Congress passed legislation to ameliorate some of BBA97's harshest fiscal consequences. As expected, profitability again started to increase. Nevertheless, the most recent decline in profitability started in 2006, long before the most recent recession started.

Although parallel profitability numbers are lacking at a more fine-grained level, approximate measures such as gross operating surpluses suggest that profits are higher in the ambulatory health sector than in health facilities (figure 8.4b). In ambulatory care, corporate profits appear to be increasing in importance.

8.4a Health services profits have increased substantially since the advent of Medicare and Medicaid but still are below average

Profits as a percentage of industry's own national income

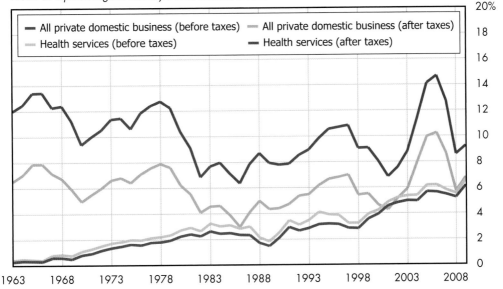

8.4b Gross operating surpluses—an extreme approximate measure of profitability—are higher in ambulatory care than in health facilities

Gross operating surplus (GOS) as a percentage of industry's own national income

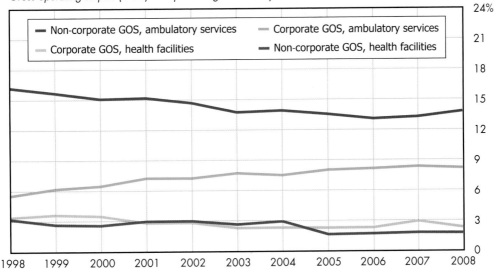

Note: GOS is the share of industry's national income remaining after deducting compensation for employees and indirect business taxes (for example, privilege licenses). GOS is somewhat more than pre-tax corporate profits because it includes net interest payments and adjustments for capital consumption and inventory valuation.

Corporate profits before taxes in the health sector are less than that of other major sectors and private businesses overall.

Before-tax corporate profits for health services are generally less than half the levels seen in private businesses as a group, even during times of recession. As illustrated in figure 8.5, in goods-producing industries (agriculture, forestry, fishing and hunting, mining, manufacturing, and construction), pre-tax profits typically are in the double-digit range, reaching as much as 20 percent in recent years. In contrast, pre-tax corporate profits in health services, while increasing, have consistently been much less than 10 percent of that industry's national income.

That said, profitability in the private economy, and major sectors such as goods and other services, are much more volatile than in the health services market. Consequently, there are brief periods during recoveries from recessions in which the share of national income going to profits in these other sectors increases more quickly than in health services. However, during the past 50 years, the secular rise in health sector profits as a share of health-related national income has been more rapid than in any other sectors.

The apparent sharp rise in profitability among all other services in 1998 might be a statistical anomaly. The BEA introduced a substantial revision in how industries were categorized, and they ceased reporting an aggregate number for "Services." Thus, since 1998, the total for services had to be derived by adding component parts. However, certain services (for example, information services) now appear in other BEA-reported aggregates. Conversely, some services appearing in the component parts might previously have been included in a different industry. Thus, the trend between 1998–2008 is more likely to be accurate than is the size of the large estimated increase between 1997 and 1998.

To avoid confusion, corporate profits shown here reflect the definitions used by the BEA. The BEA makes several adjustments (for example, inflation adjustments) to what are known as "book profits" that corporations report to stockholders in various financial reports. For most purposes, the adjusted BEA numbers are technically superior to these book amounts, but the adjustments also are arbitrary to some extent.

8.5 Pre-tax profits as a share of income are lower in health care than in goods-producing industries but are comparable to non-health services

Profits before taxes as a percentage of industry's own national income

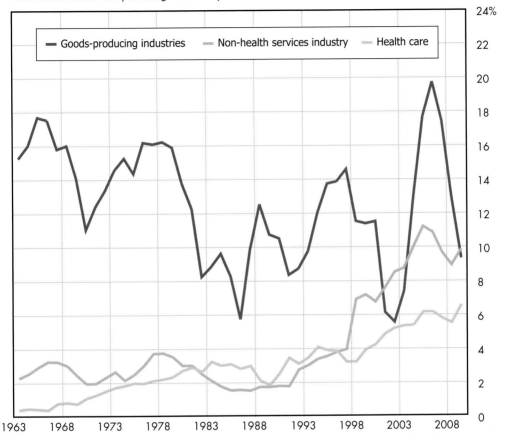

Note: The industry classification system changed in 1998, substantially changing the components of the non-health services industry. Although every effort has been made to retain comparable industries within this category over time, this classification change might account for at least some of the apparent gap that appeared that year between health care and the rest of the services industry.

Publicly traded health services companies generally have lower profits than do other firms listed on the stock market.

Even among publicly traded companies, industries having to do with health services tend to have lower rates of return than most other industries. Profitability for health services generally was less than in other major sectors of the economy (refer to figure 8.5). Some might view this as misleading because so much of the health industry is comprised of non-profit or government health providers.

An arguably fairer apples-to-apples comparison would be to restrict the comparison to for-profit firms within each sector. The most readily available numbers are rankings among Fortune 500 firms grouped by major industry (approximately 50 such industries are included in these rankings). This clearly is not complete because it ignores small- and medium-sized firms. Nevertheless, the Fortune 500 typically accounts for the lion's share of output in a given industry. Thus, these rankings provide an approximate idea of how health care firms compare to the rest of the economy. In figures 8.6a–c, the numbers in each bar show the ranking of each industry relative to all major U.S. industries. Although industry rankings were not reported with the most recently released 2009 and 2010 profit numbers, they are not likely to be sharply different from the rankings for prior years.

I start with health services industries and then turn to goods-producing components of health care (pharmaceuticals and medical equipment) in figures 8.7a–c. There are three standard measures of profits. In each case, profits are defined as the difference between revenues and costs, but the denominator used to calculate the profit rate differs. Return on revenue (ROR), what many call "profit margin," calculates profits as a percent of total revenues. Most health services industries have single-digit RORs of less than 5 percent (figure 8.6a).

When profits are divided by assets, that is, the overall capital invested in a given company, the result is return on assets (ROA). Assets equal both equity (for example, stocks) and debt. Such returns also are typically at single-digit levels for health services industries (figure 8.6b). The final measure divides only by equity, that is, to exclude debt. Using the return on equity (ROE), the health services industries attain double-digit levels of returns, but again these typically rank them in the bottom half of industries overall (figure 8.6c).

8.6a Profit margins generally are highest for "health insurance and managed care" and lowest for health care wholesalers for all health-related services

Profits as a percentage of revenue (return on revenue [ROR]), Fortune 500 publicly traded companies

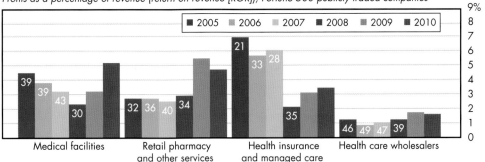

Note: Data labels indicate industry's ranking within Fortune 500 on ROR for year shown (rankings not available for 2009 or 2010). Although the number varies slightly by year and profitability measure, approximately 50 industries are included in each year's ranking.

8.6b Retail pharmacies generally have the highest return on assets and medical facilities the lowest for health-related services

Profits as a percentage of assets (ROA), Fortune 500 publicly traded companies

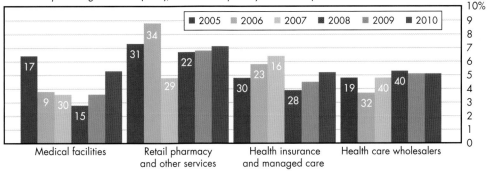

Note: Data labels indicate industry's ranking on ROA for year shown (rankings not available for 2009 or 2010). Although the number varies slightly by year and profitability measure, approximately 50 industries are included in each ranking.

8.6c Return on equity generally exceeds 10 percent among health-related services industries

Profits as a percentage of equity (ROE), Fortune 500 publicly traded companies

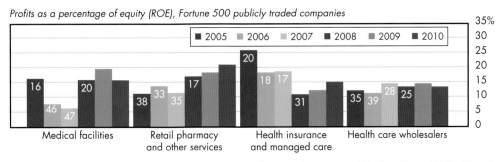

Note: Data labels indicate industry's ranking on ROE for year shown (rankings not available for 2009 or 2010). Although the number varies slightly by year and profitability measure, approximately 50 industries are included in each ranking.

Pharmaceutical and medical devices have higher profits than do most industries, reflecting returns for discovery and innovation.

Pharmaceuticals and medical devices typically rank among the top 10 most profitable industries in America. This is true whether profits are measured as a return on revenue (figure 8.7a), return on assets (figure 8.7b), or return on equity (figure 8.7c). Occasionally, one of these two industries ranks first among all industries in some measures of profitability (figure 8.7b).

Several reasons explain why these two health industries are so much more profitable than the various health-related services industries just examined. First, as shown previously, both industries consist entirely of for-profit firms, creating an arguably more competitive environment. Although there are mixed findings regarding performance of for-profit versus non-profit or government-owned enterprises, almost all comparisons agree that rates of return (however measured) are higher in for-profit firms relative to the not-for-profit counterparts.

Second, patents play a far more important role in pharmaceuticals and medical devices than in the rest of the health care sector. By design, patents are structured to encourage innovation by permitting their owners to earn monopoly returns for a limited time. Although the nominal patent term is 20 years, more than half of this time is typically lost before Food and Drug Administration (FDA) approval due to the lengthy time required for clinical trials and regulatory review.

Third (and related), pharmaceutical R&D especially is a complex, costly, risky, and time-consuming process. Including the costs associated with hundreds of compounds that do not succeed, as well as the cost of capital (financial resources) that is unavailable for other uses during this lengthy process, more than $1 billion is spent to bring a single new drug to market. Absent the incentives provided by the patent system, there is no question that the amount of pharmaceutical R&D would be considerably less. Concomitantly, the number of new drugs discovered would be fewer. Thus, high profits represent the price paid for the benefits of new discoveries.

Whether profits are higher than needed to bring forth an optimal level of innovation is a perennial question. Several different analyses have concluded that the high level of pharmaceutical profits only slightly exceeds the industry's cost of capital. Briefly, investors demand higher profits to invest in an industry where returns on R&D are so risky.

8.7a Pharmaceuticals and medical devices typically rank in the top 10 among all industries in their return on revenue

Profits as a percentage of revenue (ROR), Fortune 500 publicly traded companies

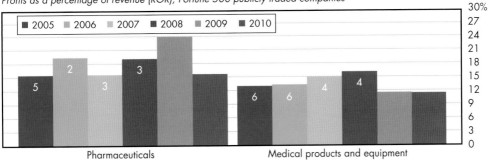

Note: Data labels indicate industry's ranking on ROR for year shown (rankings not available for 2009 or 2010). Although the number varies slightly by year and profitability measure, approximately 50 industries are included in each ranking.

8.7b Returns on assets for pharmaceuticals and medical devices place them among the top 10 industries in the United States

Profits as a percentage of assets (ROA), Fortune 500 publicly traded companies

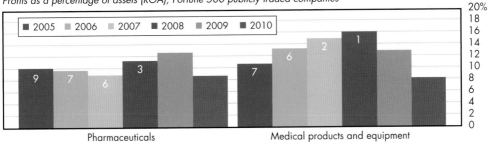

Note: Data labels indicate industry's ranking on ROA for year shown (rankings not available for 2009 or 2010). Although the number varies slightly by year and profitability measure, approximately 50 industries are included in each ranking.

8.7c Both pharmaceuticals and medical products have somewhat lower industry rankings on return on equity than other measures of profit

Profits as a percentage of equity (ROE), Fortune 500 publicly traded companies

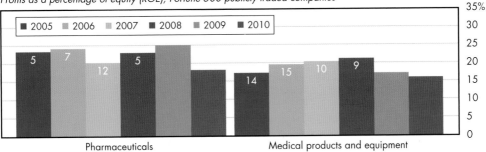

Note: Data labels indicate industry's ranking on ROE for year shown (rankings not available for 2009 or 2010). Although the number varies slightly by year and profitability measure, approximately 50 industries are included in each ranking.

CHAPTER 9

Productivity in the Health Sector

Only recently has the increase in real health services output exceeded the increase in the input of labor or the combined increase in the inputs of labor and capital. Output per unit of input is called productivity.

In 2007, the output of real health services in American health facilities was approximately double its level 20 years earlier. What was behind this production increase? To what extent did it reflect the use of more factors of production or inputs—the number of persons employed and the amount of capital they had to work with—and to what extent did it reflect greater efficiency in the use of inputs, that is, increased productivity? Measuring productivity growth is important because if productivity declines, the nation will require ever-increasing amounts of labor and capital to produce the same level of health output. This either will slow down or might even reverse the rise in general living standards.

The basic facts about the growth of output and input are compiled by the Bureau of Labor Statistics (BLS). Unfortunately, these facts are limited both in scope—covering only health services—and time—going back to only 1987. Typically, the growth of output is compared with the growth of labor input, which is measured in simplest terms by changes in employment and annual hours worked. Labor hours for health facilities rose just over 60 percent during these 20 years, approximately 2.5 percent annually (figure 9.1a). Output grew 3.4 percent a year. These numbers suggest a rise in labor productivity of 0.9 percent annually (3.4 minus 2.5).

However, this particular measure ignores other important factors that contribute to production, including the physical facilities themselves, equipment, inventories, and land. With these taken into account, combined inputs for health facilities rose 140 percent during these 20 years, approximately 4.4 percent annually. This growth implies a *decline* in productivity more broadly measured.

A similar result, though less extreme, occurred in the ambulatory health services industry. Over the entire period since 1987, output rose at almost the identical rate as labor input, although declining labor productivity occurred during the entire 1990s (figure 9.1b). Output grew somewhat faster than among health facilities, but combined inputs grew faster still, again implying declining productivity.

9.1a In hospitals and nursing homes, real output increased faster than labor hours over the past decade but more slowly than all inputs combined

Indexes: 1987=100

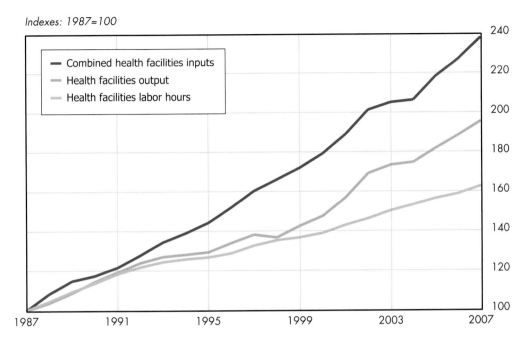

9.1b Over the past 20 years, total inputs for ambulatory health care outpaced growth in output even as growth in labor hours slowed

Indexes: 1987=100

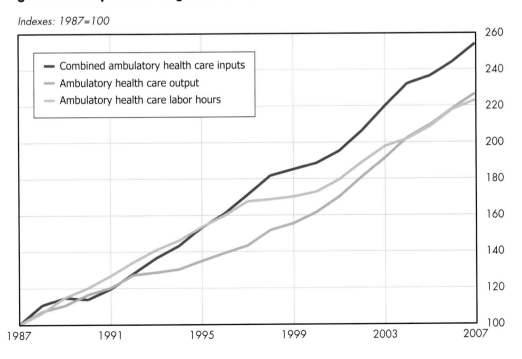

Productivity growth is less in the health sector than in private business in general.

Ambulatory care output per unit of input was less in 2007 than it had been 20 years earlier (figure 9.2a). This is only one way of measuring productivity. Even in terms of output per hour, productivity in the ambulatory health care industry generally declined into the 1990s and generally rose thereafter. Even so, hourly productivity in 2007 was almost identical to its 1987 level. In contrast, productivity grew much more steadily in the private sector overall during the same period. Hourly productivity climbed by approximately 60 percent while output per unit of input increased approximately 25 percent.

In health facilities, hourly productivity has tended to increase, especially since 1998. However, when capital inputs are taken into account, output per unit of input actually had fallen more by 2007 in health facilities than in ambulatory health care services (figure 9.2b).

In the goods-manufacturing portion of the health industry, productivity trends are somewhat like those in the private economy overall. For manufacturers of medical equipment, the growth in hourly productivity and output per unit of input has easily exceeded the average levels experienced in the private sector (figure 9.2c).

In pharmaceuticals, 2007 output per hour was approximately at the same level as in 1987. However, this combines a sharp drop in productivity in the late 1980s followed by rather steady annual increases thereafter. Pharmaceutical manufacturers saw a slight increase in output per unit of input at the start of this period, with generally falling productivity levels thereafter.

Falling productivity does not connote falling output. Output was increasing in all these health subsectors during this time. Because inputs into production also were increasing either more quickly or at approximately the same rate, productivity growth generally was more anemic in health care than elsewhere in the private economy. However, readers are cautioned that estimates of productivity are highly dependent on accurate price measurement. Accurate estimates of price changes are more challenging for health care than for most other goods and services because for the latter, it is easier to account for changes in quality.

9.2a Since 1987, low or negative productivity growth in ambulatory health care contrasts with steadier private-sector productivity gains

Indexes: 1987=100

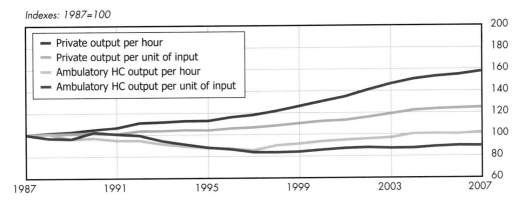

9.2b Over 20 years, hourly output of health facilities increased even as productivity per unit of input declined, and then remained relatively flat

Indexes: 1987=100

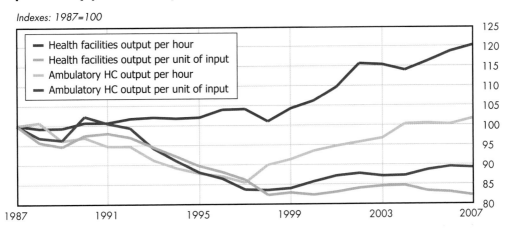

Note: Health facilities = hospitals and nursing and residential care facilities; outpatient = ambulatory health care services.

9.2c Productivity has increased much faster in the medical device industry than in the pharmaceutical industry, where output per unit of input is decreasing

Indexes: 1987=100

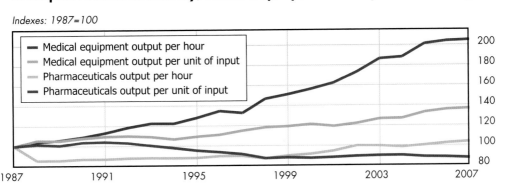

Productivity tends to be lower in the health sector despite more education among health workers compared with those in the rest of the economy.

Of those who work in the health industry, 75 percent of men and 50 percent of women have at least a college degree (figure 9.3a). Conversely, compared with the work force in general, a much lower share of health sector workers have less than a high school diploma or have graduated only from high school without any additional schooling. In the general economy, increased education of the work force has been an important source of growth in output. That is, higher levels of education have tended to contribute to productivity growth. Thus, low productivity growth in health care exists despite high levels of worker education.

Earnings tend to rise with educational attainment. Compared with males whose highest level of education is a high school diploma, male health workers who have a bachelor's degree have average annual incomes that are twice as high. Males who have advanced degrees earn five times as much as high school graduates (figure 9.3b).

Many labor economists believe that individuals who have higher education levels earn more because they produce more. Education brings more skill and knowledge to the individual. A more educated person can perform several different tasks and has greater awareness of other job opportunities. A contrary view maintains that high school diplomas and college degrees are credentials, useful for hiring but not necessarily for measures of what people actually produce on the job, when hired. To an employer, a person who has a degree might seem well motivated and reliable, that is, likelier to have characteristics considered desirable in an employee than an equivalent individual who has no degree. In a heavily regulated industry such as health care, credentialing might have as much to do with professional rent-seeking behavior as it does with higher productivity. It is difficult to isolate a pure "education effect" on output because of the difficulty of measuring personal characteristics and because other attributes, such as experience, are closely related to education.

Whether it reflects lagging productivity or something else, recent growth in health sector earnings has been slower than for other workers (figure 9.3c).

9.3a For both men and women, education levels are much higher in health services than among employees in other industries

Percentage of workers with education level shown (March 2009)

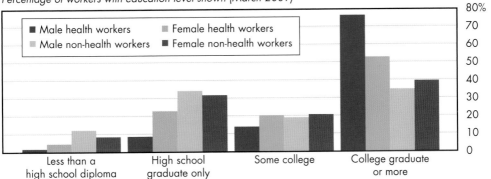

- ■ Male health workers
- ■ Female health workers
- ■ Male non-health workers
- ■ Female non-health workers

Less than a high school diploma   High school graduate only   Some college   College graduate or more

9.3b Average earnings for full-time, year-round employees in the health industry generally increase with education

Index: Average earnings for full-time year-round male workers with high school diploma = 100

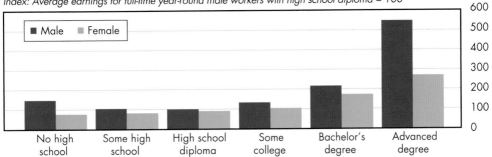

- ■ Male
- ■ Female

No high school   Some high school   High school diploma   Some college   Bachelor's degree   Advanced degree

Note: Earnings are for 2008.

9.3c Recent growth in health sector earnings has been slower than for other employees, except those who have the least education

Annual growth in mean earnings of full-time year-round workers 18 and older, 2003–2009

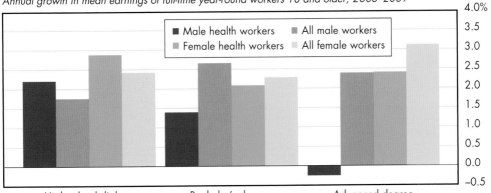

- ■ Male health workers
- ■ All male workers
- ■ Female health workers
- ■ All female workers

High school diploma   Bachelor's degree   Advanced degree

Information capital per hour has risen far less slowly in ambulatory health services than in private business overall.

Information capital stock in the health services sector has approximately quadrupled in the 20 years since 1987 (figure 9.4a). Such capital stock includes computers, software, and communications equipment. It also includes traditional office equipment. As with many other data series presented up to this point, this one is restricted to ambulatory health services and health facilities. The picture might well be different were parallel numbers available for pharmaceutical and medical device manufacturing.

More important, in the health sector, the BLS also includes medical instruments, whether as small as a pair of surgical clamps or as large as a PET scanner. With the huge growth in medical equipment (the industry's output more than doubled from 1987–2008), this large increase in information capital for medical services might not be that surprising. Indeed, excluding the "other office equipment" category, the total amount of information stock held in the form of computers, software, and communications equipment is less than $40 billion. This is 10 times the inflation-adjusted level of spending reported in 1987 but amounts to less than four cents per dollar of annual health services industry output.

A better metric compares real information capital to labor hours, because these too have grown since 1987. In the private sector overall, real information capital per hour quadrupled over the subsequent 20 years (figure 9.4b). For much of this period, the same metric for health facilities grew practically in lockstep with private business. After 2003, real information capital per labor hour grew somewhat faster in health facilities than in the rest of private industry. The growth rate for health facilities was almost triple the increase seen in the ambulatory health services industry.

Selected provisions of health reform are intended to stimulate greater investments in electronic medical records and other forms of health information technology. How much such infusions of new information capital will affect the relative growth trends shown is unclear. That is, this will increase the aggregate amount of information capital. But some of this might be labor-saving. So, the rate of growth in real information capital per hour might be slower or faster than in recent decades, depending on the extent to which capital substitutes for labor.

9.4a Information capital stock in the health services sector has quadrupled during the past 20 years

Billions of 2000 dollars

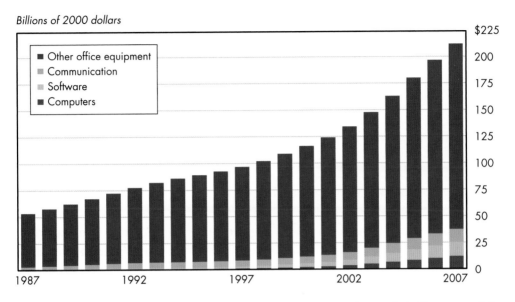

Note: All growth rates calculated through the end of the last year shown in each interval. Health services includes private sector ambulatory health services, hospitals, nursing and residential care facilities. It does not include pharmaceuticals, medical devices, health insurance, or government hospital workers. However, *other office equipment* includes medical and non-medical instruments used in the health services subsector.

9.4b Since 1987, real information capital per hour in health facilities grew almost three times as fast as in ambulatory health care services

Indexes: 1987=100

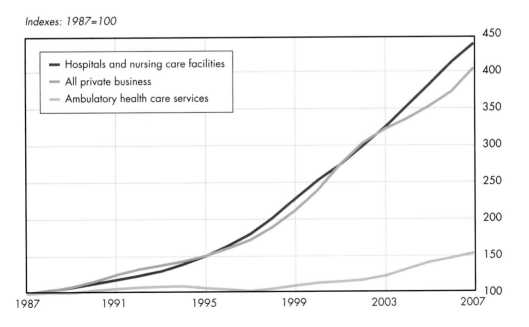

Expenditures for R&D have expanded our scientific and technological knowledge; this has contributed to the increase in health sector productivity.

Relative investments in R&D appear to be less in the health sector than in private business overall. By one traditional measure—the ratio of R&D capital to productive capital stock—R&D investments are approximately five times as large in the private sector as in the health services industry (figure 9.5a). Ignoring details of measurement, productive capital stocks simply are a way of measuring the total amount of capital available at any given time, accounting for the fact that all other things being equal, new capital is more productive than old capital.

By some measures, growth in capital stock is higher in some health-related industries than in the general economy. Unless R&D investments also increased at a similarly accelerated rate, the ratio of R&D to capital stocks would tend to decline even if investments in R&D were growing at identical rates in health care compared with the general economy.

Thus, a more "neutral" comparison would be to measure R&D relative to total output. When done, the health sector looks much more comparable to the general economy (figure 9.5b). There have been periods such as 1960–1979 in which relative R&D investments have been higher in health care. However, using this same measure, the current level of R&D in the overall economy is approximately 50 percent higher than in health care.

Neither of these measures proves that the health sector invests "too little" in R&D. First, they are only approximate measures. Second, the measure that compares R&D to productive stocks is limited to one component of the health industry, leaving out the subsector—pharmaceuticals—that arguably is the most important from an R&D perspective. Finally, whether an investment in R&D makes sense in any industry depends on the technological opportunity set available at that time. The expected rate of return to such investments often can depend on advances in basic science (for example, nanotechnology) that are beyond the control of any given industry. As long as there are differences in such rates of return, disparities in the rate of R&D investment are unavoidable.

9.5a The ratio of R&D capital to productive capital stock is approximately five times as high in private business as in health services

Net stock of R&D capital per $1,000 of productive capital stocks

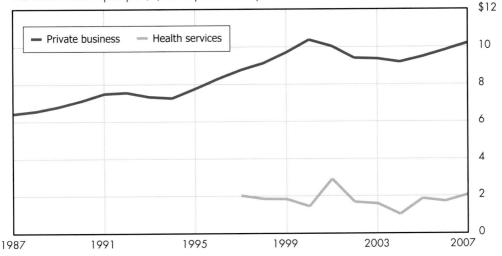

Note: All growth rates calculated through the end of the last year shown in each interval. Health services includes private sector ambulatory health services, hospitals, nursing and residential care facilities. It does not include pharmaceuticals, medical devices, health insurance, or government hospital workers. The data for health services did not begin until 1997.

9.5b The ratio of R&D capital to GDP is higher than the ratio of health care R&D to NHE; the opposite was true from 1960 to 1979

Net stock of R&D capital per $1,000 of GDP or NHE

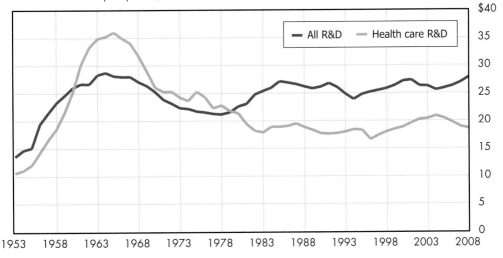

Note: R&D expenditures include both private and public sector spending, regardless of where the R&D was actually conducted.

Since 1982, increased personal health spending alone can explain approximately 80 percent of the decline in personal savings. Although U.S. health spending matches its gross annual savings, most of the nation's major competitors save much more than they spend on health care.

For at least 25 years, rising health expenditures generally have been matched by a parallel decline in the personal savings rate (figure 9.6a). Capital stocks are the accumulation of investment flows, the financing of which depends on savings. Total savings for the nation encompass private savings, government savings, and foreign investment.

Measured relative to disposable (post-tax) personal income, the personal savings rate generally was on an upward path for 35 years starting in 1947 (figure 9.6a). Taken together, Americans typically saved more than they spent on personal health care during this period. After 1982, there was a sharp reversal in this trend. The savings rate generally declined even as personal health spending continued to rise. Mathematically, the positive slope of the personal health spending line is almost as steep as the negative slope of the personal savings line. Statistically, approximately 80 percent of the variation in the personal savings rate can be explained simply by knowing the share of disposable income allocated to personal health spending.

On average, gross annual saving in the United States is almost identical to its level of national health expenditures. In contrast, the savings rate among the rest of its G7 competitors generally is much more than their spending on health care (figure 9.6b).

The relationship between savings and health spending is not nearly as tight at the cross-national level as it is within the United States over time. Although the nation that has the lowest share of GDP devoted to health spending also has the highest savings rate (Japan), the nation that has the next-lowest health spending also has a savings rate almost identical to that of the United States (the UK). In terms of comparable purchasing power, U.S. GDP per capita is much higher than among its biggest competitors. To match U.S. savings in real per capita terms would unavoidably require these nations to devote a higher share of GDP to savings.

9.6a The shares of income for personal health care and personal savings increased before 1982, but savings generally declined thereafter

Percentage of disposable personal income

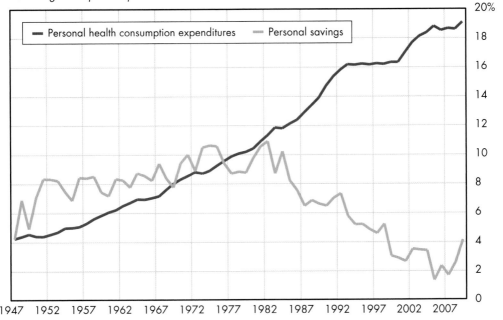

9.6b Health spending matches gross annual saving in the United States; in most other G7 countries, the national savings rate is much higher than their NHE

Percentage of GDP (2007)

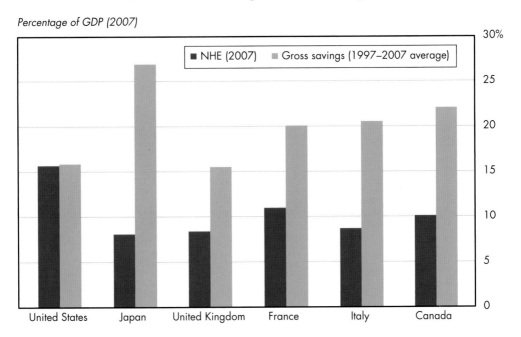

In many parts of the health sector, output generally has increased more slowly than the combined inputs of labor, capital, and other factors of production.

For much of the past 20 years, overall productivity growth has been negative for ambulatory health care and health facilities. Only in the last decade has multifactor productivity increased slightly in the ambulatory health services sector (figure 9.7a). Various factors of production such as labor, capital, and even information capital are discussed previously in this chapter. However, other inputs into the production process affect the level of output that is attainable. These include energy, materials, and purchased services (for example, legal services), among others. The various inputs are combined, based on their relative contribution to the cost of production. Thus, the net increase in inputs essentially is a weighted average of changes in all the various factors of production. For example, conceivably, efficiency improvements in the energy sector would result in a net decrease in energy inputs required to produce a unit of health output. Thus, the multifactor measure of inputs would have to combine negative growth in energy inputs with positive increases in other factors of production.

Viewed from this perspective, multifactor productivity generally has been declining in the pharmaceutical industry during the past 20 years (although this might have reversed itself since 1998). In sharp contrast, multifactor productivity in the medical device industry has grown by more than 30 percent during this period. This productivity outpaced the rate of increase in multifactor productivity in the private sector (figure 9.7b).

These disparate trends reinforce a general point that should have been increasingly clear as this chapter has evolved. The health industry comprises several subsectors that vary greatly in terms of the relative importance of labor, capital, and other factors of production, but also in terms of the degree that changes in such factors contribute to changes in overall output. The goods-producing portions of health care typically are different from the services-producing health industries. Even within the health services sector, health facilities are different from the components of ambulatory health services in terms of various productivity trends. This makes it difficult to generalize about the health industry as a whole.

9.7a Multifactor productivity growth has steadily increased in ambulatory care over 20 years but is negative for health facilities

Compound annual rate of change in multifactor productivity

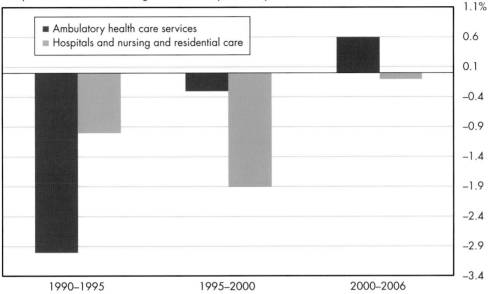

Legend:
■ Ambulatory health care services
■ Hospitals and nursing and residential care

Y-axis: 1.1%, 0.6, 0.1, −0.4, −0.9, −1.4, −1.9, −2.4, −2.9, −3.4

X-axis: 1990–1995, 1995–2000, 2000–2006

9.7b Multifactor productivity has decreased in pharmaceuticals even while increasing in the medical device industry more quickly than in the private sector

Multifactor productivity indexes: 1987=100

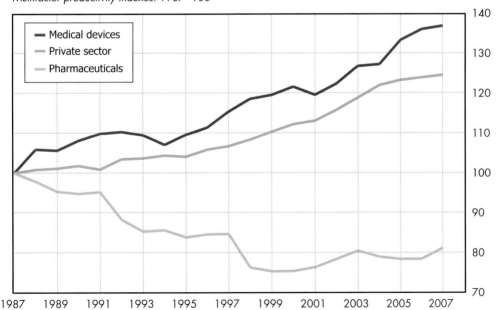

Legend:
— Medical devices
— Private sector
— Pharmaceuticals

Y-axis: 140, 130, 120, 110, 100, 90, 80, 70

X-axis: 1987, 1989, 1991, 1993, 1995, 1997, 1999, 2001, 2003, 2005, 2007

The Labor Force and Employment in the Health Sector

Since 1930, if health services employment had increased only as fast as in the rest of the economy, the health sector would have employed nearly 11 million fewer workers in 2009. Employment has increased faster in ambulatory health services than in hospitals or nursing homes.

In every decade since the 1930s, total health services employment has increased two to three times as fast as the number of workers in the general economy or private business (figure 10.1a). The numbers exclude workers in the goods-producing part of the health industry, along with employment by health insurers. It is uncertain whether inclusion of such workers would appreciably alter the data. Because the general population grows at approximately 1 percent a year, the numbers in figure 10.1a also illustrate the ratio of health services growth to the overall population. In none of those 80 years has health sector growth been less than two percent a year; in the 1970s, the annual increase reached almost seven percent. These general trends are quite consistent with previous information about growth in health care expenditures relative to the economy (refer to figure 1.5a).

In light of the surge in spending that occurred in the aftermath of the arrival of Medicare and Medicaid in the mid-1960s, the extremely high relative growth in health sector employment might not be surprising. However, even in the 1950s, the health sector work force also grew three times as quickly as employment in private businesses overall. The 1980s were characterized by increasing concerns about rising health expenditures; indeed, this became an important issue in the 1992 election and a failed effort at health reform in 1993–94. Conversely, the late 1990s saw a noticeable slowdown in health spending, yet that increase in health industry employment relative to the rest of the economy during that decade was practically the mirror image of the pattern in the 1980s.

Since 2000, growth in health sector employment reached its lowest level since the 1930s in absolute terms. Yet this growth rate nevertheless was triple the rate of increase in both overall civilian employment and private business employment during that period.

Employment consistently has grown faster in ambulatory health services than in health facilities (figure 10.1b). The annual rates of increase for all services except hospitals has declined for each of the snapshots shown in the figure. However, the rate of increase became larger for hospitals, but the *absolute* rate of increase for hospitals is lower than for ambulatory health services for all years, even 2000–2008. The introduction of Medicaid fueled a nursing home boom that lasted more than a decade.

10.1a For 80 years, growth in health services employment has greatly exceeded the rate of growth in the number of all employees, as well as for all workers in private business

Compound annual growth rate in number of full-time-equivalent (FTE) employees (percent)

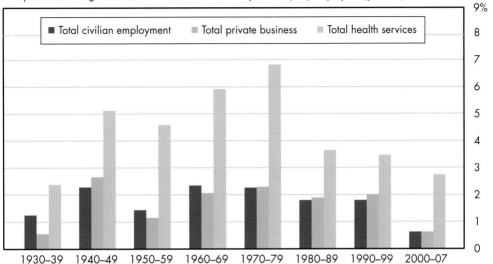

Note: All growth rates calculated through the end of the last year shown in each interval. Health services includes private sector ambulatory health services, hospitals, nursing and residential care facilities. It does not include pharmaceuticals, medical devices, health insurance, or government hospital workers.

10.1b Employment growth has steadily become smaller since 1972, except in hospitals, where the employee growth rate increased starting in 2000

Compound annual growth rate in number of total employees (percent)

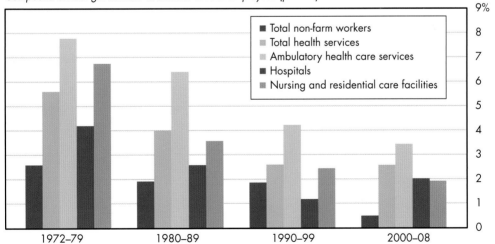

Note: All growth rates calculated through the end of the last year shown in each interval. Health services includes private sector ambulatory health services, hospitals, nursing and residential care facilities. It does not include pharmaceuticals, medical devices, health insurance, or government hospital workers.

The health sector as a share of total employment is higher in the United States than in other industrialized countries. The industry's growth relative to all employment appears comparable with other G7 nations in recent years.

The share of civilian employment in the health and social work sector is higher in the United States than in other nations in the G7 (figure 10.2a). Nevertheless, compared with 1995, all these major competitors experienced, along with the United States, an increase in health sector employment relative to all civilian workers. It is worth noting that in the three OECD countries most comparable to the United States in terms of standardized per capita health expenditures (Norway, Switzerland, and the Netherlands), health employment exceeds 11.5 percent of total employment; in Norway it equals 20 percent. The U.S. level is assuredly not the highest in the world.

These data have three limitations. First, they combine health sector workers with veterinary workers and those doing other types of social work services. In the United States, "social assistance" makes up approximately 15 percent of the total for health services and social assistance. This is a catch-all category for various services: emergency and other relief, vocational rehabilitation, child day care, and other individual or family services. Unfortunately, data do not show whether this 15 percent share is similar in other G7 countries (a higher share would make the differences between the United States and other nations even more than shown). Second, reporting gaps for the United States, Japan, and France preclude an exact comparison of numbers, especially for 1995 (figure 10.2a note). Finally, the data shown are self-reported estimates from population surveys. In the United States, such self-reporting for health care is one-seventh higher than are more precise counts obtained through detailed employer surveys.

These limitations inhibit our ability to get precise cross-sectional comparisons between the United States and other nations. Nevertheless, it is possible to compare how employment in this health sector and social work aggregate grew relative to civilian employment overall in each country. In the United States, health sector and social work employment grew 1 percent a year faster than did civilian employment (figure 10.2b). This was much slower than in Japan and the same as the experience in the UK and Italy, but the U.S. increase was approximately double the added growth rate in health workers in France and Canada, relative to the whole work force.

10.2a Employment in the health and social work sector has a higher share of total civilian employment in the United States than in other G7 nations

Health and social work sector employment as a percentage of total civilian employment

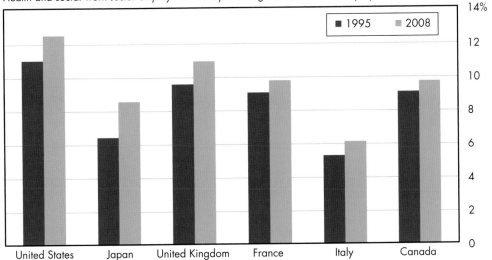

Note: Health and social work includes human health activities, veterinary activities, and social work activities. For the United States and Japan, the 1995 figure is imputed from 2003, which is the earliest year with data reported for this measure. In France, data refer to employees only (excluding the self-employed). This underestimates by about 10 percent the total number of people employed in health and social services.

10.2b U.S. growth in health sector employment relative to total employment has been approximately the same as in the other G7 countries

Compound annual growth rate (CAGR) in number of health/social work employees minus CAGR in number of all civilian workers, 1995–2008

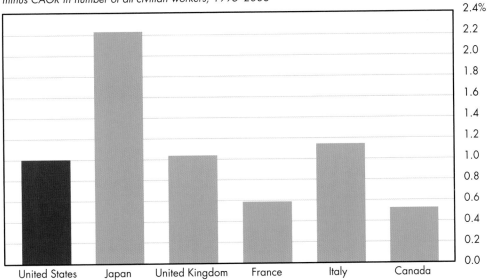

Whether the opportunity cost of health sector employment in the United States is more or less than in the rest of the G7 depends on how it is measured.

Health expenditures are not a good measure of whether the burden of medical care is more or less in the United States, compared with its major competitors. If markets are less competitive in health care due to regulation or other forces, this will result in higher prices. Thus, for each unit of resources used (for example, an hour of labor), spending might be more in medical care than if the identical resource were used elsewhere in the economy. Briefly, spending might be much more than costs.

However, because higher prices result in income to someone (for example, doctors, drug company shareholders), decreasing the medical prices might change the distribution income in the economy. Nevertheless, it will not make Americans better off in the aggregate (every dollar of income "won" by buyers would be matched by a corresponding loss by the sellers of medical services).

Two methods provide an approximate measure of the opportunity cost of health services labor across countries. One approach calculates the percentage of the population employed in health care. This method assumes that the cost to any economy of diverting a worker into the health care sector is approximated by GDP per worker in that economy. However, this would be a poor approximation for doctors, whose value to the economy presumably would be much higher than average GDP per employee even if they were employed elsewhere. Taking this into account—by weighting employment by the average ratio of doctor compensation to nurse compensation in the countries shown in figure 10.3a—the U.S. share of employment is higher than in its competitors, but not by much.

Another approach assumes that the opportunity cost of health workers is the same elsewhere as in the United States. When applying U.S. prices to the number of physicians, nurses, and other workers, the opportunity cost of medical labor is lower in the United States than in any of its major competitors (figure 10.3b). That is, after accounting for the higher prices paid for medical labor in the United States, the level of potential output these nations give up to produce health care is greater than in the United States.

Neither of these exactly measures U.S. comparative performance. However, the truth is likely to fall somewhere in between these estimates.

10.3a The opportunity cost for health employees is only slightly more in the United States than in the rest of the G7

Weighted health employment as percentage of total (2006)

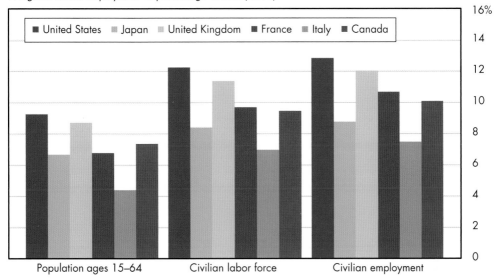

Note: Weighted figures are calculated by multiplying the number of general practitioners, specialists, and all other doctors times their respective salary ratios (see below) and adding this to the total number of non-physician health sector employees. The salary ratios were calculated as the average ratio of compensation for doctors relative to nurses for nine countries (six shown plus the three more with the highest level of health spending per capita: The Netherlands, Norway, and Switzerland). The ratios were: 1.8 for GPs, 2.8 for specialists, and 3.0 for all other MDs.

10.3b When U.S. prices are applied to health sector employment, the United States has a lower relative share of GDP spent for doctors and nurses

Standardized spending on medical labor (U.S. prices) as percentage of GDP (2006)

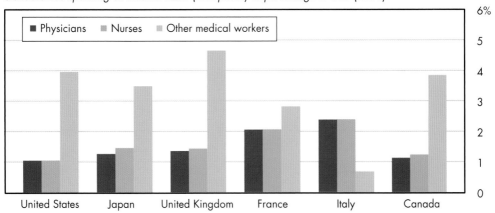

Note: Standardized spending is calculated using U.S. levels of compensation for general practitioners, MD specialists, and nurses (both standardized spending and GDP measured in 2006 U.S. dollars, purchasing power parity).

Females account for more than 75 percent of health sector employees but constitute fewer than half of employees in the goods-producing part of the health sector.

Although females make up fewer than half of all civilian workers, they comprise more than 75 percent of workers in the health sector (figure 10.4a). This share varies dramatically across different components of the health industry. In the goods-producing part of the industry—manufacturing of pharmaceuticals, medical equipment, and supplies (which together make up only 6.5 percent of health sector employment)— the female share is slightly less than among all civilian workers.

In the services part of health care, the share of female workers is dramatically higher. In home health care, nine of 10 workers are women. In nursing-care facilities, seven of eight workers are female (although in residential facilities that do not provide skilled nursing care, the female share is less than 75 percent). Most ambulatory health services have a workforce in which women make up 75 percent of employees. Hospital workers have approximately the same share of female workers.

The differences in share of females are even wider at the individual occupational level. Women make up 88 percent of health care support occupations such as nursing and home health aides, compared with fewer than 75 percent of workers in health care practitioner and technical occupations. In the five health-related occupations that have the highest share of females, women make up more than 90 percent of employees (figure 10.4b). Also shown are registered nurses (RNs), who make up the single largest occupation in health care, almost 90 percent of whom are female.

The five occupations in which women are least represented include four that require doctoral training; these include chiropractors (22 percent), physicians and surgeons (32 percent), dentists (44 percent), and pharmacists (48 percent). Although some pharmacists have only bachelor's degrees, all newly minted pharmacists now must have a doctorate. However, these numbers are gradually changing. Currently, females comprise half of all medical students; chiropractics is also seeing an increase in the female share of graduates.

10.4a Females account for more than 75 percent of health sector employees compared with fewer than half of civilian employment overall

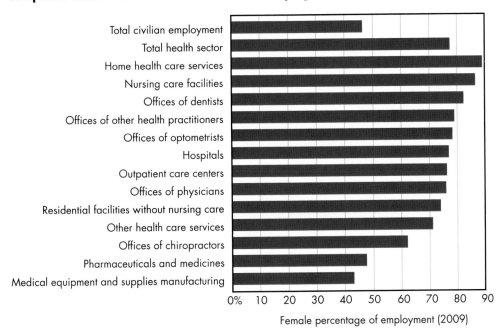

Female percentage of employment (2009)

10.4b Females tend to be concentrated more in health care support occupations than in health care practitioner or technical occupations

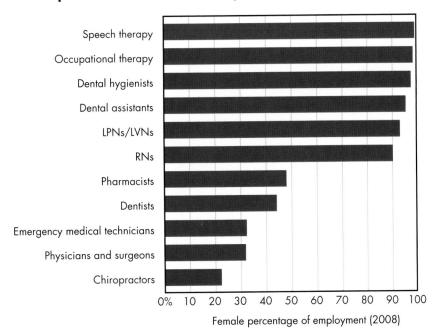

Female percentage of employment (2008)

Note: LPN = licensed practical nurse; LVN = licensed vocational nurse; RN = registered nurse.

Compared with employees in general, the work-year per full-time equivalent worker is several hundred hours shorter for health services employees. Recently, annual work hours per employee generally have declined in long-term care facilities while increasing in hospitals.

The average health care worker spends fewer hours a year working than do employees in private business or all civilian workers (the latter includes government employees). This statement is valid regardless of whether hours per worker or average annual hours per full-time equivalent (FTE) worker are counted (figure 10.5a). Within the health services industry, hospital workers have the longest work-years, followed by ambulatory health care services employees and those in nursing and residential care facilities. These respective differences are less than the difference in hours worked in health care compared with the total economy.

Annual hours worked in the goods-producing part of the health sector, including manufacture of pharmaceuticals and medical equipment, are much more than in the general economy. In pharmaceuticals, the length of the work-year peaked in 2002 but has declined subsequently, even though the total number of employees in the industry continues to grow (except for the years 2008 and 2009, which reflects the economic slow-down).

In the hospital industry, the work-year has generally increased since 1987, but hospital employees also saw a sharp increase in their annual hours starting in 2002 (figure 10.5b). This increase likewise occurred despite rising numbers of hospital employees. Changes in the length of the work-year have been more modest in ambulatory health care services, and nursing and residential care facilities. Since the start of the 21st century, there has been a general, modest decline in the length of the work-year among employees of nursing homes. In contrast, the length of the work-year generally has risen in the ambulatory care sector for approximately 20 years.

10.5a Across the health services industry, annual hours per employee are shorter than in private business or the general economy

Average annual work hours per employee (2009)

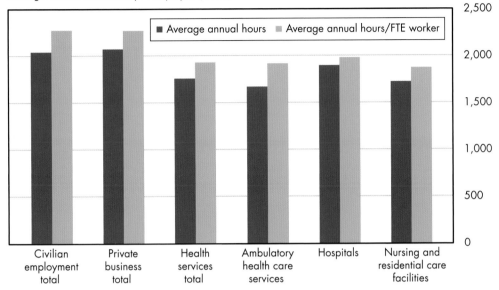

■ Average annual hours   ■ Average annual hours/FTE worker

| Civilian employment total | Private business total | Health services total | Ambulatory health care services | Hospitals | Nursing and residential care facilities |

10.5b Annual hours per employee have declined in long-term care facilities during the past decade but have generally risen in hospitals

Average annual work hours per employee

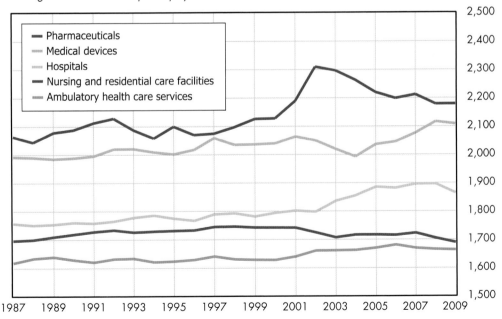

— Pharmaceuticals
— Medical devices
— Hospitals
— Nursing and residential care facilities
— Ambulatory health care services

Increased longevity and a shorter working life have lengthened the period of retirement for men but not for women.

Since 1900, male life expectancy at age 20 has risen by 14 years, yet working-life expectancy currently is *lower* than it was when Theodore Roosevelt first was elected president. Working-life expectancy for men generally declined slowly but steadily starting in 1950, although it has increased slightly since 1990.

A baby born in 1900 had a life expectancy of only 47 years. A baby born in 2007 has a life expectancy of 77.9 years. The health sector cannot take credit for this entire 30-year increase in life expectancy. Public health measures such as improved sanitation and clean drinking water surely played a role. For the same reason, everyone believes that the rapid growth in the health care sector in the United States contributed to these remarkable gains in years of life.

At the start of the last century, a man age 20 could expect to live an additional 42 years, during which he could expect to work 38 years (figure 10.6a). The period of retirement was thus short. By 2004, life expectancy for a typical 20-year-old man had climbed to 56 years, yet his expected working-life expectancy still was 38 years! With a longer life expectancy and no change in working-life expectancy, the expected duration of retirement rose to 18 years, a considerable increase over four years a century earlier. Another way to look at this is to consider that in 1900, a man surviving to age 20 could expect to work 90 percent of his remaining life; by 2004, that share was less than 65 percent.

Women have a different course. Female life expectancy has risen even more than for men over the same period—from 44 to 61 years for a woman age 20 (figure 10.6b). Working-life numbers for women also rose more rapidly, as women's participation in the labor force has increased. In 1940, the average woman at age 20 could expect to be actively working in paid employment for only 12 years—less than 25 percent of her remaining years of life. This was 28 years fewer than the comparable number for men. By 2004, this male-female difference had decreased to only five years.

Despite these changes, men today have 11 more working years than women do. Women spend far more time in paid employment than a century ago, but such work accounts for only approximately half of their adult lives.

10.6a The health sector helped contribute to increasing male life expectancy over the past century, yet working-life expectancy declined

Additional years of life expectancy at age 20

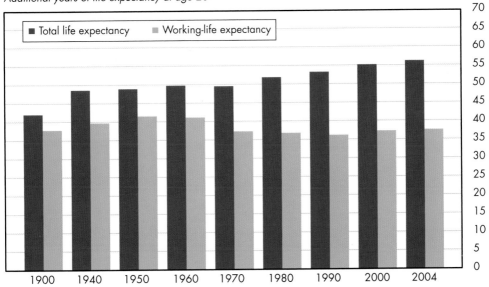

10.6b Increased life expectancy for females generally has been accompanied by rising working-life expectancy

Additional years of life expectancy at age 20

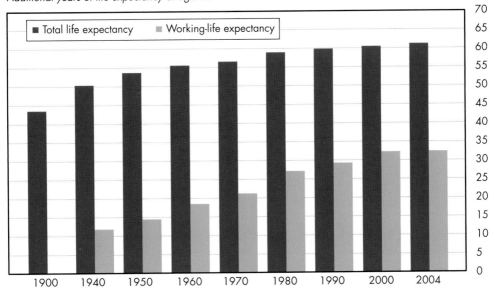

Note: Working-life expectancy not available for females in 1900.

CHAPTER 11

Personal Incomes and Health Care

For the average American worker, growth in real hourly earnings has in recent decades lagged behind growth in real compensation per hour, due in part to rising health costs.

Inflation-adjusted hourly wages in 2008 were 2.8 times as high as they were 60 years earlier. This has occurred despite rapid growth in supplements to wages and salaries, including employer-provided health coverage, payroll tax deductions for health-related purposes such as Medicare and workers' compensation, and other fringe benefits.

The data in figure 11.1 include only the employer's contribution toward health insurance and social insurance. Thus, the 1.45 percent employer contribution for Medicare is included but not the parallel contribution made by the employee that appears as a deduction on most employee paychecks. Likewise, the "hidden" employer contribution to employer-sponsored health insurance is included, but not the employee share of the premium (which again shows as a paycheck deduction that reduces the monetary compensation that otherwise would go to the employee).

This calculation uses the PCE price deflator to remove the effect of inflation. For several reasons, the PCE price deflator is superior to the more commonly reported CPI. It more accurately reflects changes in the purchasing power of U.S. workers. Figure 11.1 is indexed to hourly earnings rather than total compensation. Thus, it also shows how much cash earnings would have increased had there been no increase in wage and salary supplements over the past 60 years. In that case, earnings would have been 3.5 times as high.

The exact percentages are not important. As an approximation, almost half the increase in compensation for wage and salary supplements was health-related. The lion's share of these health-related add-ons was for group health coverage. Because Medicare payroll taxes support the care of today's Medicare beneficiaries, some might question whether this is an employee "benefit" at all. However, from a social contract point of view, it does not matter whether individuals are literally banking for their own future retiree health expenses or merely making their contributions into a pool in exchange for a promise to receive such benefits in the future. The purpose is unquestionably health-related.

11.1 Rising health-related supplements are an important reason real hourly earnings have grown less quickly than average compensation

Inflation-adjusted hourly wages index using PCE deflator: 1948=100

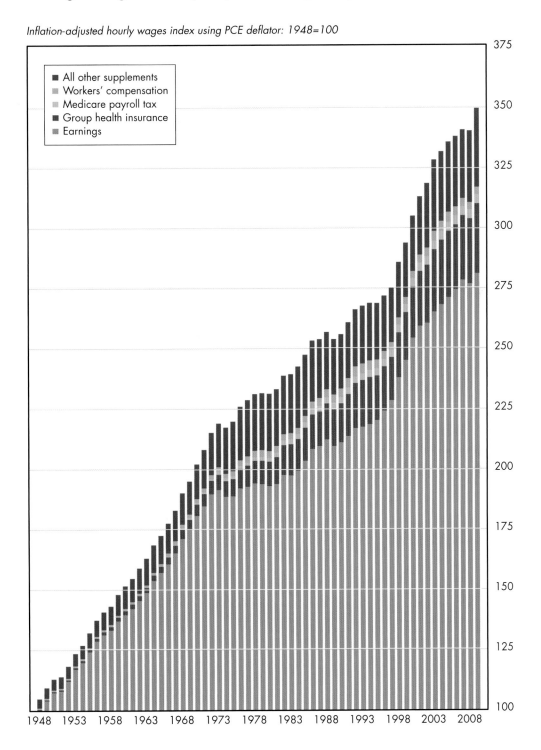

Employee compensation in the health services industry is much more than the average for other service industries but only slightly more than the average for all workers.

In the health services industry, the average compensation per FTE worker is more than $10,000 higher than for other workers in the service industry (figure 11.2a). It is lower than compensation in private goods-producing industries but slightly higher than the average for all private-sector workers. Both higher cash payments and fringe benefits contribute to the health care's margin of advantage.

Because detailed data are not available, these numbers exclude workers in the pharmaceutical and medical device industries. They also do not count government workers who might be employed in hospitals or other government-owned facilities. However, average compensation for all types of government workers is much higher than in the private sector (figure 11.2a, right axis). Therefore, inclusion of public sector health workers might increase the health industry average overall rather than reduce it. This is not certain because some of the difference in public versus private compensation relates to differences in the skill mix used in each sector.

The average compensation for health services masks some sizable differences across different parts of the industry. Average compensation for nursing and residential facilities is only approximately half the level seen in ambulatory health care services such as physicians' offices (figure 11.2b). In the former facilities, a relatively large portion of the workforce is performing custodial care that requires less skill and training than is required for many of the highly specialized personnel used in hospitals, for example.

Currently, one of every nine private employees works in the health care industry, a fraction that the BLS projects will grow over the next decade. Of the 12.2 million FTE private workers in the health sector in 2008, 40 percent work in ambulatory health care services, slightly more than 30 percent work in hospitals, and the remainder work in nursing homes and residential care facilities. It is somewhat more difficult to forecast health services employment under the health reform law. Total health spending is expected to rise. However, stringent limitations on Medicare payments, for example, have raised the prospect that some health facilities will be forced out of business altogether.

11.2a Average compensation in the health care industry is higher than in the rest of the service sector but lower than for public employees

Annual compensation per FTE worker (2008 dollars)

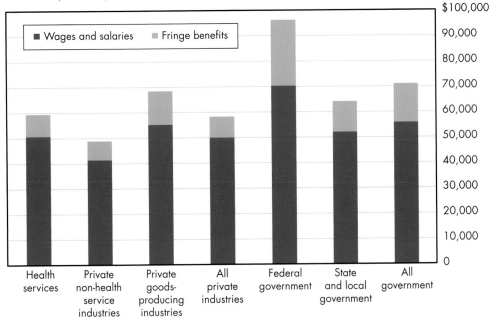

11.2b Average annual compensation is much lower in long-term care facilities, such as nursing homes, than elsewhere in the health sector

Annual compensation per FTE (2008 dollars)

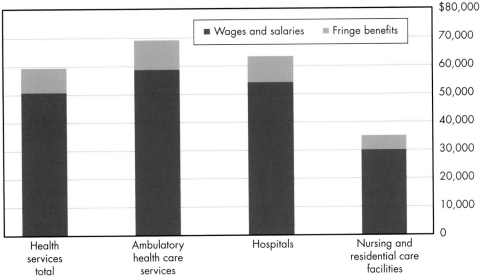

Real compensation per hour has increased more slowly in the ambulatory health sector than in the rest of the economy.

In terms of worker purchasing power, real (inflation-adjusted) hourly compensation in ambulatory health care has matched changes in hourly output over the long haul (figure 11.3a). This might seem unremarkable except that it deviates from the experience in the private sector generally. In most of the economy, inflation-adjusted hourly compensation increased in the 20 years starting in 1987. However, it did not rise as quickly as changes in real hourly output over the same period.

In ambulatory health services, real hourly compensation rose far more rapidly than either hourly compensation in the rest of the economy or hourly output in that industry. Subsequently, however, compensation steadily declined from its "excess" level in 1992 to a level more comparable with the change in hourly output by 2007. This is more in line with conventional economic theory that wages generally will reflect the productivity of labor. However, this compensation index measures wages in terms of worker purchasing power (as previously written, by dividing by the PCE price deflator to remove the effects of general inflation).

An alternative approach divides by the price of business output. This reflects the price of what a worker can produce in an hour. Doing this (figure 11.3b), the private sector shows a much tighter fit between changes in hourly output and what is paid to labor (although in recent years, compensation again has begun to lag behind higher productivity).

The facts in the ambulatory care sector are quite different. Although labor productivity increased by 10 percent over this period, hourly compensation declined by approximately the same amount. This reflects the fact that prices in the ambulatory health care sector have outpaced worker productivity gains. If prices rose in parallel with productivity gains—as apparently they do in the private sector generally—then real compensation for ambulatory services workers would have risen 10 percent also.

Briefly, real hourly compensation has risen less rapidly in the ambulatory health sector than in the rest of the economy. This reflects the reality that hourly productivity gains in that sector likewise have been less.

11.3a In terms of employee purchasing power, real hourly compensation in ambulatory health care matches changes in hourly output over the long haul

Indexes: 1987=100

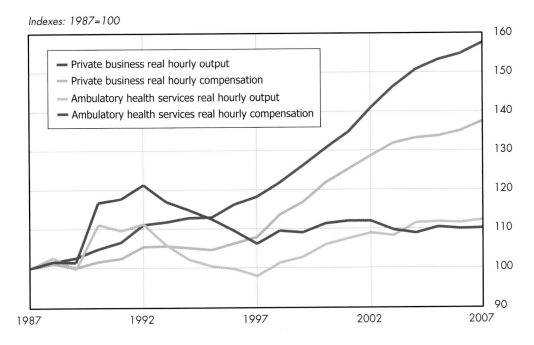

11.3b Relative to the price of hourly output, real hourly compensation in ambulatory health services has decreased since 1992; it rose in private business overall

Indexes: 1987=100

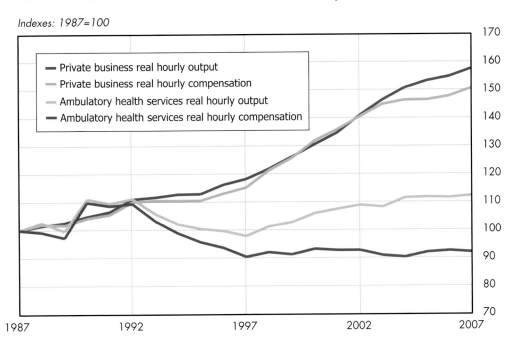

Health professionals in the United States have much higher relative incomes than do their counterparts in other industrialized countries.

In general, the United States pays higher prices for health labor than are paid elsewhere. The price differential varies a great deal, depending on the category of health professional examined. The average annual remuneration of physician specialists in the United States is more than six times the nation's GDP per capita (which was approximately $46,000 in 2009). Physician specialists in OECD countries for which such data are available also are well paid, but the comparable ratio to GDP per capita is less than four to one (figure 11.4a). Alternatively, even accounting for the fact that the United States has higher wages and GDP per capita than the OECD comparators have, U.S. specialists, relatively speaking, are paid 50 percent more than their counterparts in competitor nations receive.

A similar result with less pronounced differences can be told for general physicians. In the United States, their relative compensation is the same as the average compensation of specialists in the OECD. Generalist physicians in the OECD earn on average less than three times per capita GDP in their own country. Thus, U.S. physician generalists are paid in relative terms almost 50 percent more than physicians in other industrialized nations receive.

The U.S. pay differential shrinks further in the case of nurses. U.S. nurses, on average, are paid approximately 50 percent more than GDP per capita, whereas in the OECD they are paid approximately 10 percent more on average. Thus, a typical U.S. nurse earns approximately 30 percent more than do counterparts in the OECD.

More detail illustrates some of the variation masked by using averages. The annual compensation for nurses employed in American hospitals is almost 2.5 times as high as that for the average U.S. worker (figure 11.4b). This is the same as the relative compensation of nurses in the UK. Although relative nurse pay is lower in some other countries (Finland and Norway), it is higher in Australia, Denmark, and Ireland. U.S. health workers generally are compensated well in absolute and relative terms. Even so, this does not imply that U.S. prices for health labor necessarily are the highest in the world when taking into account the earnings or resources available to the rest of a nation's workers or population.

11.4a Physicians and nurses are paid relatively more in the United States than in other OECD countries, but the largest pay differential is for specialists

Ratio of annual compensation to own country GDP per capita (2006)

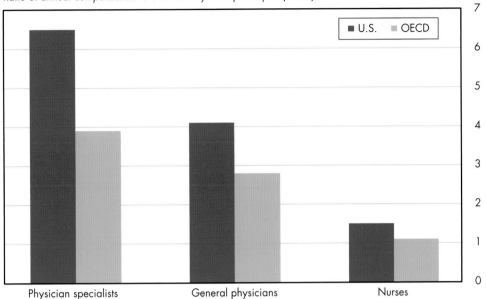

11.4b Nurses in American hospitals are paid more than twice the average employee wage, but that is also true elsewhere

Ratio: annual compensation of salaried hospital nurses relative to all workers (2007)

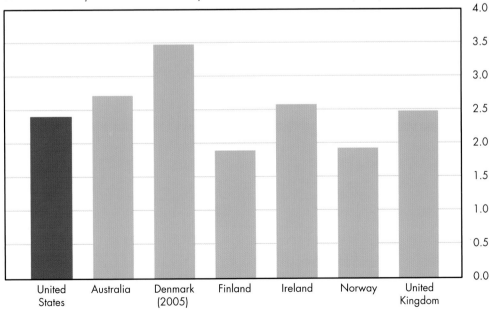

Physicians in the United States enjoyed rising rates of return for medical education for decades. Although such returns might have fallen recently, they appear to be similar for those who pursue careers in law or business.

The annual rate of return to investment in physician education currently is at double-digit levels. Approximately 50 years ago, earlier studies found that such rates of return were much less than 10 percent (figure 11.5a). The numbers represent the hours-adjusted annualized rate of return on medical education over a doctor's working lifetime. The investment in medical education includes direct costs (tuition, books, and so forth) and indirect costs, that is, the income foregone by attending school/residency rather than working.

The return on this investment is the higher annual compensation physicians receive relative to what similar individuals receive on average during each year of their career. The hourly adjustment is important because physicians work longer hours than the average worker does. The rate of return is annualized to make it the same as other investments. For example, from 1900–2009, the total rate of return for the Dow Jones Industrial Average (DJIA) was 9.4 percent.

These data are approximations because such information for every category of physician is not available. Each of the studies that constitute the data displayed in figure 1.5b differs in its methodological details. However, they suggest that a typical physician earns a healthy rate of return compared with investing comparable resources in the stock market. These sizable rates of return appear somewhat less than for other professional degrees such as MBA or law degrees (figure 11.5b). Dentists and physician specialists have comparable rates of return, but primary care doctors have lower—albeit still impressive—rates of return. This is consistent with the general impression that primary care doctors are "underpaid" relative to specialists. The study shown defined procedure-based medicine as surgery, obstetrics, radiology, anesthesiology, and medical subspecialties. Trends for these other professions are not available, but CEO compensation has increased considerably, relative to that of average workers (figure 11.5c).

These comparisons suggest that high prices for health labor in the United States might simply reflect higher returns to skilled labor across the board. If doctors were paid much less, more people might get MBAs or law degrees instead. This might reduce health spending, but reasonable people might disagree on whether it would improve social welfare.

11.5a The annual rate of return for medical education appears for some specialists to have increased over many decades

Hours-adjusted annualized internal rate of return on educational investment over a working lifetime

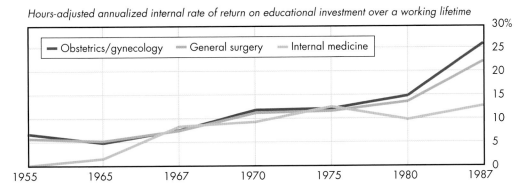

Note: The interval between years is not equal. Each year represents a different study. These studies have similar but not identical methodologies.

11.5b Physician specialists have higher educational rates of return than primary care doctors have, but these rates are lower than those for lawyers or for those who have MBA degrees

Hours-adjusted annualized internal rate of return on educational investment over a working lifetime

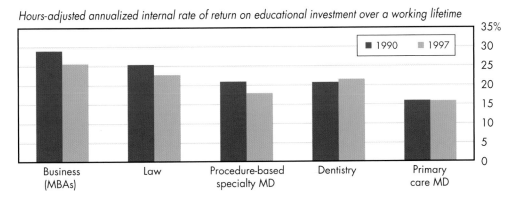

11.5c Increasing returns for physician education have occurred during a period in which CEO compensation also has been rapidly rising

Ratio: median CEO compensation compared with average U.S. worker compensation

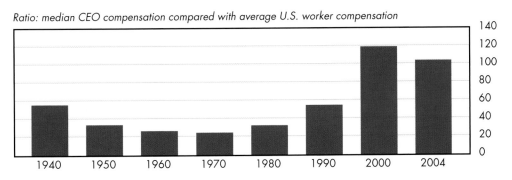

CHAPTER 12

Distribution of Health Services

1 percent of the population accounts for approximately 25 percent of health spending; 5 percent accounts for almost half.

The 1 percent of the population that has the highest annual health expenses accounts for almost 25 percent of health spending (figure 12.1a). Their annual spending in 2010 likely exceeded $125,000. Those in the top 5 percent account for just less than half of all spending, with average annual expenditures that exceed $50,000. With the average U.S. worker earning less than $50,000 a year, these numbers demonstrate the desirability of some kind of health insurance coverage. Few but the wealthiest families are in a position to self-insure spending at these amounts.

At the other end of the distribution, individuals in the bottom half of spenders account for only 3 percent of annual health costs. Their average annual spending is less than $350. Leaving aside administrative costs, an actuarially fair premium to cover only the catastrophic expenses of the top one percent would be almost $1300 a year. To cover the risk of being in the top 5 percent would require annual premiums of approximately $2,800. The challenge in a voluntary health insurance system is to convince a sizable share of those who have expected expenses of less than $350 to spend almost $3,000 to secure protection against risks that have only a 5 percent chance of occurring. The more low-risk individuals who opt out, the higher will be the premiums needed for those who remain. This greatly exaggerates the challenge when people are separated into different age groups. In that case, the difference between the lowest and highest spenders shrinks considerably.

Only selected snapshots in time are available The concentration of health spending might have become somewhat larger between 1963 and 1996 (figure 12.1b). However, there is evidence that it has fallen slightly in subsequent years. All the data from 1996 through 2007 come from the same household survey. Thus, one cannot dismiss the changes observed prior to that as an artifact of differences in methods of collecting this kind of statistics. Only one data point (from 1928) shows that the top 5 percent of spenders accounted for just over half of spending. This situation is almost identical to the share of spending accounted for by the same group 40 years later. In light of the enormous changes in technology that occurred in the intervening decades, there is no reason to expect such stability in the degree of health expenditure concentration.

12.1a One percent of the population accounts for approximately 25 percent of health spending; 5 percent accounts for almost half

Estimated per capita spending (2010)   *Percentage of total health spending (2007)*

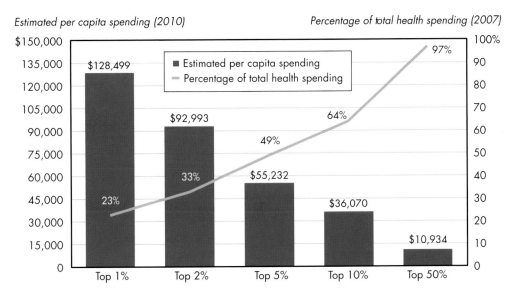

Distribution of population ranked by annual per capita health spending

Note: Percentages are for the civilian, non-institutionalized population based on Medical Expenditures Panel Survey (MEPS) data for 2007. 2010 per capita spending has been calculated from 2007 figures, adjusted to account for increased personal health spending per capita and to reduce differences between MEPS and NHE estimates.

12.1b The concentration of health spending has been stable over decades, but there is some indication it has declined recently

Percentage of total annual health spending accounted for by group

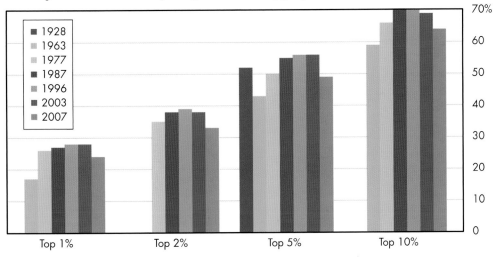

Distribution of population ranked by annual per capita health spending

After accounting for all hidden costs and subsidies, the net burden of paying for health care is 2.5 times as much for the very lowest-income families compared with the very highest-income families.

Households at the bottom of the income distribution devote more than 40 percent of their income to paying for health care (figure 12.2a). The corresponding number for those who have the highest incomes is approximately 15 percent. Thus, the relative burden (measured in terms of shares of income) is approximately 2½ times more for the first group compared with the last.

These data account for the entire burden of health spending for families in each income group. The spending data shown include the readily visible amounts paid by the family for out-of-pocket spending and premiums but also the hidden costs, such as the net employer share of premiums after subtracting any tax subsidies for health coverage. The hidden costs also include each family's estimated share of various payroll, income, and other taxes used to finance Medicare, Medicaid, and other health care spending.

Two points are worth noting. First, the burden at the lowest end of the distribution would be considerably less if it were based on actual annual expenditures by these households rather than income (which is negative or zero for a non-trivial number of households in the lowest-income bracket). Second, tax-financed health care is to some considerable degree targeted for those who have lower incomes (refer to figure 4.2b). Therefore, a measure of actual expenditures for health care (including tax-subsidized care) would result in a ratio that would likely be much higher. Thus, the *net* burden is considerably more evenly distributed than if families had to pay for all health expenses entirely on their own.

Out-of-pocket spending accounts for more than 30 percent of this burden for the lowest income families compared with less than 5 percent for those with the highest incomes (figure 12.2b). Conversely, health-related taxes make up more than 80 percent of the burden at the highest end of the income distribution compared with just over 20 percent for those at the lowest end. The premium share of the burden increases to the middle of the income distribution but declines thereafter.

12.2a The net burden of health-related expenditures is approximately 2½ times as large for extremely low-income families compared with extremely high-income families

Spending as percentage of family income (2002)

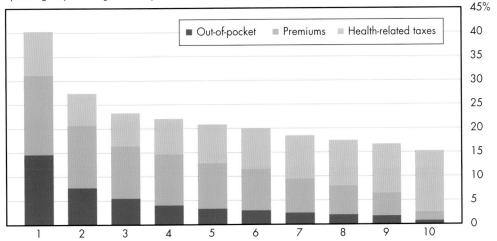

Income decile (1 = 10 percent of households with lowest incomes)

Note: The family burden of health expenditures includes out-of-pocket spending; premium payments for group and non-group health insurance (including the employer share) and Medicare Parts B and D; and health-related taxes, including payroll taxes for Medicare Part A and the family's share of other taxes used to pay for publicly-financed health care.

12.2b Even for the lowest-income families, health-related taxes account for more than 20 percent of the net burden of paying for health care

■ Out-of-pocket   ▨ Premiums   ▥ Health-related taxes

Distribution of net burden of health spending (2002)

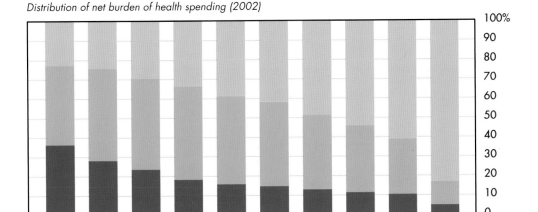

Income decile (1 = 10 percent of households with lowest incomes)

The net burden of paying for health care has increased. The relative burden for low- versus high-income families appears relatively stable in recent decades.

Over the past 25 years, the direct visible burden of health spending has decreased for those in the lowest fifth of households ranked by income (figure 12.3a). For those in the higher income brackets, this burden has increased slightly (second highest quintile) or remained stable (top quintile). These data count only out-of-pocket spending and direct premiums paid by the family.

Moreover, a different scenario emerges if measures include health spending relative to annual consumption expenditures instead of income (figure 12.3b). Incomes can greatly vary from year to year and many economists believe that actual expenditures more closely reflect a family's permanent income. That is, if a family experiences a decline in income perceived to be temporary (for example, a lost job or a decision to return to school), it likely will borrow temporarily to avoid a steep decline in lifestyle that otherwise would result from limiting spending to income. From this perspective, the direct health spending burden is quite similar across households with widely varying incomes. However, according to this measure, this burden also has been rising for most income groups.

Note that switching from income to consumption reduces the burden in the lowest income quintile by approximately eight percentage points. This reduction would be even larger for the lowest decile rather than quintile because, by necessity, anyone who has a negative or zero income would be forced to borrow. Thus, the 40 percent net burden shown previously would be much lower using an arguably more accurate measure of permanent income.

The most complete way to look at burdens considers both hidden and unhidden costs and subsidies. One snapshot used methods similar (though not identical) to the net burden estimates described previously in figure 12.2a. Interestingly, this 1989 analysis also found approximately a two-and-a-half to one ratio between the net burden at the bottom compared with the top 10 percent of the income distribution (figure 12.3c). The absolute level of these burdens was approximately half the levels observed in 2002. The net burden rose almost equally across the income distribution. Consequently, the relative burden grew neither larger nor smaller during this period. No good way exists to determine whether this pattern is typical for the period that preceded it, or whether it has continued until the present.

12.3a Direct health spending has been declining as a share of family after-tax income for families with the lowest incomes

Direct health spending as a percentage of family income

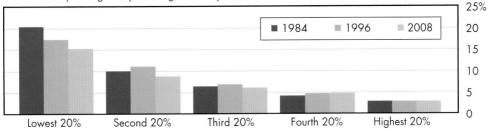

Income quintile before taxes

12.3b The burden of health spending is far smaller when compared with consumption rather than with spending

Direct health spending as a percentage of family consumption expenditures

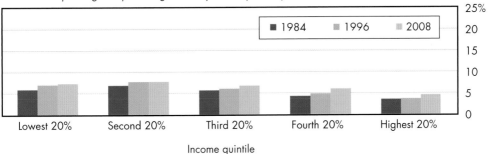

Income quintile

Note: Direct health spending includes only the family share of premiums paid for private or public health insurance, along with all out-of-pocket spending on medical services.

12.3c Since 1989, the total net burden of health-related expenditures has approximately doubled at both ends of the income distribution

Net burden of health spending as percentage of family income

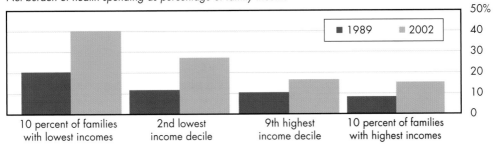

Note: The net burden of health spending includes out-of-pocket spending; premium payments for group and non-group health insurance (including the employer share) and Medicare Parts B and D; and health-related taxes, including payroll taxes for Medicare Part A and the family's share of other taxes used to pay for publicly financed health care.

Per capita health spending generally increases with age; annual health costs for the elderly are at least four times as high as for children and young adults.

Total health spending by the "oldest old" is approximately nine times as much as is spending by school-age children (figure 12.4a). These numbers are for only the civilian non-institutionalized population. Because approximately one in six of the "oldest old" (age 85 and over) are in nursing homes and the average annual cost of a nursing home stay exceeds $75,000, this ratio would be considerably higher were costs of the nursing home population included.

The relatively low expense for children helps explain why it has been easier politically to secure expansions in Medicaid and SCHIP coverage for children rather than for non-elderly adults. Expenditures at childbirth are one important reason why pre-school health spending is higher than for school-age children. Forty percent of births are covered by Medicaid, which contributes to higher spending in the postnatal period, especially for newborns who otherwise would have been uninsured.

Conversely, the relatively low spending among those ages 18–34 helps explain why these so-called "young invincibles" tend to have a much higher rate of being uninsured. In the group market, premiums are community-rated, which often makes them not a particularly good deal for young adults unless the employer substantially subsidizes the premium. In some states, the non-group market also faces community-rating restrictions or what is called "modified community rating." In many of these states, insurers can offer different rates based on age but within rating bands. The new health reform law will do the same. The difference between premiums for the most expensive age category and the lowest ages cannot vary by more than a factor of 3:1, even though it is clear from figure 12.4a that actuarially, the cost difference between age categories is substantially greater. The consequence will be higher rates for young adults than they would otherwise face in a less regulated environment.

Between 1977 and 2004, the average annual increase in expenditures declined for every major age category (figure 12.4b). These declines were much greater for children and the elderly than for other groups. Should the health reform law be fully implemented, this downward trend might reverse itself for two reasons. First, the expansion of coverage to tens of millions of uninsured will boost their previous levels of spending. Second, various regulations are having the effect of increasing premiums in the short run.

12.4a Annual health spending increases sharply by age; health costs for the "oldest old" are approximately nine times as high as for school-age children

Per capita health spending (2007 dollars)

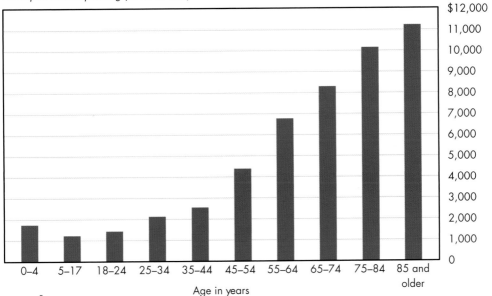

Age in years

12.4b The rate of increase in per capita health spending declined for all age groups between 1977 and 2004, though at varying rates

Compound annual growth rate in per capita health spending

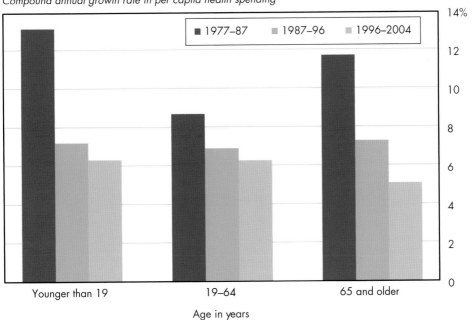

Age in years

During their reproductive years,
women's health costs are much higher than are men's
and only slightly higher in early retirement.

When spending by gender is separated, the rise in spending with age no longer is inexorable. In reproductive years, women's health expenditures are approximately twice as large as that for men (figure 12.5). In 2007, the average childbirth cost $8,800. Because the average fertility rate is 2.1 births per female age 15–44, this alone would add more than $500 a year to annual spending by females. Figure 12.5 is indexed to health spending for males age 18–24 rather than in raw dollars. This difference between men and women during childbearing years is approximately $1,000; thus, childbirth accounts for much but not all of the difference.

Female health spending also is slightly more in the early years of retirement, but for the "oldest old," there is a dramatic shift. Men's health spending soars to more than 15 times the level of their 18 to 24-year-old counterparts, but women's spending actually declines. Recall that these data exclude the institutionalized population. Because women have a higher rate of nursing home use compared with men at all ages 65 and older, inclusion of nursing home costs likely would yield a different result. With 16 percent of oldest-old women in nursing homes and average nursing home costs of approximately $75,000 a year, this alone would add more than $10,000 to their per capita spending but only half that amount to men's.

Much of the male-female difference in spending at age 85 and older relates to the high cost of dying. Decedents cost approximately 50 percent more than do survivors of the same age and diagnosis. However, they cost several multiples of the spending made by the *average* survivor at any given age (decedents are more likely to be sick). Because female life expectancy at age 85 is more than 20 percent higher than that of men's, a higher share of remaining lifetime health costs for males will consist of decedent spending.

End-of-life costs account for approximately 10–12 percent of all health spending. The exact fraction that is publicly financed is unknown. Approximately 80 percent of decedents qualify for Medicare, of whom 20 percent also qualify for Medicaid. Assuming that 100 percent of costs for "dual eligibles" and only half of costs for Medicare eligibles are covered by public insurance, this would imply that taxpayers fund approximately half of end-of-life care. The true number likely is higher.

12.5 From childbirth through reproductive years and in early years of retirement, health spending for females is higher than for males

Index: 100=annual per capita health spending for males 18–24 (2007)

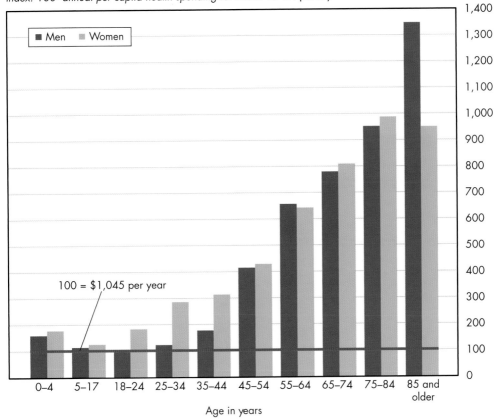

Age in years

Regional differences in both health spending per capita and income per capita have widened somewhat since 1980. Before that time, per capita income differences had been narrowing for at least 50 years.

There is approximately a 40 percent difference between the regions having the highest and lowest health expenditures per capita (figure 12.6a). New England's per capita spending is more than 20 percent higher than the national average, and spending in the Rocky Mountain states is approximately 15 percent less than the U.S. average. This overall difference is approximately the same today as it was in the year Medicare and Medicaid started.

What has changed, however, are the relative ranks of some of the regions. The most dramatic change occurred in the Far West region, which in 1966 had the second highest level of per capita health spending, barely behind that of New England. In the decades that followed, the region's spending fell from 15 percent above the national average to approximately 10 percent below the average by 2004 (the latest year these data are available). The Rocky Mountain region also improved its relative position by approximately 10 percentage points.

In contrast, the Southeast climbed from having expenditures 25 percent below the nation's to an amount that by 2004 was only 5 percent lower. New England reduced its relative spending from 1966 to the early 1980s but thereafter gained approximately 15 percentage points relative to the U.S. average.

No single explanation for these trends exists. The Far West result was driven largely by California, which in the 20 years before 2004, arguably had the most competitive health care system in the country. New England is notable for generally having taken a more regulatory approach to health cost containment (refer to figure 14.3). These contrasting approaches to health regulation surely are not the only explanation for these large changes. However, the differences in approaches were so stark that it seems unlikely that they contributed nothing to New England's now having a level of health spending that is 35 percent higher than that of the Far West.

During at least half of the twentieth century, per capita incomes across regions had been converging until the mid-1970s, after which they grew somewhat (figure 12.6b). As an approximation, health spending per capita has mirrored this trend.

12.6a Regional differences in per capita health spending narrowed from 1966 to approximately 1985 and widened thereafter

Index: per capita health spending by location of service (100=U.S. average)

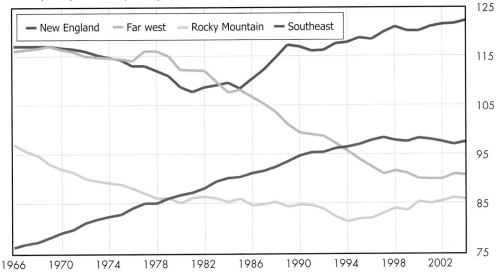

Note: Data not available for years 1967–68, 1970–71, or 1973–75, so they have been interpolated to avoid distorting the length of the bottom axis.

12.6b Regional income disparities have narrowed considerably over the past 80 years but have widened somewhat since 1979

Index: per capita income (100=U.S. average)

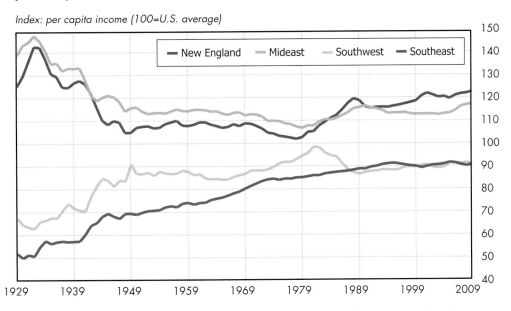

Note: New England = CT, ME, MA, NH, RI, VT; Southeast = AL, AR, FL, GA, KY, LA, MI, NC, SC, TN, VA, WV; Mideast = DE, DC, MD, NJ, NY, PA; Southwest = AZ, NM, OK, TX.

Regional differences in the financial burden of health spending narrowed between 1980 and 1987 but have increased in subsequent years.

What matters more to citizens and policymakers is the relative burden of health spending rather than its absolute level. An approximate measure of this burden examines state health spending as a share of gross state product (the state equivalent of gross domestic product). In contrast with per capita spending, this measure declines with per capita income (figure 12.7a). That is, the states with the highest per capita incomes tend to have lower health spending burdens. The best-fitting prediction line explains only 37 percent of the differences across states; thus, many other factors must determine the size of any given state's health spending burden. Recall that Mississippi had the lowest health spending per capita, but its relative spending burden is higher than any other state's except Maine.

However, even according to this view, several states in the Northeast region other than Maine have burdens visibly higher than would be predicted from their level of income. Whereas California had a level of per capita spending almost 20 percentage points lower than would be expected from the state's per capita income, its burden is only 10 percentage points lower.

At the regional level, one explanation why New England's per capita health spending grew so high is that it could afford to do so. Although its per capita spending was 22 percent higher than the national average in 2004, its burden was only 6 percent higher (figure 12.7b). Even under this alternative view, the Far West made dramatic gains relative to the nation. Its burden was the same as the national average in 1980 but by 2004 had fallen to 15 percentage points below that average. For the regions as a group, differences declined quickly between 1980 and 1987. In those years, all regions had burdens within 7 percent of the U.S. average.

Subsequently, the spread between the regions has grown to approximately 25 percentage points between the Far West and the Southeast, which has a burden approximately 15 percent above the average.

12.7a Differences in per capita income alone account for more than 30 percent of differences in health spending burdens across states

Index: health spending as a percent of gross state product, 2004 (100=U.S. average)

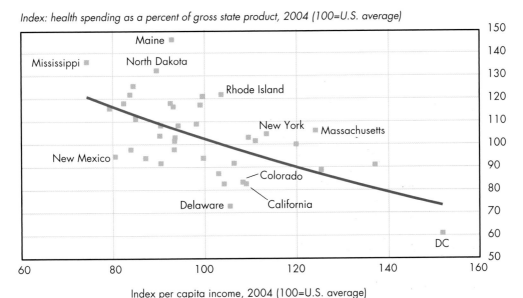

Index per capita income, 2004 (100=U.S. average)

12.7b In only 25 years, there have been large changes in the relative burden of health spending across regions

Index: health spending as a percentage of gross state product (100=U.S. average)

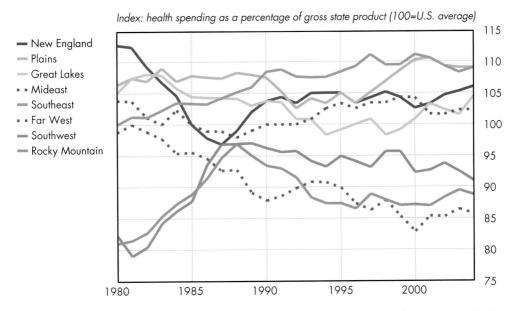

Note: New England = CT, ME, MA, NH, RI, VT; Far West = CA, NV, OR, WA, AK, HI; Rocky Mountain = CO, ID, MT, UT, WY; Southeast = AL, AR, FL, GA, KY, LA, MI, NC, SC, TN, VA, WV; Mideast = DE, DC, MD, NJ, NY, PA; Southwest = AZ, NM, OK, TX; Great Lakes = IL, IN, MI, OH, WI; Plains = IA, KS, MN, MO, NE, ND, SD.

CHAPTER 13

Poverty and Health

Millions of people no longer would be categorized as poor if medical expenditures were handled differently when measuring poverty.

The term *poverty* not only implies having less income than someone else in similar circumstances or less income than one would like, but it means an economic condition of sufficient concern to elicit sympathy from others, and possibly to raise the question of social action to correct it. No single definition is possible. Whether one falls below this threshold varies by country, historical epoch, and even among citizens of the same country at a single time.

Scientists or economists cannot define poverty. They can describe only whatever definition is being measured. Others would have to decide whether that measure conforms to what they have in mind when they think of poverty. Figures 13.1a and 13.1b show the percentage of the U.S. population living below poverty according to various definitions. These data do *not* encompass the full range of possibilities. They highlight how measured poverty rates depend on the alternative manner in which experts have suggested medical expenses should be treated. These definitions include:

A. The official standard—cash income below the official threshold of three times the cost of minimum food needs in 1963, adjusted by changes in the consumer price index

B. Similar to A, but adding the value of health insurance supplements

C. Similar to B, but adding the cash value of Medicare benefits

D. Similar to C, but adding the cash value of Medicaid benefits

E. One standard recommended by the National Academy of Sciences (NAS) in which a family's actual medical out-of-pocket (OOP) expenses, inclusive of health insurance premiums, are subtracted from income (compared with a poverty threshold that excludes medical spending). Note that the NAS method differs from the official standard in other respects.

F. An alternative standard recommended by NAS in which expected medical out-of-pocket costs are added to the poverty thresholds

Using definition D reduces measured poverty by approximately one-ninth. This is a modest relative change, but it would reduce the estimated number of poor in the United States by approximately 4.5 million in 2008 (figure 13.1a). However, how medical expenses are treated in the definition of poverty has only a negligible impact on measured trends in poverty rates (figure 13.1b).

13.1a Taking into account medical expenditures decreases the estimated number below poverty by up to 4.5 million people

Total number below poverty line, in millions (2008)

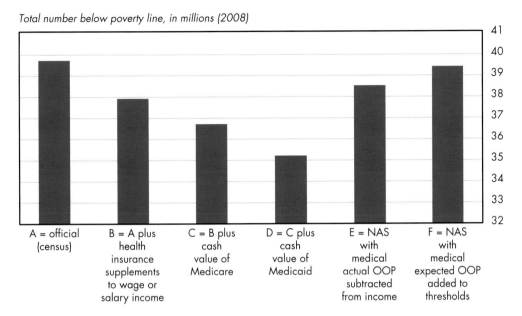

| A = official (census) | B = A plus health insurance supplements to wage or salary income | C = B plus cash value of Medicare | D = C plus cash value of Medicaid | E = NAS with medical actual OOP subtracted from income | F = NAS with medical expected OOP added to thresholds |

13.1b How medical expenses are treated in measuring poverty has a negligible impact on measured trends in poverty rates

Percentage of US population below poverty line

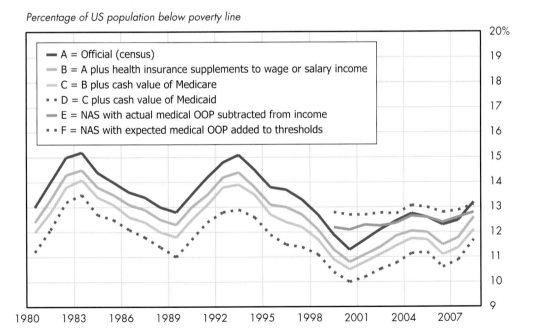

Note: NAS series not available prior to 1999.

Approximately half of those below poverty
are covered by government insurance
(primarily Medicaid). Approximately 30 percent
are uninsured. The chances of being uninsured
decline steadily with increasing income.

Only approximately half of those counted as poor have government insurance (primarily Medicaid). Approximately 30 percent are uninsured (figure 13.2a). Many assume that Medicaid covers the poor. In fact, however, eligibility for Medicaid historically has been restricted to certain categories of individuals: children, pregnant mothers and newborns, single parents, disabled, and the elderly. Thus, in most states, someone not fitting one of these categories can never qualify for Medicaid, even if they have no income or have medical bills that exceed $100,000.

Many near-poor can qualify for Medicaid. Although thresholds vary by state, federal law requires states that participate in Medicaid to cover pregnant women, infants and children to 133 percent of poverty, and children age 6–19 at 100 percent of poverty. Most states choose to cover them at a much higher level (for example, 185 percent of poverty and some as high as 300 percent of poverty). Most states cover the elderly and disabled who are between 75 and 100 percent of poverty. A few states have elected to provide optional coverage to other groups, for example, unemployed parents. Others have either gotten federal waivers or used state-only funds to cover all individuals below poverty. The new health reform law eradicates these categorical distinctions and if fully implemented will provide Medicaid coverage to all Americans living at less than 133 percent of poverty.

The chances of being uninsured drop steadily as incomes rise, and the chances of having private coverage increase with income. Public coverage can be viewed as filling the gap; because the figure focuses on the non-elderly population, most of this public coverage is through Medicaid. However, there is considerable evidence of "crowding out" of private insurance by Medicaid; one should *not* infer that absent government help, the uninsured rate for the poor would exceed 80 percent, for example.

More than half of the uninsured and 60 percent of those who have government insurance have incomes less than 200 percent of poverty (figure 13.2b). Conversely, among those who have private insurance, approximately only one in eight is poor or near poor.

13.2a Approximately half the non-elderly poor have government insurance, while 30 percent are uninsured; the uninsured rate declines with income

Percentage of U.S. population younger than age 65 with coverage shown (March 2008)

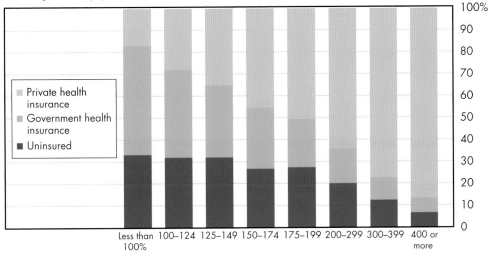

Family income as a percentage of poverty (2007)

13.2b More than half the uninsured and 60 percent of those who have government insurance have incomes below 200 percent of poverty

Percentage of U.S. population younger than age 65 (March 2008)

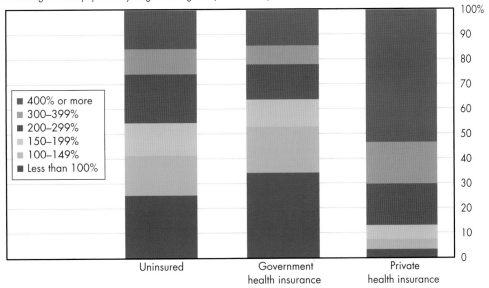

Note: Individuals who have both government and private health insurance were placed in the government health insurance category.

Health status generally is worse among those who have lower incomes; poverty status explains only some of the health status differences related to race.

It has long been known that the poor generally are in worse health than is the rest of the population. Numerous methods can measure health status. Although not perfect, self-reported health status is a surprisingly good measure. Careful studies show that self-reported health status does a good job of predicting future mortality. That is, those who report their health status as "poor" are far more likely to die within the next year than are those who view their health as "good" or "excellent."

Using this measure, only approximately 40 percent of the poor say that their health is excellent compared with almost half of the near-poor and almost seven in 10 of those who have incomes above 200 percent of poverty. Conversely, more than 25 percent of the poor are in fair or poor health compared with fewer than 10 percent of those above 200 percent of poverty (figure 13.3a).

This relationship works in both directions. Some people are poor because of poor health. Poor health might prevent them from working or lower the amount that they can earn. Poverty itself can contribute to poor health. Those who live in poverty are more likely to be concentrated in areas that have higher crime rates, for example, putting them at risk of a violent injury that might permanently compromise their health for the rest of their lives. Likewise, poor people are more likely to drive less expensive, lighter cars that put them at higher risk of an auto-related injury. For many reasons too complicated to explain here (and too poorly understood), smoking rates and obesity also tend to be higher among those who have the lowest incomes.

Those who have the greatest general, objective need for health services also are least able to pay for such care. Consequently, how to finance such care is a social problem faced by all nations.

Socioeconomic factors explain only some of the persistent health differences across racial and ethnic groups. Even after accounting for higher poverty rates among blacks and Hispanics relative to whites, health status differences remain among these groups (figure 13.3b). The degree of these disparities grows smaller as incomes rise. Thus, economic growth and rising incomes will help naturally dissipate many disparities. However, they cannot be expected to disappear entirely even if incomes were equalized.

13.3a Based on self-reported health status, the percentage of people in fair or poor health is highest among the poor and near-poor

Percentage of individuals (March 2009)

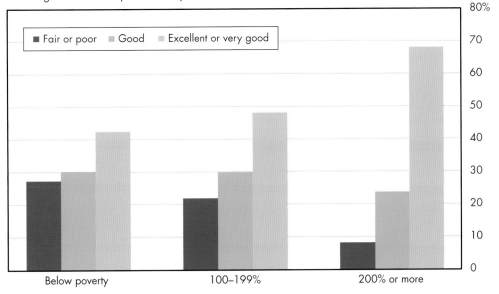

Family income as a percentage of poverty (2008)

13.3b In all poverty categories, Hispanics have the best self-reported health status, followed by whites, while blacks have the worst self-reported health status

Percentage of individuals reporting poor or fair health (2003)

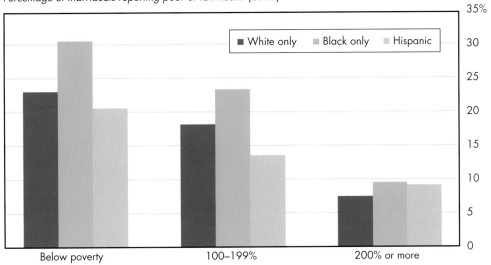

Family income as a percentage of poverty (2002)

Poor children are much less likely to have private coverage than any other age group. Almost seven in 10 poor children have Medicaid/SCHIP coverage.

Among poor children, the number who have no coverage exceeds the number who have employer-based health coverage. As figure 13.4 illustrates, in the general population of children there is a six to one ratio between the number who have employer-sponsored insurance and those who have no coverage. Even so, the chances of being uninsured among poor children are approximately 30 percent the level among non-elderly adults who are poor. In contrast, the shares of poor and near-poor children who have employer-sponsored health plans are almost identical to those of their counterparts age 18–64.

Filling the gap is Medicaid/SCHIP coverage held by almost seven in 10 poor children and almost six in 10 children who are near-poor. The pervasiveness of Medicaid/SCHIP coverage among children in the lowest income households results in 30 percent of children overall who have Medicaid. This is triple the rate seen among non-elderly adults. These numbers understate the true extent of potential coverage. Careful studies show that approximately 25 percent to almost half of uninsured children qualify for Medicaid or SCHIP but their parents decline to enroll the children.

Medicaid "crowd-out" is sizable. In the most recent major expansion of Medicaid/SCHIP for children before the new health reform law, the CBO estimated that 30 percent of those who obtain new government coverage would otherwise have had private coverage. This does not mean that they literally dropped private coverage to get onto Medicaid (although some do). Generally, "crowd-out" consists of formerly uninsured individuals who otherwise eventually would have obtained some form of private coverage but for the opportunity to enroll in Medicaid or SCHIP.

Numerous studies have confirmed, using many measures, that access to care for those who have Medicaid is worse than for those who have private coverage. There is solid empirical evidence that low Medicaid fees adversely affect physician participation in the program, including pediatricians or others who might treat children. Medicaid on average pays less than 60 percent of the price of medical services delivered by physicians in the private sector and less than 75 percent of Medicare fees.

13.4 Children below poverty are only 25 percent as likely as the general population to have employer-sponsored health coverage

Percentage of individuals who have coverage (March 2008)

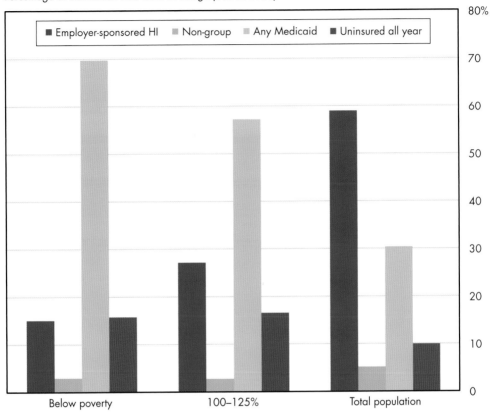

Family income as a percentage of poverty (2007)

Note: Medicaid includes coverage through SCHIP.

Fewer than one-third of non-elderly adults who are poor are covered through Medicaid. More than 40 percent are uninsured. Although more than 90 percent of the elderly poor have government coverage, approximately three in 10 have some sort of private insurance.

Twenty percent of poor adults younger than age 65 have private health insurance coverage (figure 13.5a). Among those who have incomes from 100–125 percent of poverty, this amount is approximately 30 percent. Yet slightly more than 40 percent of both groups were uninsured. Approximately one in 20 individuals in both low-income groups had non-group coverage; thus, this cannot explain the difference. This percentage was not much different from the share of the total adult population younger than age 65 having non-group coverage.

Differences in government coverage explain why the uninsured rate for the poor is almost equal to that of the non-poor despite lower rates of private coverage. Approximately 30 percent of poor adults have some sort of public coverage, most of which is through Medicaid. For the near poor (up to 125 percent of poverty), only one in four have government coverage. As with children, Medicaid accounts for most of this public coverage.

Private coverage among the elderly (age 65 or older) below poverty is approximately 50 percent higher than it is for children or non-elderly adults (figure 13.5b). One in 20 elderly adults below poverty is uninsured because Medicare is available only to those who have a qualified wage history or those able and willing to pay premiums for their coverage.

Approximately 25 percent of poor persons who are elderly are "dual eligible" for Medicare and Medicaid. Approximately 20 percent of these live in nursing homes or other long-term-care facilities. Consequently, approximately 45 percent of spending for this group is for long-term care. Medicare covers acute care services, with Medicaid covering any beneficiary premium payments (for Parts B or D) and cost-sharing obligations (deductibles and coinsurance). All told, Medicare finances approximately 65 percent of acute care spending for "dual eligibles."

In contrast, Medicare does not pay for long-term care. It pays for only sub-acute care, that is, time-limited home health or nursing care services needed for rehabilitation following a hospital stay. As a result, Medicaid finances $5 of every $6 in long-term care and sub-acute care services.

13.5a Poor adults younger than the age of 65 are more than three times more likely to be uninsured all year than to have employer health coverage

■ Employer-sponsored health insurance   ■ Non-group   ■ Any Medicaid   ■ Uninsured all year

Percentage of individuals who have coverage (2008)

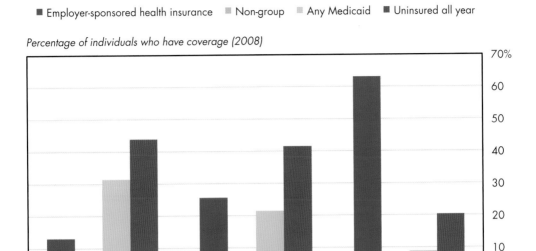

Family income as a percentage of poverty

13.5b A large fraction of the elderly has supplemental Medicare coverage through employers or non-group plans

■ Employer-sponsored health insurance   ■ Non-group   ■ Any Medicaid   ■ Uninsured all year

Percentage of individuals who have coverage (2008)

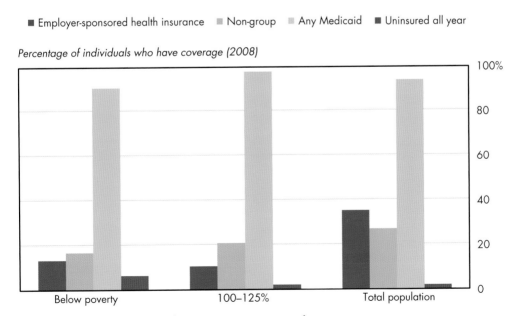

Family income as a percentage of poverty

CHAPTER 14

The Structure of the Health Sector

More than half of U.S. health sector workers are employed by firms that have fewer than 500 workers. The share of employment accounted for by large firms varies significantly across health industry subsectors.

More than 70 percent of health sector firms employ fewer than 10 employees (figure 14.1a). This is almost identical to the number for all U.S. private businesses. However, only approximately 10 percent of all health sector workers are employed by such firms, somewhat lower than for private business overall. In fact, relative to all private businesses, health sector workers are somewhat "underrepresented" in all firm-size categories up to 500 workers. In contrast, almost 40 percent of health care employees work in organizations that have 500 or more employees—almost double the national average. In both health care and private industry, such firms account for much less than 1 percent of all firms. This is almost invisible in figure 14.1a.

At one further level of detail, hospitals, the insurance industry, and pharmaceutical industry represent subsectors in which more than half of workers work in the largest firms. In hospitals, fewer than one in six workers works in facilities that have fewer than 500 employees (figure 14.1b). Not surprisingly, there are few hospitals with fewer than 100 workers. In the insurance industry—specific figures for health insurance are not available—more than half work in the largest firms, but another fourth work in medium-size firms of 100–499 employees. On the goods-producing side of health care, more than half of pharmaceutical manufacturing employees but fewer than 30 percent of medical equipment manufacturing workers work in the largest firms (figure 14.1c).

Note that there is no consensus about the dividing line between *large-* and *medium-size* firms. Some draw the line at 100 or 200 workers, but under virtually all definitions, a firm that has 500 or more workers is a large employer. Using the most expansive definition—a cut-off at 100 workers—99 percent of hospital workers, nine in 10 pharmaceutical industry workers, and approximately 75 percent of health insurance workers would be counted as employed by large firms. Over the past 30 years, the percentage of workers accounted for by health services has risen in all firm sizes; such growth has been fastest among the largest organizations.

14.1a Compared with all private-sector workers, a much higher share of health services employees work for large firms

Percentage of total firms or employees within an industry working in firm size (2007)

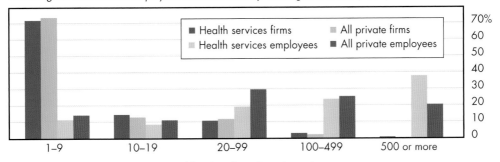

Size of firm (number of employees)

Note: Health services employees include those in ambulatory health care services, hospitals, and nursing homes and other residential care facilities.

14.1b More than half of hospital and health insurance employees work for firms that have 500 or more employees

Percentage of employees within an industry working in firm size (2007)

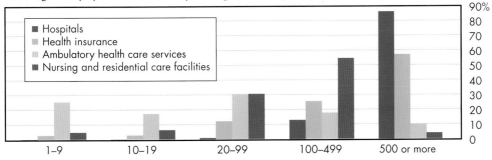

Size of firm (number of employees)

14.1c In the goods-producing area of the health sector, most employees work in medium- or large-size firms

Percentage of total employees within an industry working in firm size (2007)

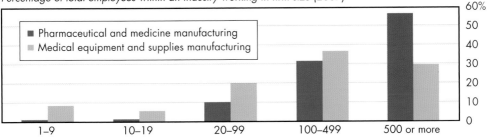

Size of firm (number of employees)

Seemingly high levels of concentration in the health insurance industry might not accurately depict its competitiveness. Concentration is increasing for both hospitals and health insurers.

By conventional measures, the health insurance industry is highly concentrated. Some experts worry that lack of competition might result in higher premiums for health coverage than would otherwise prevail in a more competitive market. Economists measure concentration using what is called a Herfindahl-Hirschman Index (HHI). The calculation involves squaring the market shares of each competitor in a market and adding the results. For a monopolist having a market share of 100 percent, the HHI would be 10,000 (100^2 = 10,000). Ten competitors each with equal market shares would produce an HHI of 1,000 (10×10^2). For purposes of antitrust regulation, the Federal Trade Commission (FTC) currently views areas with an HHI of 2,500 and more as *highly concentrated*. Transactions that increase the HHI by more than 100 points in highly concentrated markets presumptively raise antitrust concerns.

Using an HHI threshold of 1,800 that the FTC used prior to August 2010, in more than 90 percent of metropolitan statistical areas (MSAs), the market for insurers offering fully insured HMO or PPO plans is highly concentrated. A related measure shows that in more than 90 percent of MSAs, a single insurer for these products accounts for 30 percent of the market (figure 14.2a). In more than 60 percent of markets, the dominant insurer has more than half of all market shares, and in 25 percent of MSAs, this share exceeds 70 percent.

However, other studies have found much less concentration (figure 14.2b). Moreover, all the foregoing calculations focus on the fully insured market, ignoring self-funded health plans. Most large employers self-fund their health benefits: They absorb the risk and hire a health insurer or third-party administrator to pay claims. Approximately 60 percent of employer coverage is through such plans. Having market power does not mean it can be exercised. The modest profitability levels for health insurers described previously are not consistent with insurers having a widespread ability to demand supra-competitive prices. Although these measures do not paint a completely accurate picture of competitiveness in the health insurance industry, they do suggest that concentration might be increasing.

14.2a By conventional measures, many metropolitan areas appear to have high levels of insurance company concentration

Percentage of MSAs with concentration level

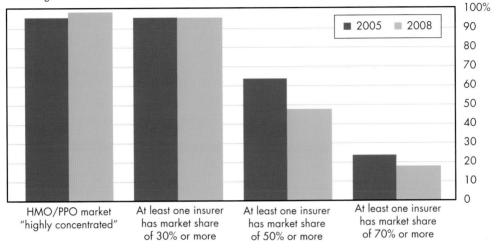

Note: At the time of this analysis, the threshold for "highly concentrated" was a Herfindahl-Hirschman Index score of 1,800 or higher. Since August 2010, the FTC has this threshold at a score of 2,500 or higher. The denominator for the percentages shown was 313 MSAs in 2005 and 359 in 2008.

14.2b It appears that concentration is rising in both the hospital industry and HMO industry

Percentage of MSAs with concentrated or highly concentrated markets

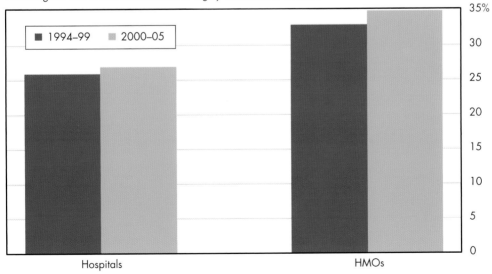

Note: At the time of this analysis, the threshold for "highly concentrated" was a Herfindahl-Hirschman Index score of 1,800 or higher; "concentrated" is defined as an HHI of 1,000–1,800. Since August 2010, the FTC has the first threshold at a score of 2,500 or higher and the second at 1,500–2,500.

The health sector is more highly regulated than almost any other segment of the U.S. economy. However, the extent of regulation varies widely across states.

For decades, experts have regarded the health sector as one of the most highly regulated areas of the U.S. economy. State governments license many health providers. In more than 65 percent of states, hospitals, and/or nursing homes must secure a certificate of need—that is, the state's permission—before building or expanding a health facility or adding equipment to it. Health insurers cannot operate in a state without its approval and in some cases, review of its premium rates. FDA approval is required to bring drugs and medical devices to market. Finally, in many states, special rules or limits govern how the courts handle medical liability cases compared with how a bread-and-butter tort case would be adjudicated.

Even this incomplete description of regulation shows that states play an important role in regulation of health services. Consequently, differences across states in the scope and stringency of various health services regulations are quite large.

Figure 14.3 illustrates a flavor of this diversity. As with any index, this one cannot count every possible aspect of regulation. Moreover, even if it could, reasonable people might disagree on how to combine the various scores for potentially dozens of different areas of health services regulation. Should the score assigned to health facilities regulation receive the same weight as the score for regulation of health professionals? With this caveat, this particular ranking seems to show that states in the Rocky Mountain and Far West regions *generally* regulate health services less (or less stringently, depending on the particular area of regulation being examined) than do states in the Northeast or even Southeastern regions.

If fully implemented, the new health reform law will do two things. First, it will significantly increase the amount of health services regulation. Second, it will shift more regulation to the federal level. States still will play a role in implementing the details of how, for example, state health exchanges will work. However, they will do so under a new set of "rules of the road" established by the federal government.

14.3 **States that have the least amount of health services regulation in 2007 are predominantly located in the South and west of the Mississippi River**

Regulation ranking (1 = least)   0–9   10–19   20–29   30–39   40–50

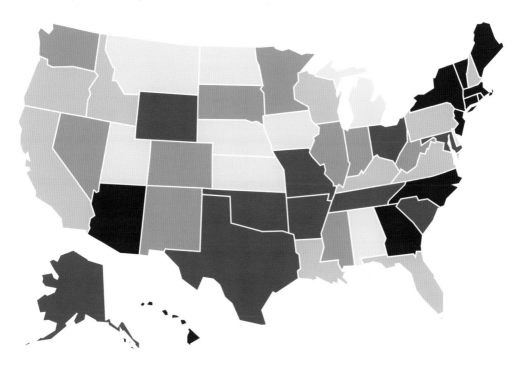

Unionization rates in the health industry are comparable to the economy-wide rate. The unionization rate within some health occupations is much higher.

The percentage of health industry workers who are union members appears to be the same as the national rate of unionization among all workers. At the industry level, the available data combine health services workers with other social assistance workers. Because the latter group constitutes only 15 percent of the combined total, it is unlikely that the numbers shown in figure 14.4 would change much if unionization in the health industry were measured more precisely. That said, at least part of the apparent steep decline in unionization for this group between 1992 and 2000 might be a statistical artifact. During that time, a major change occurred in how industries are categorized; the groups being compared in these two years are not identical in composition. It seems likely that there was a decline in unionization but perhaps not to the extent shown. The apparent rise in unionization from 2000 to 2007 cannot be explained in a similar fashion. It likely is genuine (though small).

Unionization data also are available at a more detailed level for health-related occupations. Shown are the numbers for the broad aggregates used by the BLS to describe health sector workers. Thus, among health care practitioner and technical occupations, the unionization rate is approximately double the rate for all health services. Moreover, this rate appears to be increasing over time. In contrast, unionization seems to be declining among health support occupations (again, with the caveat that the steep decline from 1992–2000 likely is exaggerated). "Personal care and service occupations" is another imprecise aggregate. It includes personal and home care aides, but these constitute only approximately one-sixth of the workers in this category. It also includes those who provide personal care services such as haircuts or manicures. Unionization within this group is similar to the economy-wide average and might possibly be increasing. Because identifiable health workers account for a much smaller group within this total, it is conceivable that these numbers would be different with numbers that are more detailed.

14.4 Health industry unionization rates appear to be the same as those elsewhere, but among some health occupations, unionization is much greater

Percentage of workers in industry/occupation who are union members

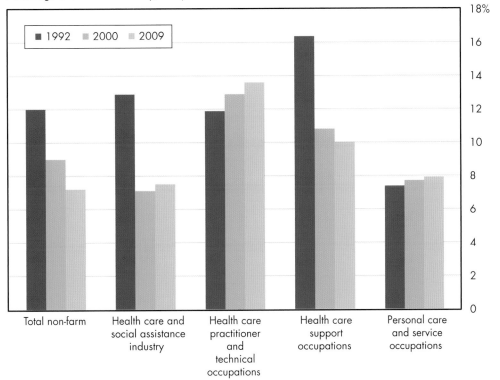

CHAPTER 15

Health, Wealth, and Debt

Since the early 1950s, real health spending per capita has grown approximately twice as fast as real per capita net worth.

Since 1952, inflation-adjusted health spending per capita rose much faster than per capita net worth or GDP (figure 15.1a). Net worth is the excess of assets over liabilities. According to Federal Reserve data, the net worth of U.S. households at the end of 2008 was $56 trillion. The nation's net worth includes the net worth held by households and non-profit organizations. This represents the total wealth of the nation because assets held at the household level reflect any net worth held by corporations and non-corporate businesses.

Over 55 years starting in 1952—that is, excluding the most recent economic downturn—net worth increased at an annual rate of 7.3 percent, as compared with an increase of 6.8 percent in GDP. Adjusting for general inflation and population growth, these numbers decline to 2.5 percent and 2.0 percent, respectively. These numbers imply that on a per-person basis, real wealth doubles every 29 years and real GDP doubles every 35 years.

Real per capita health spending grew 4.5 percent over the same period. This was 80 percent faster than the pace at which net wealth increased. This pace implies a doubling of real per-person spending (in general purchasing power terms, *not* medical dollars) every 16 years.

A clearer way to see this difference is to calculate health spending for every $100 of net worth. When Mr. Eisenhower was elected president in 1952, this ratio was $1.29 in spending per $100 of wealth. By 2007, this amount had increased to $3.86 (figure 15.1b). Because of the steep decline in net worth from 2007 to 2009, coupled with ever-rising health costs, this ratio had reached $4.80 by the end of 2009. Health spending does not put us in danger of eradicating national wealth, but it is steadily chipping away at it, decade after decade. Health spending has not yet resulted in a reversal of real gains in national income (GDP) (refer to figure 20.4a). Likewise, increasing medical costs have not prevented real national wealth from increasing. However, less rapid increases in health spending in principle might have allowed for more rapid gains in wealth.

15.1a Since 1952, inflation-adjusted health spending per capita increased much faster than per capita household net worth or GDP

Index of real amounts per capita, 2005 chained dollars: 1952=100

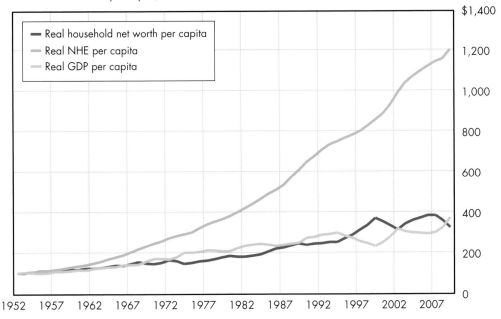

15.1b Health spending per dollar of wealth has almost quadrupled over more than 50 years

Health spending per dollar of net worth held by households and nonprofits

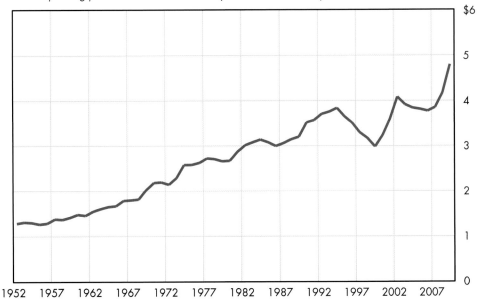

A relatively small fraction of American households incurs annual health expenditures that exceed their net worth.

For low-income families, the cost of having one member in the top 10 percent of health spending would exceed their net worth. Thus, low-income households are more vulnerable to bankruptcy risk from medical expenses. The question is how large a risk they face.

Our conventional sources of health spending at the household level do not provide information on household wealth. Therefore, as an approximation, available information on the distribution of net worth across households was compared with the average per capita spending amounts for individuals in particular parts of the spending distribution (refer to figure 12.1a). This gives an approximate sense of the vulnerability to bankruptcy risk, but it is not equivalent to determining that a specified fraction of low-income families actually undergoes a bankruptcy caused by medical bills.

As an example, a low-income household having just one member whose medical spending fell into the top 1 percent of spending, would, on average, incur medical bills more than five times their net worth (figure 15.2). This is no guarantee of bankruptcy because if they are Medicaid-eligible, their third-party coverage finances all or almost all of such bills. Likewise, if such a family had private medical insurance, much of this hypothetical burden would be shifted onto others. Even if such a family were entirely uninsured, the safety net absorbs a considerable fraction of health expenditures (refer to figure 3.9b).

For a middle-income family, having one member in the top 1 percent would result in bills almost equal to the family's net worth. Again, whether this circumstance would actually force the family to declare bankruptcy would depend on the particular situation. A large public or teaching hospital might be in a better position to write off an expensive stay than would a small community hospital with low or negative operating margins. In contrast, for the highest income families, paying the bill theoretically ought to be relatively easy even if they lacked insurance and were responsible for the entire bill. It would wipe out 20 percent of their net worth, but presumably, this would not trigger bankruptcy.

15.2 For low-income families, the cost of having one member in the top 10 percent of health spending would exceed their net worth

Simulated spending as a percentage of family net worth (2008)

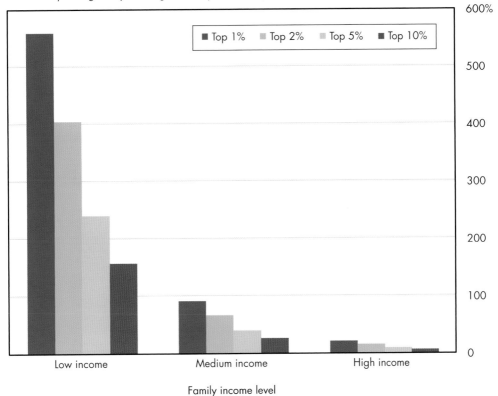

Family income level

Note: Simulated spending estimated assuming one family member had health spending in the top 1, 2, 5, or 10 percent of individuals ranked by expenditures. Figure 12.1a shows the estimated annual amount of spending for each of these percentiles.

"Medical" bankruptcies account for 25 percent to possibly 35 percent of all bankruptcies in the United States.

Families whose principal reason for debt relates to medical bills account for approximately 25 percent of all bankruptcies. Other experts have suggested that this number might be much more than this, but this assumption uses an overly broad definition of a *medical bankruptcy*. The numbers shown in figure 15.3 represent evidence from the first study that separates the problem of paying medical bills from other problems that bankruptcy filers face, including loss of employment, low income, or other sources of debt, particularly credit card debt. According to this study, even if medical bankruptcy were defined to include all families having *any* medical debt, such families would account for just over 35 percent of bankruptcies.

Poor health can result in loss of income or even loss of a job—an impact that can greatly exceed the effects of medical bills. Thus, even for families whose debt primarily relates to medical bills, there is no guarantee that bankruptcy could have been avoided had their medical bills been eradicated, that is, paid by someone else. The average amounts of the medical bills involved in bankruptcy cases are surprisingly small. One study by the U.S. Department of Justice (DOJ) found that only 11 percent of bankruptcy filers had medical bills in excess of $5,000. Medical debt accounted for 50 percent or more of total unsecured debt in only one of 20 cases. Across all filers, medical debt averaged only approximately 6 percent of all unsecured debt.

The limited available evidence suggests that fluctuations in the cost of health care are *not* linked to increases or decreases in bankruptcy rates. There has been a secular increase in bankruptcy filings entirely independent of increases in medical expenditures. There is more mixed evidence about whether bankruptcy rates have been affected by trends in insurance coverage. Approximately 60 percent of bankruptcies are filed by families who have health insurance. Thus, if the new health reform law results in expanded coverage, in principle this will reduce bankruptcy risk. The new law eliminates ceilings on lifetime coverage and places maximum limits on out-of-pocket spending. This too will lower bankruptcy risk, but for all the reasons reviewed, it seems unlikely that bankruptcies would decline by 25 percent.

15.3 Approximately one-fourth of bankruptcies are related primarily to medical debts; medical debts are a factor in just over one-third

Percentage of bankruptcies related to families with medical debts (1994–96)

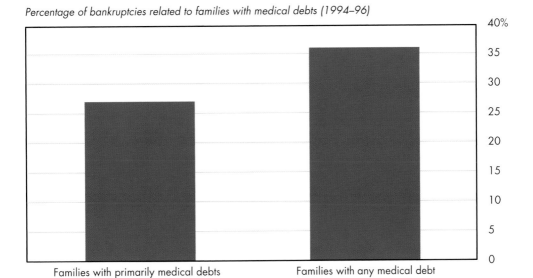

Families with primarily medical debts   Families with any medical debt

CHAPTER 16

Economic Fluctuations and Health

Aggregate health spending growth appears to be largely independent of fluctuations in the business cycle.

Over the past 60 years, growth in health spending has persisted even during periods of economic contraction (figure 16.1). No particular pattern to its growth exists during periods of contraction relative to adjacent periods before or after a recession. During the 1990s, somewhat more regularity appeared in this pattern, with growth in health spending generally higher during downturns than during the periods that preceded or followed. Even this cycle appears to have been broken in the most recent downturn because Medicaid spending has grown less rapidly than during 2001–2007.

Unlike the unemployment rate, government spending and other key economic indicators, health expenditures are not reported monthly (a notable exception is Medicaid spending, although monthly dollars are available only with a considerable time lag). Thus, the data shown have been generated assuming a uniform monthly rate of growth between years. This assumption permits a calculation of estimated spending at the start and end of each period of downturn or recovery, but it is quite possible that growth in spending was higher or lower during the months of an economic slowdown compared with the remaining months in a given year. The picture is only an approximate gauge of how spending actually changes on a monthly basis.

During recessions, mortality due to motor vehicle accidents (because people drive less), homicides (reflecting less crime in general), and workplace injuries all decline. To the extent such mortality reductions are matched by similar reductions in morbidity due to motor vehicle accidents, crime, and occupational injuries, these should reduce the amount of medical spending. However, any such reduction is not apparent in the numbers shown in figure 16.1.

16.1 Aggregate health spending growth appears to be largely independent of fluctuations in the business cycle

Compound annual growth rate

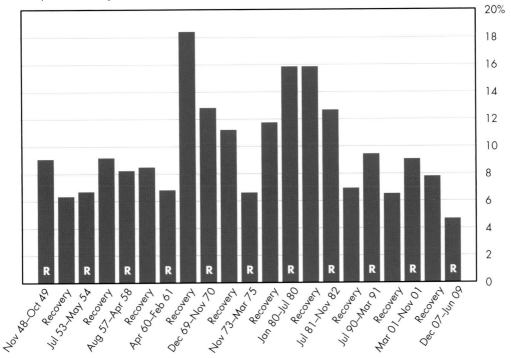

Note: R = recession.

Medicaid expenditures tend to be more countercyclical than are other components of NHE, generally rising faster during recessions than during recoveries.

When health spending is separated into Medicaid and "everything else," a slightly more cyclical pattern emerges (figure 16.2). In some recessions—notably those during the late 1960s and early 1990s, growth in Medicaid spending has far outpaced spending for other health care services. The size of this growth differential was much larger during the downturn than in the period either before or after. Other social welfare spending, certainly unemployment benefits, but also Food Stamps and other forms of cash or in-kind assistance, tend to be more cyclical than Medicaid is.

Some of the program's tendency to serve a countercyclical function has been masked by some large changes in Medicaid policy that had the effect of escalating Medicaid spending during years of economic growth rather than during downturns. Arguably, the political will to enact such Medicaid expansions was greater during times of relative "plenty." For example, starting in the mid-1980s, a series of expansions over many years targeted children, pregnant women, and infants. Likewise, enactment of SCHIP in 1997 to expand further the coverage of children occurred during a period of rapid economic expansion. This had the effect of exaggerating Medicaid's relative rate of growth (compared with all other health spending) during the 1990s and thereby making it appear larger than the growth differential that occurred during the 2001 economic slowdown.

16.2 Medicaid spending occasionally is more countercyclical than other health spending is, increasing relatively faster in downturns

Compound annual growth rate

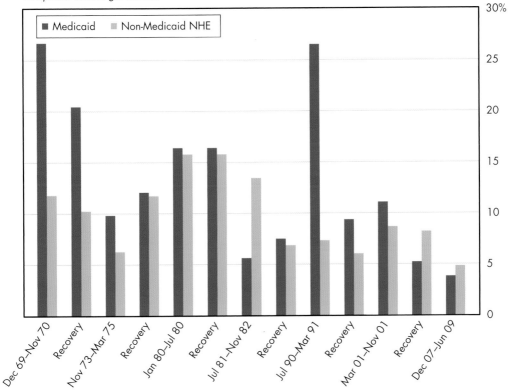

Unemployment rates for workers in the health sector are lower for males but not for females, compared with workers in the rest of the economy.

For almost 50 years, unemployment rates among males working in hospitals or other parts of the health services industry have been lower than for their counterparts in the rest of the economy (figure 16.3a). Since at least 1994, male unemployment rates in non-hospital health settings have been somewhat higher than for those working in hospitals. Before, the reverse was true. For these data, non-hospital health settings include nursing homes in addition to physician offices or other ambulatory settings. Note also that the unemployment rates shown are for experienced workers only, not for new workers or those reported as being "not in labor force" because of school, an inability to find work, or other reasons.

The picture for females is quite different. For female health services workers outside of hospitals, the unemployment rate has routinely been higher than for females elsewhere in the economy—typically by two to three percentage points (figure 16.3b). For female hospital workers, the pattern is the same as just described for males. Since at least 1994, female hospital workers have had a somewhat lower unemployment rate than have all females. In the limited data from the 1960s and 1970s, the reverse was true, with female unemployment among hospital workers being one to two percentage points higher than the rate for women generally.

Both worker hours and employment have been increasing in the hospital sector in recent years (refer to figure 10.1b). This indicates the strong demand for hospital labor, which is reflected in their lower unemployment rate. The reason is less clear as to why the pattern for women has diverged so significantly from that of men. In all periods, women have a lower general unemployment rate than men. However, unemployment in non-hospital health services is routinely higher for women than for men in all of the annual data. Within the hospital industry, female unemployment rates were somewhat higher than were men's decades ago. More recently, female unemployment rates have been less than male unemployment rates by approximately 1 percent. Why women now have attained a margin of advantage over men in the hospital sector but not in the rest of the health services industry is not well understood.

16.3a Unemployment rates among males who work in health services are lower than for males overall; this has been true for decades

Average annual unemployment rate within industry

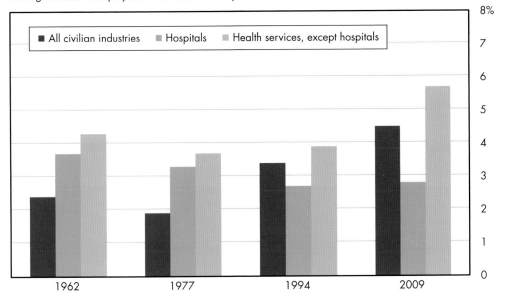

Note: Unemployment figures are for experienced workers only, not new workers or those reported as being "Not in Labor Force" because of school, an inability to find work, or other reasons.

16.3b Unemployment rates among females who work in health services, but not hospitals, are higher than for females overall; this has not always been true

Average annual unemployment rate within industry

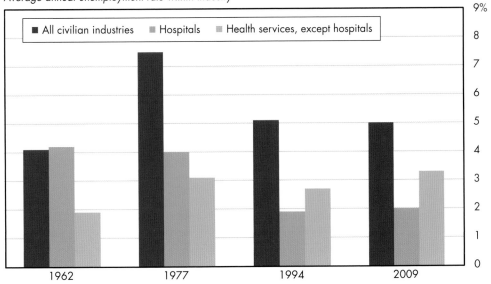

CHAPTER 17

Health Services and Quality of Life

The value of a typical American's stock of health at birth is several multiples of his or her lifetime earnings.

The health capital (value of their health) for average individuals in the United States is several times as large as expected lifetime earnings. This calculation converts future earnings to a present value, using a real discount rate of 3 percent. This is approximately equivalent to the inflation-adjusted rate of return paid on long-term U.S. Treasury bills. Most economists believe that this approximates the *social discount rate*, that is, the degree to which the value of a future dollar declines compared with today's dollar. A 3 percent rate implies that a dollar one year from now is worth only 97 cents in today's dollars. Another way to think about it is that 3 percent represents the amount people would have to be paid today to get back a dollar in one year.

There obviously is a great deal of variation across different individuals in lifetime earnings. Calculating from available evidence about earnings by age in 2005 dollars discounted back to the present, the average U.S. citizen will earn approximately $1 million or more over a lifetime. Figure 17.1 illustrates how this average varies by gender and race. Lifetime earnings represent a conservative estimate of the value of a human life. Economists have used various methods to calculate the willingness-to-pay value of a human life. For example, consider workers in risky jobs who are willing to be paid $10,000 more a year in exchange for a 1 percent increase in their risk of dying on the job in any given year. This implies that collectively, such workers are willing to be paid $1 million in exchange for one of them dying. Their willingness-to-pay value for life is said to be one million dollars. Based on this kind of real-world evidence about willingness to accept higher pay in exchange for loss of a *statistical life,* the present value of a life at birth averages almost five million dollars (there is wide variation in this number across studies). Due to differences in life expectancy, this value varies by race and gender.

Willingness-to-pay encompasses both the expected amount of future earnings (because these future earnings have value to the earner), as well as the intangible value of life. Thus, subtracting expected earnings from the willingness-to-pay value of a life, the result is the intangible value of each U.S. worker's stock of health when born. This is invariably much larger than lifetime earnings.

17.1 The average American's stock of health is several multiples of lifetime earnings

Net present value using 3 percent discount rate (millions of 2005 dollars)

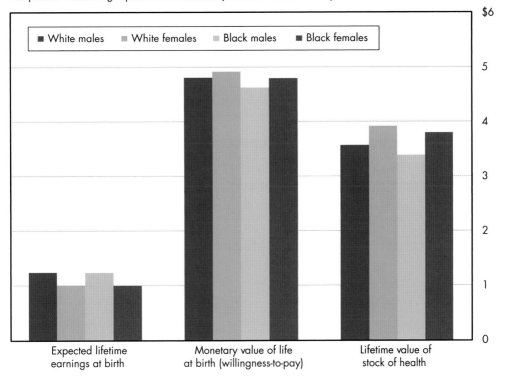

Note: Lifetime value of stock of health = willingness-to-pay value of life at birth minus expected lifetime earnings at birth.

In price measurement, the treatment of innovations or new products is perhaps the most difficult aspect of handling quality change.

For decades, medical prices have outstripped general inflation. Price trends vary by medical service, with prices for some services rising much faster than for others. When the BLS measures prices for other commodities, it is straightforward to measure how the price of a discrete item, such as an apple, changes over time.

This task is much more difficult in health care. The price of a hospital room, for example, does not include the much larger costs of actually occupying a bed. Moreover, even if the price could be precisely calculated, a hospital stay today is a dramatically different product than it was 50 or even 30 years ago. Unless the BLS can account for changes in technology and quality of care, the measured price of hospital care will give an exaggerated picture of how "pure" prices are rising over time.

Even if that task could be performed perfectly, such prices do not represent what is important: How much is the cost of treatment increasing? Even if we knew all the services needed for treatment, the answer depends on whether we assume that bundle of services is fixed over time or can be adjusted to account for actual changes in medical practice (figure 17.2a). Prescription drugs are another good example. Increases in the price of a particular drug are reasonably straightforward to measure. However, the average cost of the "blue pill" is not a good indicator of how much more patients have to pay for treatment for two major reasons. First, if a drug goes off-patent, generic competitors will appear with lower prices. Even for brand names for which there is not yet a generic substitute, there can be competitor drugs similar enough in function whose prices might be rising much more slowly. This could result in many patients switching to those alternatives if prices of the blue pill got too high.

When the price of treatment is taken into account, for example, the cost per day to treat depression or high cholesterol, rising drug *prices* (that is, the price of blue pills) can easily co-exist with falling *costs* for treatment (figure 17.2b). For social welfare, knowing how the price of various medical treatments is changing is a far better indicator than knowing how the price of individual components of a given treatment is changing. In a highly innovative medical system, new competing treatments appear all the time as do changes in the mix of resources required for a given treatment. Systematic price measurement of treatments is in its infancy.

17.2a The price of heart attack treatment increased from less than 10 percent to more than 35 percent, depending on how prices are measured

Index: 1983=100

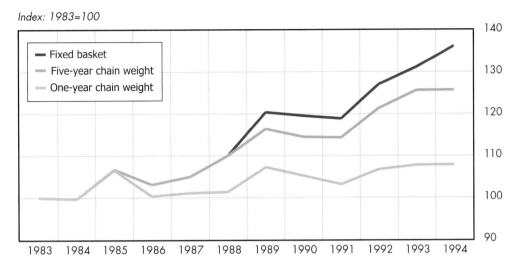

Note: The fixed basket price index is calculated assuming the bundle of services needed for treatment is unchanged over time. The chain-weighted price indexes allow the bundle to change at specified intervals based on actual practice patterns.

17.2b After patent expiration, there has been a 51 percent reduction in the daily cost of therapy after 24 months

Percent change in wholesale cost per day (24 months post event)

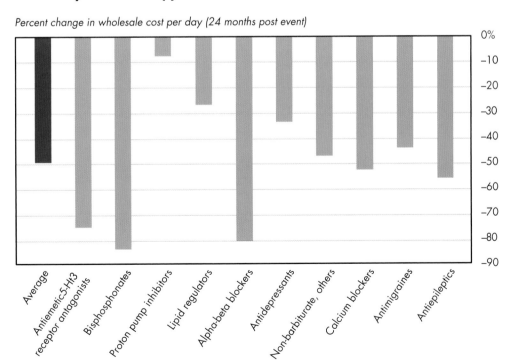

Technology has been an important driver of health spending. However, measuring its precise role has been difficult.

Technology accounts for as much as 25 percent to 60 percent of the rise in real per capita health spending from 1960 to 2007. It is impossible to be more precise about technology's role because it is not feasible to measure price changes accurately enough to distinguish between pure price changes and changes in the quality of the health care good or service being sold. This makes it difficult to determine how much of rising health costs is due to actual changes in output versus higher prices. Economists have resorted to trying to bound this uncertainty using different assumptions. For example, if there are zero changes in productivity, then it is easy to calculate changes in output based on measuring changes in inputs.

Another important factor driving health spending is that as incomes increase, the inclination to use health care appears to increase. This greater demand occurs not only in terms of the use of health services but also in terms of the quality of care. Experts disagree on how much increase in demand for medical services can be expected for every $1,000 increase in per capita income.

Figure 17.3 shows the impact of various assumptions about these issues. Using high-impact assumptions about rising incomes and demand for health care and conservative assumptions about productivity growth, that is, zero, the estimated magnitude of the role of technology in driving health spending is the smallest. Using the opposite assumptions about income and productivity growth (that is, that productivity grows in step with productivity trends in the general economy), the role of technology appears much larger.

Under any of these assumptions, rising medical prices account for only approximately 3 percent to 15 percent of rising real per capita health spending. Despite the aging of the U.S. population, demographic factors likewise account for only 3 to 6 percent of rising health costs. In contrast, expanded insurance coverage accounts for a relatively larger share of the change in real per capita health spending than either of these other two factors. Some experts assign a far larger role to health insurance due to ample evidence that it drives decisions to acquire and use new technology.

17.3 Technology and other factors might account for 25 to 60 percent of the increase in real per capita health spending from 1960–2007

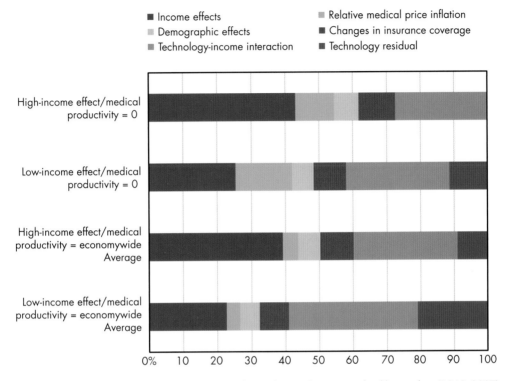

Share of average annual growth in real per capita health spending (1960–2007)

If premature mortality and morbidity are measured in terms of lost production, the social burden of illness has increased since 1963; however, if the intangible value of human life is taken into account, the social burden of illness has declined despite the large increase in health expenditures during this period.

Despite all the medical progress made during the past 50 years, the economic burden of illness appears to be increasing from a cost-of-illness perspective. The aggregate economic burden of illness consists of three components. The first are direct costs, that is, all of NHE, because in one way or another, these expenditures aim to prevent or ameliorate the effects of poor health. Under a broad definition of the health system, non-medical expenditures such as highway barriers could be included if their principal purposes are to save lives. However, the data shown in figures 17.4a and 17.4b are restricted to NHE.

The second component is morbidity losses. In figure 17.4a, these are measured in terms of productivity losses, that is, lost income attributable to workers who are sick. The final component is mortality losses. These also consist of productivity losses except that they are from premature death rather than illness. For simplicity, rather than convert all these dollar amounts to a current-year equivalent, the burdens are expressed as a percentage of GDP. Direct costs—the focus of much of this book—have risen quite rapidly since 1963.

During the same period, mortality losses declined steadily. By 2007, they were just over half of the 1963 level. Morbidity losses did not decline as steeply as mortality losses but did decline between 1963 and 1980. Unfortunately, there are no 2005 data for this measure. However, the rise in direct costs was so rapid between 1980 and 2005 that an unequivocal conclusion is that the aggregate social burden of illness in the United States has increased over the past 50 years. That is, even assuming that morbidity losses had been eradicated by 2005, the sum of direct costs and mortality losses exceeds the total for all three components of the social burden of illness. This increasing economic burden can be attributed solely to increasing health spending in the United States.

However, when the intangible value of human life is taken into account, this conclusion is reversed (figure 17.4b). That is, the value of mortality gains has more than offset the increase in health spending. No good way exists to estimate morbidity losses over time using this approach, but because morbidity was declining as a percent of GDP in terms of lost output, the same would be true were these improvements in health valued in willingness-to-pay terms.

17.4a The economic burden of illness has increased since 1963, even though the loss related to premature death and morbidity has declined

Economic burden of illness as a percentage of GDP

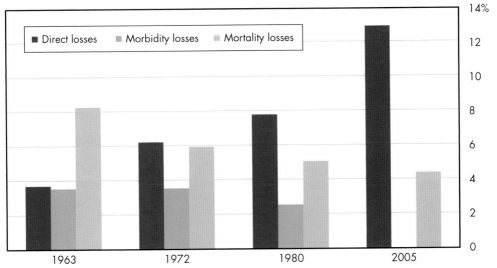

Notes: Direct losses = NHE. Morbidity losses = lost earnings due to illness. Mortality losses = lost earnings due to premature death.

17.4b In willingness-to-pay terms, the social burden of illness has declined since 1963, even though medical spending has increased

Social burden of illness as a percentage of GDP

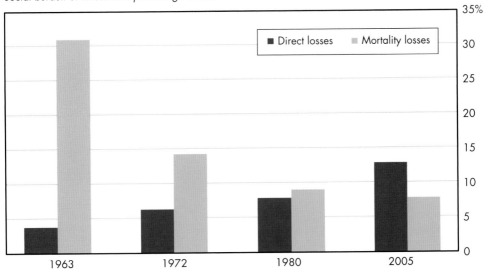

Notes: Direct losses = NHE. Mortality losses = willingness-to-pay value of premature death.

CHAPTER 18

U.S. Health Care in a Global Economy

The United States leads the world in medical innovation.

The United States has contributed to more of the leading diagnostic and therapeutic innovations in medicine than has any other nation. Even combining the European Union (EU) and Switzerland, which collectively have approximately one-half billion residents, the United States outpaces this set of nations as a group by a considerable amount (figure 18.1a).

There is no one way to measure the nation's worldwide role in medical innovation. Figure 18.1a is based on a widely cited study of the most important medical diagnostic and therapeutic innovations developed between 1975 and 2000. These were systematically evaluated by leading primary care physicians and ranked by the effect of these innovations on patients. For some innovations, more than one country deserves credit. Even so, the United States was the country of origin for 20 of the top 27 such innovations. This is almost 50 percent more innovations than from the EU and Switzerland combined, even though these countries collectively have a population that is approximately 65 percent more than in the United States.

Researchers in the United States also were partially or solely responsible for nine of the top 10 such innovations. This again is much more than the contribution made by the EU and Switzerland collectively. Superiority in the United States can be measured in other ways. Of 99 recipients of the Nobel Prize in medicine and physiology since 1948, 60 were from the United States and 41 were from EU countries, Switzerland, Canada, Japan, and Australia. This group of countries collectively has a population more than twice that of the United States. Much of the funding for basic research in the United States comes from the National Institutes of Health (NIH), which spends approximately seven to 10 times as much as the countries in Europe spend. The 30 billion dollars in NIH funding excludes a similar amount spent by the private sector on some basic (but mostly applied) research. In the context of these enormous investments, the U.S. lead in innovation might not be that surprising.

The United States also is superior to the EU and Switzerland in terms of the top 29 pharmaceutical innovations developed in the 40 years starting in 1968 (figure 18.1b). This dominance in pharmaceutical innovation can be attributed to the sizable investments made by the pharmaceutical industry into R&D. The United States also dominates global funding for pharmaceutical R&D (figure 18.2a).

18.1a The United States has less than 65 percent of the population of the EU and Switzerland but has produced approximately 50 percent more top medical innovations

Number of top medical innovations (1975–2000)

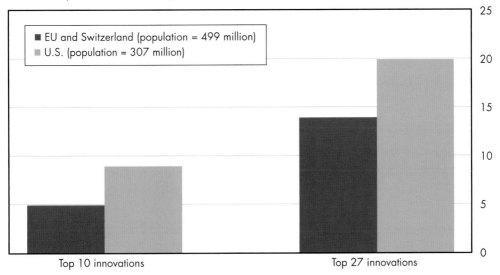

Note: More than one country shares the credit for some innovations. Population figures are for 2009.

18.1b The United States is responsible for more major pharmaceutical innovations than the EU and Switzerland combined

Number of top 29 pharmaceutical innovations (1968–2007)

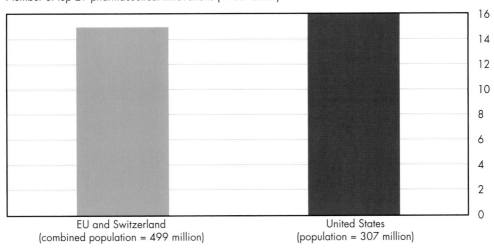

Note: More than one country shares the credit for some innovations. Population figures are for 2009.

Among the top 10 global funders of pharmaceutical R&D, the United States accounts for more than 50 percent to 65 percent of total spending.

The U.S. dominance in pharmaceutical research can be measured in two ways. First, among the 10 countries that rank highest in pharmaceutical R&D expenditures, the U.S. share has ranged from more than 50 percent to 65 percent of the collective R&D spending by this group (figure 18.2a). This has been true since at least 1990. Unfortunately, information is available for only four of these countries for 1980; thus, it is not possible to attain certainty about the U.S. share that long ago.

Of course, the United States has a substantially larger population than any of the others on this list. Thus, an arguably better comparison examines pharmaceutical R&D spending per capita (figure 18.2b). Doing so reveals that only Denmark has higher relative spending on pharmaceutical R&D than does the United States; in 2006, Denmark ranked sixth on the top-ten list cited (figure 18.2a).

Some demand-side factors might affect where pharmaceutical companies are located. However, location decisions of major pharmaceutical companies also are driven by the availability and cost of the scientific research personnel required to conduct R&D, and by government regulations that affect how R&D is conducted.

Another factor that has fueled U.S. pharmaceutical R&D relates to generic competition. The Hatch-Waxman Act enacted in 1984, designed to promote the use of generics, and the rise of managed care formularies have been cited as the principal drivers of growth in the U.S. generic drug industry. Unless there are externalities (my taking a drug benefits or harms someone else's health), competition should lead to the desired result of pushing drug prices down to the marginal cost of producing them. It likewise will encourage a socially optimal level of consumption, that is, where the marginal benefit of consumption equals the marginal cost of supplying a drug. Numerous studies have shown that following the expiration of patents, prices fall toward marginal costs (the more generic competitors, the more prices fall). Generic competition thus forces brand-name pharmaceutical manufacturers to invest in R&D to ensure a steady pipeline of new products under development.

18.2a Among the top 10 global funders of pharmaceutical R&D, the United States accounts for more than half to two-thirds of total spending

Percentage of aggregate R&D expenditures

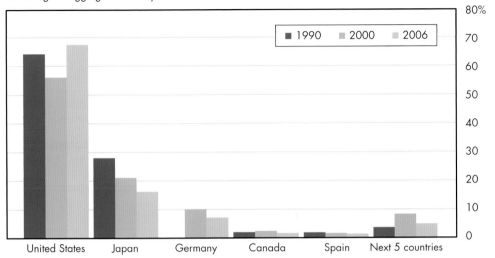

Top 10 global funders of pharmaceutical R&D
(listed [left to right] by 2006 R&D expenditures in U.S. dollars PPP)

Note: Data not reported for selected years in selected countries. Shares are of summed totals for countries that reported data.

18.2b On a per capita basis, U.S. spending on pharmaceutical R&D is exceeded only by Denmark

Per capita pharmaceutical R&D expenditures (U.S. dollars, PPP)

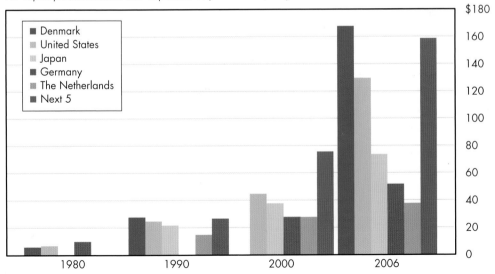

Despite its global dominance in pharmaceutical R&D, the United States accounts for a small share of pharmaceutical exports among industrialized nations. Conventional measures of U.S. trade provide an incomplete picture of the contribution of the health sector to imports, exports, or the country's overall balance of trade.

U.S. dominance in pharmaceutical research is not mirrored in its shares of pharmaceutical exports. Not only is this share small—approximately 10 percent in 2006—but it has declined considerably since 1980, when it was closer to 20 percent (figure 18.3a). The United States likewise accounts for a modest share of imports—approximately 15 percent (compared with 45 percent of global pharmaceutical sales accounted for by those who live in the United States).

Measures of exports and imports are based on the location of the manufacturing facility, regardless of ownership. The approximate 10 percent export share in 2006 does *not* imply that U.S.-owned firms supplied 10 percent of pharmaceutical products purchased by other nations. Nor does it mean that U.S.-owned firms accounted for 10 percent of pharmaceuticals exported because some foreign-owned firms (for example, GlaxoSmithKline [GSK]) have U.S.-based manufacturing facilities. It simply refers to the share of pharmaceutical products manufactured on U.S. soil that cross country borders.

Health-related goods and services play a much smaller role in the U.S. trade imbalance than they do in the entire economy. In 2009, the U.S. trade imbalance (excess of imports over exports) exceeded one-half trillion dollars (figure 18.3b). Pharmaceutical, medical and dental products accounted for approximately 7 percent of this total. This was offset by a trade surplus in scientific, hospital, and medical equipment that reduced the trade imbalance by less than 2 percent. Thus, the health industry overall accounted for approximately 20 percent of the most recently measured trade imbalance.

For the limited time for which such detailed statistics are available, it appears that this share is increasing. This scenario of trade involving the health care sector is not complete. Medical tourism, for example, appears to be a rapidly growing industry. Its magnitude is not large enough yet to warrant separate tracking by the U.S. government.

18.3a Since 1980, the U.S. share of pharmaceutical exports within the OECD has been declining while its share of imports has increased since 1980

U.S. share of aggregate value of pharmaceuticals traded, in U.S. dollars, PPP

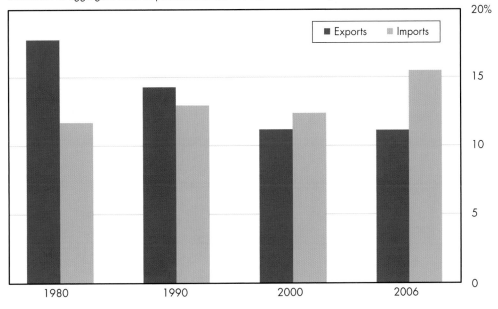

18.3b The health sector contributes a relatively small share to the U.S. trade imbalance, but it appears to be increasing

Balance of imports over exports as a percentage of U.S. net trade balance

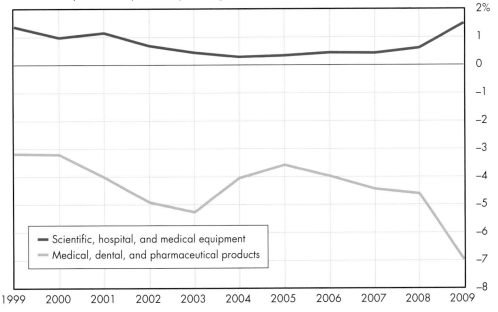

CHAPTER 19

Do Americans Get Good Value for Money in Health Care?

Health spending in recent decades appears to have been "worth it" on average, but this likely masks much wasted spending.

The United States appears to have attained good value for the money from the trillions of dollars spent on health care since 1987 (figure 19.1a). The average cost-effectiveness of this sizable expenditure is only approximate because certainty about how much of the gain in life expectancy over this period can be attributed to medical care is not achievable.

Studies of individual factors (for example, infant mortality and mortality due to heart problems) suggest that medical care improvements have been responsible for at least half of the observed mortality reductions during this time. Thus, the numbers in figure 19.1a result from an assumption that half of life expectancy gains are from expenditures on medical care, as opposed to investments in highway safety, changes in drunk driving laws, speed limits, and other non-medical factors that surely also made a contribution.

Even precisely specifying the exact contribution of health spending to better health, some might disagree about what threshold to use to distinguish spending that was *cost-effective* from that which was not. Medicare spends approximately $75,000 a year on kidney dialysis for each patient who has end-stage renal disease. Without it, such patients would die. Thus, a minimum estimate of the value of life in the United States (implied by our willingness to pay for it) is $75,000 per year. As figure 19.1a shows, spending for all age categories was less than this threshold. Thus, on average, we apparently received good value for the money from health spending.

However, not all added years of life are lived in good health (for example, added years for someone who is bedridden). A quality-adjusted life-year (QALY) is one in good health, that is, two years in bed might be viewed as one QALY. For the elderly, spending per added QALY was more than $130,000. Reasonable people can disagree about whether such spending was worthwhile.

A somewhat less-detailed analysis has examined health spending since 1960. This too shows mixed results. Spending per added year of life generally was less than the $75,000 threshold for most ages and times (figure 19.1b). Again, this suggests that health spending provided good value for the money on average, but the cost to achieve an added year of life appears to be increasing. Even being cost-effective on *average* does not mean that there is no waste or inefficiency in how we spend health dollars.

19.1a Even after accounting for the resources spent to add a year of healthy life, U.S. health spending appears to provide good value for the money

Cost per life-year gained, 1987–2000 (2000 dollars)

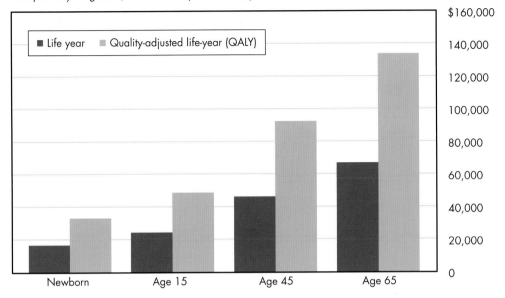

19.1b On average, increases in U.S. health spending appear to have provided reasonable value for the money

Spending per year of life gained (2002 dollars)

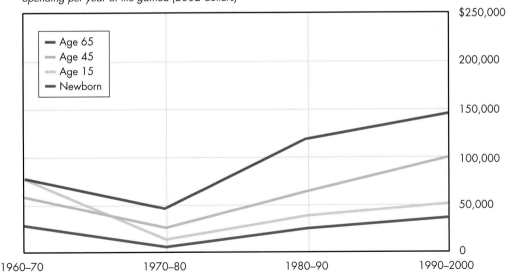

Note: Spending per year of life gained is defined by the change in spending over each decade divided by the change over the decade in expected years of life at the ages shown.

Geographic differences in broad health outcomes generally are associated with higher health spending, both across countries and within the United States. Because higher spending also is associated with higher incomes, it is difficult to untangle the separate contribution of higher income to better health.

Among industrialized nations, some association exists between expenditures on health and better health outcomes. One approximate cross-national measure of health outcomes is the number of years lost due to premature death. Because life expectancy in industrialized countries now exceeds 70 years, deaths before age 70 are *premature*. Using this metric, someone dying at age 20 would have lost 50 years of life, whereas someone dying at age 69 would have lost only one year. Giving much greater weight to deaths occurring early in life seems superior to treating all deaths equally. Adding all the years of lost life at all ages and dividing by population numbers provides a standardized measure across countries of different sizes.

Using such a measure, the burden from premature death appears to decline with increased health spending (figure 19.2a). The United States is a rather extreme outlier. It spends much more money on health care but performs much worse on this metric. Some use numbers such as these to argue that the United States does not get good value for the money compared with that of other countries.

Data from the United States illustrate the limitations of such conclusions (figure 19.2b). First, for any given level of health spending, there is almost a two-to-one difference in the premature death burden. Thus, the huge difference between Louisiana and Washington cannot be attributed to health spending because both states spend almost identical amounts. Conversely, Utah and Maine have almost identical premature death burdens, yet Maine spends almost 75 percent more on health care per resident. Washington, D.C. is an outlier to approximately the same extent that the United States is among industrialized countries. If health spending determined health outcomes, these data would imply worse outcomes with higher spending. Removing D.C.'s unique experience, health outcomes tend to improve with increasing health spending, but other factors clearly make a difference.

19.2a Years lost due to premature death are many more in the United States than in most other industrialized nations

Years of potential life lost before age 70 per 100,000 population (2006)

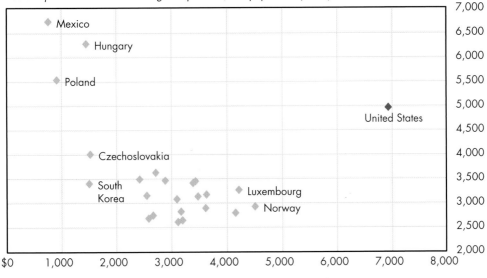

Health spending per person (U.S. PPP, 2006 dollars)

19.2b Wide differences in years lost due to premature death exist across states, even with identical health spending levels

Years of potential life lost before age 75 per 100,000 population (2004)

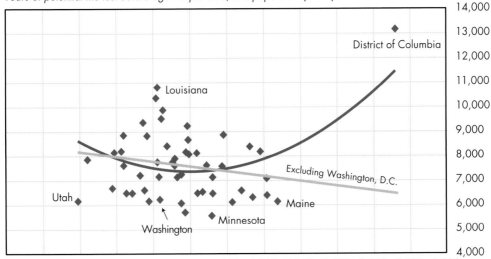

Health spending per resident in 2004 (dollars)

Note: The curved line is a best-fitting prediction line using all the states and the District of Columbia. The straight line is a best-fitting prediction line that excludes the District of Columbia.

In Medicare, there are sizable geographic variations in spending and spending growth. Only a relatively small part of geographic variations in Medicare spending can be explained by differences in health status, income, or race. Most of the difference relates to "practice style."

There is almost a three-to-one difference in Medicare spending per enrollee between hospital markets with the least amount of spending and those with the highest (figure 19.3a). These enormous differences by location are not a new phenomenon, having been observed for decades. Many factors contribute to these differences, but they are not entirely well understood. Because Medicare eligibility and benefits are the same across the entire country, these factors cannot explain the large geographic variations in Medicare spending.

The availability of resources contributes to these spending differences. Geographic areas that have more physicians or hospital beds relative to the population tend to spend more, which in turn can attract more physicians. Differences in organizational and physician decision-making, which some characterize as *practice style*, also play a critical role in these financial differences. Many discretionary decisions, such as whether a patient warrants admission to the hospital, hospital lengths of stay, whether a patient is referred to a specialist, the ordering of various tests, or how often to see chronically ill patients, collectively drive much of the variation.

Medicare's fee-for-service system also plays a role. Geographic variations in Medicare spending are not always replicated in private health plans, in which most members are in some form of managed care. Increases in Medicare spending also vary geographically. Areas that have high spending *growth* are not generally areas with the highest spending *levels*. Thus, Medicare's geographic variations might decrease over time.

Differences in income, race, and health status play a relatively minor role in explaining the geographic variations in Medicare spending (figure 19.3b). Income can explain health-spending differences across countries and individual states. However, income explains little of the difference between Medicare regions that spend more compared with those in the bottom 20 percent of spending.

19.3a Medicare reimbursements per enrollee vary substantially across hospital market areas in the United States

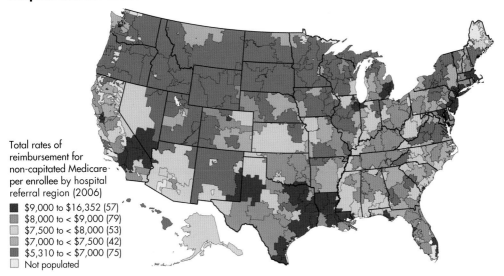

Total rates of reimbursement for non-capitated Medicare per enrollee by hospital referral region (2006)

- ■ $9,000 to $16,352 (57)
- ■ $8,000 to < $9,000 (79)
- ☐ $7,500 to < $8,000 (53)
- ▨ $7,000 to < $7,500 (42)
- ■ $5,310 to < $7,000 (75)
- ☐ Not populated

Note: Non-capitated Medicare is equivalent to fee-for-service Medicare; i.e., it excludes spending related to members of Medicare Advantage plans such as Kaiser or other HMOs. Numbers in parentheses represent the number of market areas in each category.

19.3b Differences in income, race or health explain less than half the spending differences across regions

Annual per capita Medicare spending ($ difference from quintile 1)

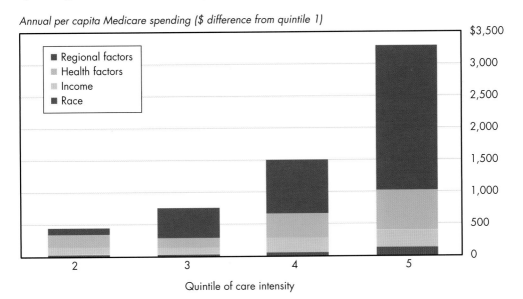

Quintile of care intensity

Note: The vertical bars show the proportion of the difference in spending between regions in each of the four top care-intensity quintiles and the regions in the lowest quintile that can be explained by differences in patients' race, income, health factors (self-reported health, presence or absence of diabetes, high blood pressure, body-mass index, and smoking history), and regional factors. All models control for age, gender, and urban or rural residence.

Health spending per capita in the United States is not necessarily more than expected relative to the pattern seen in other industrialized countries.

There is a widespread perception that the United States spends "too much" on health care. Health care is a "normal" good. As incomes increase, so does consumption of health care. Thus, an important reason that the United States has much higher health spending per person is that it also has much higher GDP per person than most other countries have. The relationship between income and health is sufficiently tight that income alone explains approximately 90 percent of the differences in health spending across countries. A statistical prediction line is one that best fits income versus health spending data for OECD countries. The United States is far above its predicted value when using such a line (figure 19.4a).

The United States is a huge country that dwarfs many of the industrialized countries of Europe, Asia, or North America. For example, if the U.S. states were countries, six would rank among the top 20 countries in the OECD in terms of GDP. Health spending per resident varies by a factor of two to one across states. Separating U.S. states (including D.C.), 13 Canadian provinces, and seven Australian states/territories, the relationship between GDP per capita and health spending per capita changes considerably (figure 19.4b). Both Nunavut in Canada and D.C. are clear outliers. Calculating the best-fitting prediction line that ignores these outliers, the line increases initially but eventually plateaus. (Were the outliers included, this line would continue to rise although much slower than as illustrated in figure 19.4a.)

This alternative S-shaped line in figure 19.4b fits the data better (it explains more of the spending variation) than does the line in figure 19.4a. Although U.S. states are both above and below the line, health spending per capita for the United States as a whole is almost exactly on the prediction line. The small difference between actual and predicted health spending illustrated in figure 19.4b does not prove that the nation's health spending is what it "should" be nor does the large difference in actual and predicted health spending in figure 19.4b. The size of the difference is sensitive to the assumed shape of the prediction line. Reasonable people can disagree about which shape more accurately predicts where other countries will be when they reach the U.S. level of GDP per capita.

19.4a **The conventional wisdom is that U.S. health spending is far above its expected level, given the nation's per person GDP**

Health expenditures per capita (U.S. PPP, 2004 dollars)

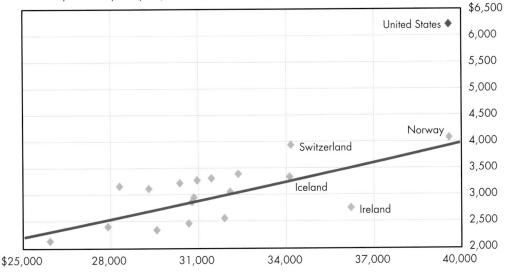

GDP per person (U.S. PPP, 2004 dollars)

19.4b **When sub-national areas are taken into account, U.S. health spending is almost exactly where it is expected to be, given U.S. GDP**

Health spending per person (U.S. PPP, 2004 dollars)

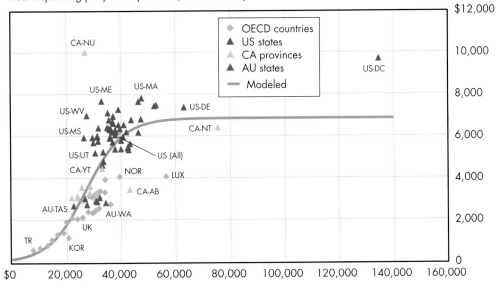

GDP per capita (U.S. PPP, 2004 dollars)

Increased spending in the United States cannot be explained by higher use of health services, although Americans do have greater access to some expensive technologies than do those in other industrialized countries.

Increased U.S. health care spending generally does not appear to be the result of more health care services use compared with use in other industrialized nations. The annual number of physician visits, for example, is as much as 100 to 200 percent higher in other G7 countries (figure 19.5a). Similarly, each one of these nations exceeds the United States in acute hospital days per person.

Pharmaceutical use, measured in grams per capita, is higher in the United States compared with other G7 countries (except France and Canada). On average, the differences are not large. Because pharmaceuticals account for only one-eighth of all health spending, these differences cannot explain per capita spending differences measured in double-digit percentages.

U.S. use of diagnostic technology (such as CAT scanners or MRI machines) and advanced medical procedures is higher than in other G7 nations, except in Germany and Japan. Examples of advanced medical procedures include percutaneous transluminal coronary angioplasty (PTCA), used to clean out clogged arteries, and coronary artery bypass graft (CABG) surgery, which also generally is used more in the United States than elsewhere (figure 19.5b). However, the aggregate spending on such procedures is not sufficient to account for spending differences as large as currently exist.

Immunization rates for children (for example, for measles, or for diphtheria/pertussis/tetanus [DPT]) and for the elderly (flu shots) generally are the same as rates in the rest of the G7 (figure 19.5c).

Health professionals in the United States generally are paid much more than their counterparts are elsewhere in the G7 (refer to figure 11.4a). Because labor costs account for such a large part of the health sector, it would be difficult to avoid higher U.S. spending levels unless the use of services by Americans was drastically lower than elsewhere. Many experts believe that the United States also pays the highest prices for medical equipment, in part because it tends to be an early adopter of new technologies. Higher introductory prices typically are paid by early adopters.

19.5a Compared with other G7 countries, the United States generally uses fewer acute care services such as doctor visits and hospital care, but not pharmaceuticals

Percentage indexes: 100=U.S. rate of use (2006)

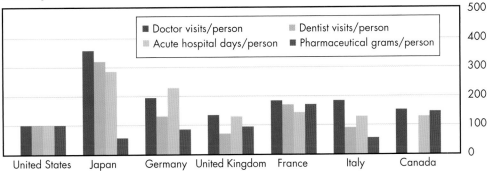

Legend:
- Doctor visits/person
- Acute hospital days/person
- Dentist visits/person
- Pharmaceutical grams/person

Countries: United States, Japan, Germany, United Kingdom, France, Italy, Canada

Note: Figures for pharmaceuticals are for 2005.

19.5b U.S. use of technology generally is much more than use by the other G7 nations, except Japan and Germany

Indexes: 100=U.S. rate of use (2006)

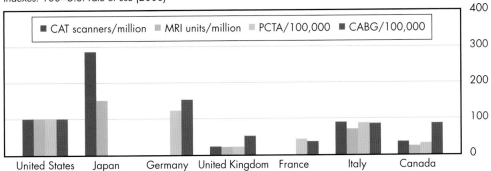

Legend:
- CAT scanners/million
- MRI units/million
- PCTA/100,000
- CABG/100,000

Countries: United States, Japan, Germany, United Kingdom, France, Italy, Canada

19.5c Immunization rates in the United States are generally the same as those in other G7 nations

Indexes: 100=U.S. rate of use (2006)

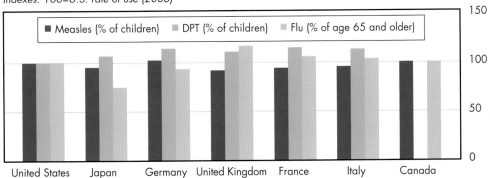

Legend:
- Measles (% of children)
- DPT (% of children)
- Flu (% of age 65 and older)

Countries: United States, Japan, Germany, United Kingdom, France, Italy, Canada

Compared with some major competitors, the United States relies more on specialists than on primary care doctors.

In the United States, seven in 10 physicians are specialists (figure 19.6a). This is higher than in France or Canada, where fewer than half of practicing doctors are specialists. However, by this same metric, U.S. reliance on specialists is only somewhat higher than in the UK, the same as in Germany, and is lower than in Japan.

In most countries, the specialty share has been increasing since 1994. In the United States, the specialty share is down slightly from its 1994 level. However, in the most recent residency match, fewer than 20 percent of medical residencies were in primary care, suggesting that absent some major change in policy, the specialty share is likely to increase in the future.

The ratio of nurses to physicians in the United States is approximately in the middle of the remaining OECD countries for which such data are available (figure 19.6b). However, Canada's ratio is 50 percent higher than in the United States and in countries most comparable to the United States in terms of health spending per capita (the Netherlands, Norway, and Switzerland), the ratio is approximately 30 percent more. No strong inferences can be made about either efficiency or quality from these comparisons, but they illustrate how differently industrialized nations organize and deliver medical care.

The new health reform law has several provisions designed to expand the supply of primary care providers. The law included (starting in 2011) a 10 percent bonus for five years under the Medicare fee schedule, to family doctors, internists, geriatricians, nurse practitioners, and physician assistants who provide 60 percent of services in qualifying evaluation and management codes. The law also requires states to increase Medicaid payment rates to Medicare levels in 2013 and 2014 for providers who deliver certain primary care services. These measures might encourage more medical students to enter these fields and also might delay the retirement of those thinking about quitting their practices.

If implemented, the new health reform law will increase demand for primary care. How much of that ultimately is provided through physicians as opposed to less expensive mid-level providers (for example, physician assistants or nurse practitioners) remains to be seen.

19.6a The United States is not alone in relying heavily on specialty physician care

Specialists as a percentage of practicing physicians

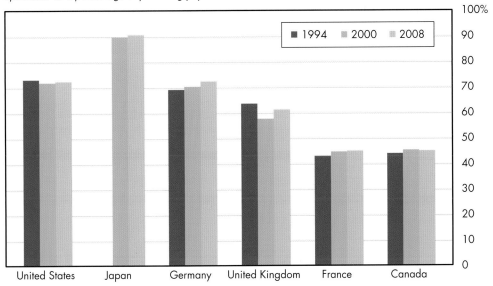

■ 1994 ■ 2000 ■ 2008

19.6b The ratio of practicing nurses to doctors in the United States is comparable to the ratios in other OECD nations

Ratio of practicing nurses to practicing physicians (2004)

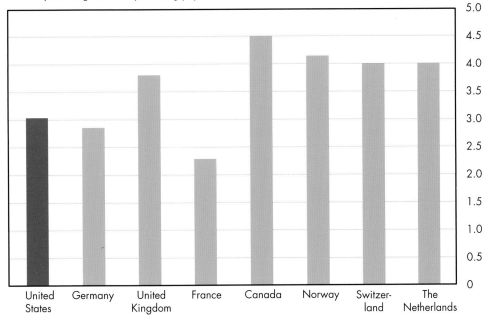

Americans pay higher prices for brand-name pharmaceuticals but lower prices for generic and over-the-counter drugs than do residents in other major industrialized countries.

U.S. pharmaceutical spending per capita is higher than in the rest of the G7. This is true whether spending is measured in terms of manufacturer prices or in terms of public prices that include wholesaler and retailer distribution margins and value-added taxes. Americans tend to use stronger drug formulations. Thus, even though U.S. prescription drug use is second lowest within the G7 based on doses per capita, the United States is exceeded only by Canada and France in terms of number of grams per capita.

Americans pay higher prices for drugs on patent, but much lower prices for generic medications and over-the-counter medications not requiring a prescription (figure 19.7a). Generic medications account for 70 percent of U.S. pharmaceuticals by volume but less than 20 percent by sales. Prices for brand-name drugs still enjoying patent protection can be set much higher. This allows the manufacturers to recoup the hundreds of millions of dollars in R&D costs that it takes on average to bring one new drug to market. Generics are less expensive in the United States because many factors in the pharmaceutical market contribute to making the generic sector extremely price competitive. Greater regulation, among other factors, contributes to higher generic prices elsewhere in the G7.

The prescription drug price index shown in figure 19.7a is a weighted average of brand name and generic prescription medications. This index illustrates that, except in Japan, the lower prices Americans pay for generics do not offset the higher prices they pay for patented pharmaceuticals. However, drugs, like most market commodities, are priced based on willingness to pay, which in turn reflects ability to pay.

Using manufacturers' prices converted to U.S. dollars at the prevailing exchange rate, the United States has higher pharmaceutical prices than any other G7 competitor except Japan. However, when this same price index is normalized to eliminate differences in GDP per capita (an approximate measure of average income), U.S. drugs are more affordable than in Japan, Germany, and Canada (figure 19.7b). Among the G7, only Italy and the UK have more affordable drugs than in the United States.

19.7a Americans generally pay more for drugs on patent than other nations in the G7 do but less for generic and over-the-counter products

Indexes: 100=U.S. (2005)

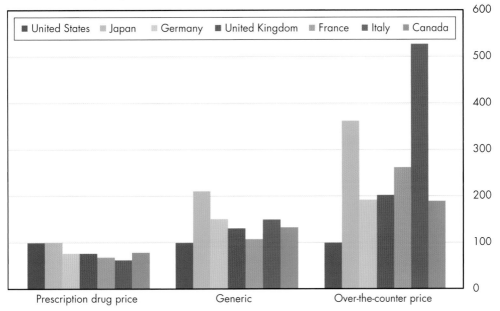

19.7b Manufacturers' prices generally are higher in the United States, but U.S. pharmaceuticals are generally more affordable because of higher incomes

Pharmaceutical price indexes: 100=U.S. (2005)

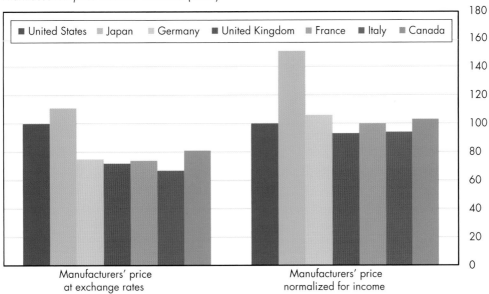

The American system of medical malpractice likely accounts for some, but assuredly not all, of the difference in health expenditures between the United States and its competitors.

The direct and hidden costs of the medical tort system amount to approximately six dollars for every $100 in NHE (figure 19.8a). The visible costs of the legal system and medical liability premiums for health facilities and health professionals equal only approximately 1 percent of health spending.

Defensive medicine, which includes any unnecessary tests or procedures that would be eliminated absent the incentives created by the medical tort system, is almost four times as much as this direct cost. These direct and indirect costs of the medical tort system can be viewed as an excise tax that increases the cost of medical care. If so, then there is another hidden cost in the form of efficiency losses arising from the lost output associated with this medical tort system "tax." There is much uncertainty around these estimates. It is possible that they are as low as two dollars for every $100 in health spending, or as high as $10.

The BEA tracks the annual level of payments for medical liability claims. The United States has experienced a series of medical malpractice "crises" starting in the mid-1970s. Relative to the amount of either total NHE or expenditures only for physician services, these medical liability payments peaked in the 1970s. Currently, these payments represent a lower share of NHE or physician spending than in 1969 (figure 19.8b). This does not suggest that the medical tort system could not be improved, only that it has been relatively worse in the past. Good cross-national estimates of malpractice spending do not exist, but OECD data indicate that the United States has the third-highest rate of deaths from medical errors per 100,000 population.

As a system for compensating victims, the medical tort system has been criticized as both inefficient and unfair. It is inefficient because fewer than 50 cents of every malpractice premium goes to paying victims. It is unfair to both patients and doctors because only a few of those injured due to medical negligence ever seek to recover damages and even fewer win awards. Conversely, many lawsuits filed involve doctors who were not negligent.

19.8a The direct and indirect costs of the medical tort system amount to approximately six dollars for every 100 dollars of health spending

Annual cost per $100 of NHE (2004)

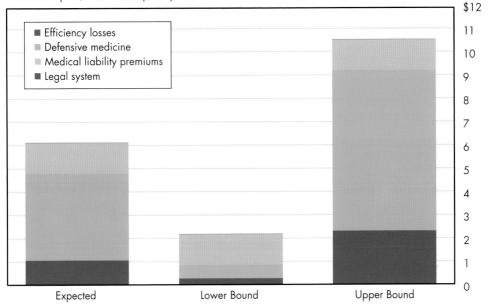

- ■ Efficiency losses
- ■ Defensive medicine
- ■ Medical liability premiums
- ■ Legal system

Expected Lower Bound Upper Bound

Note: Legal system costs are too small to be visible, but they are included in the figures shown.

19.8b Medical liability payments as a share of total or physician spending peaked in the 1970s and have declined through 2009

Medical malpractice payments per $100 of expenditures

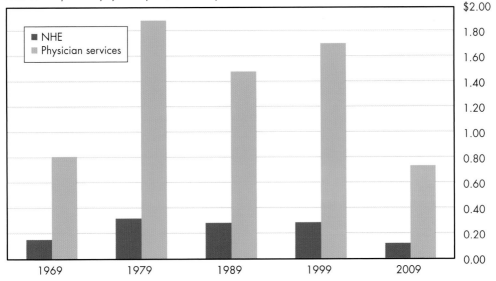

- ■ NHE
- ■ Physician services

1969 1979 1989 1999 2009

Excluding deaths due to violence, the United States generally leads the world in life expectancy at birth.

When life expectancy figures are appropriately adjusted, the United States ranks number one in the world in life expectancy at birth (figure 19.9a). Without such adjustment, the United States ranks fifteenth. The disproportionate number of U.S. deaths due to violence is the principal reason for the nation to rank so low overall. These fatalities include all gunshot-related deaths (homicides and suicides) and also deaths due to automobile accidents or other injuries. Such deaths arguably have little to do with medical system performance but instead arise from social causes, lifestyle choices, or imperfections in other public efforts to reduce such deaths, such as highway safety.

In figure 19.9a, each country was assumed to have the average fatal injury rate experienced over the 20 years examined. This has the effect of increasing life expectancy in countries that have a higher-than-average fatal injury rate, such as the United States. Conversely, it has the effect of lowering life expectancy in countries that have a lower-than-average fatal injury rate, such as Switzerland.

An OECD study shows that the availability of medical care (for example, supply of doctors and nurses relative to the population) is a relatively minor contributor to life expectancy. Increasing GDP per person by 10 percent, for example, would have almost four times as much impact on male life expectancy at birth as increasing the supply of doctors and nurses by the same percentage (figure 19.9b). In addition, increasing the level of education by 10 percent would have at least two to three times the impact as would the equivalent percent increase in doctor and nurse supply.

Changing behavior also can produce life expectancy gains that rival an increased supply of medical care services. A 10 percent reduction in smoking or excess use of alcohol (including any use of alcohol resulting in a fatal injury) would produce greater gains in male life expectancy than a 10 percent increase in the supply of doctors and nurses would.

None of these comparisons demonstrates which approach to increasing life expectancy is most cost-effective. They simply illustrate that differences in life expectancy across countries or states could arise even if they have medical care systems that are identical in performance.

19.9a When higher-than-average U.S. rates of violent deaths are taken into account, the United States leads the world in life expectancy

Mean life expectancy at birth, 1980–99 (years)

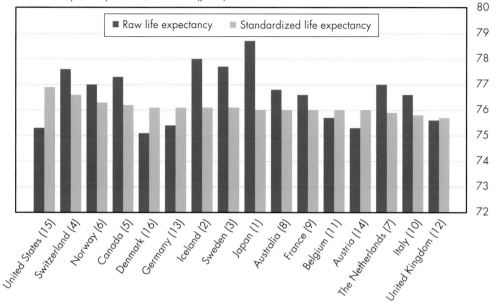

Note: Countries are ordered by standardized life expectancy derived by assigning each country the mean OECD fatal injury rate for the period shown; numbers in parentheses denote ranking on unstandardized life expectancy at birth.

19.9b Other determinants of life expectancy at birth are of equal or greater importance than the availability of doctors and nurses

Percent change in life expectancy at birth per 10 percent change in factor

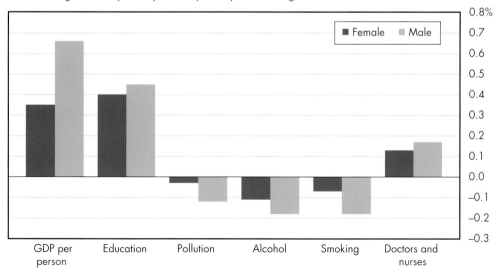

Few countries match the performance of the
United States in saving the lives of pre-term infants.
The higher rate of pre-term births in the United States
is an important contributor to its low international
ranking for infant mortality overall.

The United States ranks poorly in terms of infant mortality rates, but this too says little about the performance of its health care system. The United States has the third-highest infant mortality rate in the OECD. This rate is somewhat overstated due to differences in statistical methods for measuring infant deaths. The United States is one of only eight countries that count extremely premature infants as "live births," even though they have extremely low odds of survival.

More important, compared with most other industrialized countries, the United States has a much higher rate of premature and/or low-birth-weight infants. Although adequate prenatal care certainly can influence such rates, many other social factors also contribute. For example, low-birth-weight infants are disproportionately born to mothers from disadvantaged socioeconomic backgrounds. Adolescent pregnancies also are more likely to result in a premature birth. Even though it has been declining, the U.S. teenage birth rate far exceeds that of other G7 nations. Maternal smoking, and drug and alcohol use during pregnancy also increase the odds of a low-birth-weight infant.

A fairer comparison, therefore, examines how well the medical system performs in keeping alive infants of a given length of gestation. For all birth categories before full term (37+ weeks), the United States ranks second or third among the nine countries for which comparable data exist (figure 19.10). Unfortunately, the United States and the UK are the only G7 nations on this list.

The ability to save premature infants has increased greatly over the past few decades. For white infants, for example, infant mortality steadily declined between 1983 and 2004 despite a 20 percent increase in the percentage of such infants falling into the low-birth-weight category. This reflects sizable investments in (and wide diffusion of) neonatal intensive-care units. Careful studies suggest that since 1960, the 70 percent decline in mortality for low-birth-weight infants born in the United States was almost entirely the result of improved medical care.

19.10 The United States generally leads the world (except Sweden and Norway) in saving the lives of premature infants

Infant mortality index (U.S.=100)

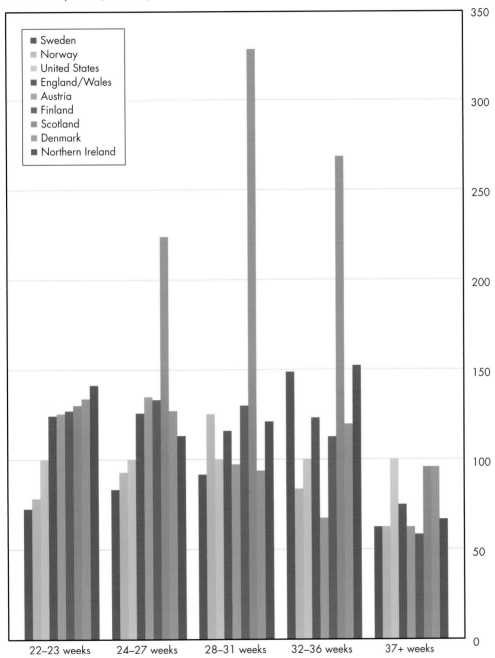

Note: Countries listed (left to right) from best to worst for infants with the shortest gestation period.

On average, Americans who have various types of cancer have markedly better chances of surviving five years compared with cancer patients in other industrialized nations. For several reasons, survival rates for blacks trail these averages.

Another area in which the U.S. medical system excels is in cancer treatment. Cancer patients live longer in the United States than in any other country in the world. For example, the United States leads the world in cancer survival rates for the leading cancers among women (figure 19.11a). In general, the survival differences between the United States and other countries are even greater for major cancers affecting males, including colon, lung, and prostate cancer.

For some of these cancers, such as female breast and cervical cancers, there is a large difference in survival rates for whites compared with blacks. If rates were standardized to account for the higher percentage of blacks in the United States relative to these other nations, the cancer survival differences would be even larger than shown.

Some of the apparently superior performance in the United States can be attributed to higher cancer screening rates (figure 19.11b). To the extent that cancers are detected earlier in their course through routine screening, this will increase the percentage of patients in whom cancer is detected who are able to survive five years.

The most important factors in cancer survival are early diagnosis, time to treatment, and access to the most effective drugs. Some uninsured cancer patients in the United States encounter problems with timely treatment and access. However, apparently a larger proportion of cancer patients in other G7 countries face similar barriers to access. For example, waiting times for specialty care are especially problematic in Canada and in the UK. Almost half the improvement in survival rates in the United States in the 1990s can be attributed to the introduction of new oncology drugs. Americans typically get more rapid access to new pharmaceuticals than do citizens in other countries. Consequently, any benefits from new oncology drugs would show up faster in U.S. cancer survival statistics than in countries that have longer lag-times for the introduction of the latest drugs.

19.11a The United States leads the world in female cancer survival rates for the leading causes of cancer deaths

Five-year female cancer survival rate indexes (U.S.=100)

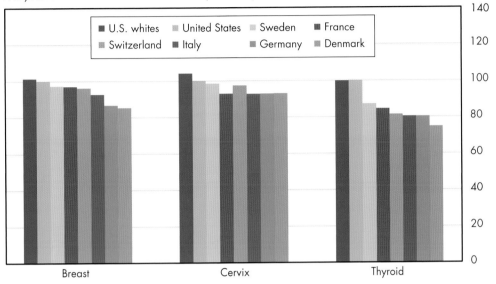

Legend: U.S. whites, United States, Sweden, France, Switzerland, Italy, Germany, Denmark

Categories: Breast, Cervix, Thyroid

Note: Countries ranked from best to worst for breast cancer.

19.11b Despite more uninsured people in the United States, cancer screening rates for adults 50 and older are much higher in the United States than in Europe

European cancer screening rates as a percentage of U.S. rates

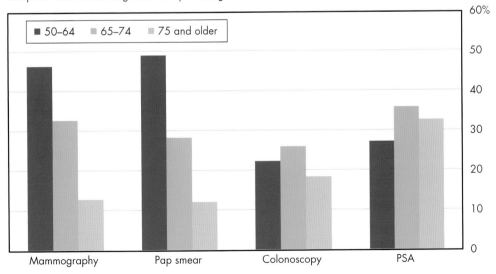

Legend: 50–64, 65–74, 75 and older

Categories: Mammography, Pap smear, Colonoscopy, PSA

Note: PSA = prostate-specific antigen test to screen for prostate cancer.

Despite its superiority in many health outcomes related to medical care, the United States has relatively more avoidable deaths amenable to health care than do many other industrialized countries.

The United States ranks nineteenth among industrialized countries in the rate of deaths amenable to health care (figure 19.12). "Amenable deaths" refer to deaths from selected causes that should not occur in the presence of timely and effective health care. Such deaths constitute approximately 25 percent of deaths for males who are younger than age 75 and approximately 30 percent of deaths in that age group for females. An important advantage of this measure is that it excludes deaths that do not necessarily reflect problems of access or quality of the medical care system. The death rates used to calculate the estimates in figure 19.12 were standardized by gender and five-year age categories. Thus, observed differences cannot be attributed to basic demographic differences in the U.S. population compared with elsewhere.

However, the numbers are *not* standardized based on race. In light of widespread racial and ethnic disparities in U.S. health outcomes—little of which reflect poor health system performance—this limitation might disproportionately cast the United States in a worse light. Moreover, the authors of the study that produced these data have cautioned, "The rate of amenable mortality is a valuable indicator of health care system performance, although it is important to note that the underlying concept should not be mistaken as definitive evidence of differences in the effectiveness of health care but rather as an indicator of potential weaknesses in health care that can then be investigated in more depth."

With these caveats, the available data show that some OECD countries have rates much lower than in the United States. For example, France and Japan have rates approximately 40 percent less than in the United States. Even the UK, which lagged behind in some of the comparisons of cancer survival rates and infant mortality by birth-weight, outperforms the United States on this metric. Second, amenable mortality rates declined only 4 percent in the United States between 1997–1998 and 2002–2003, compared with an average decline of 17 percent among all countries studied. This fact suggests that the United States is falling behind rather than catching up to its competitors on this measure.

19.12 Compared with many other OECD countries, the United States has a higher death rate from conditions amenable to health care

Index (U.S.=100) of standardized death rate per 100,000 (ages 0–74), 2002–03

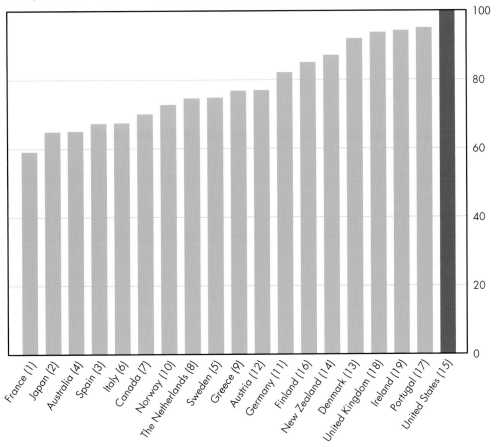

Countries ordered from best to worst in 2002–03
(numbers in parentheses denote ranking in 1997–98)

Most "avoidable" deaths are related to lifestyle or behavior.

Approximately half of premature mortality is attributable to behavior or lifestyle (figure 19.13a). These include diet, physical activity, smoking, stress, alcohol or illicit drug abuse, injury or violence, and similar factors.

Human biology accounts for 20 percent of premature deaths. It refers to the individual's genetic makeup (which includes factors with which he or she is born, or mutations acquired over a lifetime) and family history (which can contribute both to risk for disease and/or the risk of dying from it when diagnosed).

Environmental factors account for another 20 percent of premature deaths. Researchers distinguish between the social environment (interactions with family, friends, coworkers, and others in the community) and the physical environment (things that can be seen, touched, heard, smelled, and tasted, and less tangible risks such as radiation or ozone). Social institutions, such as law enforcement, the workplace, places of worship, and schools, also are part of this environment. Housing, public transportation, and the presence or absence of violence in the community are other important components.

Access to medical care itself accounts for only 10 percent of premature mortality. The data shown are only approximate. First, they are estimates made 35 years ago. Second, the experts that developed them examined only the 10 leading causes of death in the United States, not all causes of death. Third, clearly important interactions exist between the categories. For example, behaviors can have a reciprocal relationship to biology, meaning that each can react to the other. For example, smoking (behavior) increases the odds of a heart attack (biology). A heart attack then can motivate an individual to stop smoking (behavior).

Even a cursory examination of the underlying causes of death in the United States underscores the importance of behavior and lifestyle (figure 19.13b). Smoking, poor diet and inactivity, and alcohol consumption alone accounted for approximately 40 percent (almost one million) of total deaths in the year 2008. The health care system is most directly implicated in deaths due to prescription drug non-compliance (125,000), non-preventable adverse patient events (116,000), infectious diseases excluding HIV (65,000)—some of which are avoidable—and preventable medical errors, both non-negligent (37,000) and negligent (34,000); together these account for 15 percent of all deaths.

19.13a Approximately half of premature mortality relates to behavior/lifestyle; only 10 percent relates to medical care

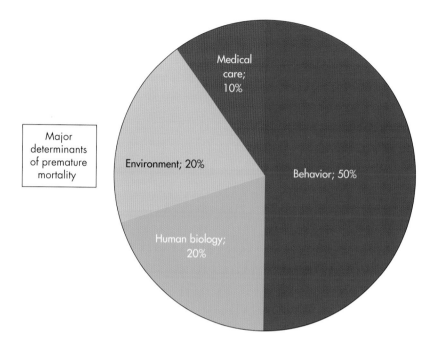

Major determinants of premature mortality

Medical care; 10%

Environment; 20%

Behavior; 50%

Human biology; 20%

19.13b Changes in behavior/lifestyle would have a sizable impact on mortality rates in the United States

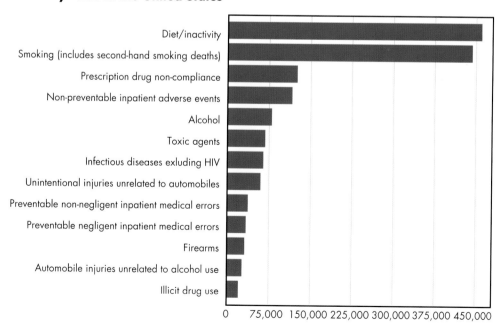

Diet/inactivity

Smoking (includes second-hand smoking deaths)

Prescription drug non-compliance

Non-preventable inpatient adverse events

Alcohol

Toxic agents

Infectious diseases exluding HIV

Unintentional injuries unrelated to automobiles

Preventable non-negligent inpatient medical errors

Preventable negligent inpatient medical errors

Firearms

Automobile injuries unrelated to alcohol use

Illicit drug use

0   75,000   150,000   225,000   300,000   375,000   450,000

Total U.S. deaths (2008)

The nation's obesity rate is the highest in the world, but smoking is somewhat less common among adults in the United States compared with most other industrialized countries. There are big differences in obesity and smoking rates across states.

The United States by far has the world's highest rate of obesity (figure 19.14a). More than 30 percent of all women in the United States are obese (based on measurements, not self-reports). Within the G7, the two countries ranking just behind the United States (the UK and Canada) have male and female obesity rates that are only approximately 25 percent. Japan's measured obesity rate for men and women is less than 5 percent.

Unfortunately, measured obesity rates for all G7 countries are not available. The difference can be considerable. In Canada, for example, the measured obesity rate is 50 to 60 percent higher than the self-reported rates for men and women. The rates shown for Germany, France, and Italy might therefore be much higher than illustrated.

Smoking is the single largest cause of death in the United States, even though the nation has one of the lowest smoking rates among industrialized countries. There are many ways to measure smoking, but this metric counts the percentage of adults age 15 and older who self-report that they are daily smokers. Using this metric, adult smoking rates in Japan and France are more than 50 percent higher than current rates in the United States. In fact, none of the G7 countries for which this information is available has a lower smoking rate than in the United States.

Smoking and obesity both contribute considerably to premature mortality in the United States. Obesity-related and smoking-attributable medical costs each amount to approximately 6 percent of national health spending.

However, differences in obesity and smoking rates within the United States itself rival cross-national differences in such rates among the G7 countries. States exhibit less than a two-fold difference in obesity rates (figure 19.14b) but a three-fold difference in smoking rates (figure 19.14c). This highlights the diversity of the United States in terms of these particular unhealthy behaviors. It also highlights the limitations of national averages when making cross-national comparisons.

19.14a The United States has far higher obesity rates but much lower smoking rates than do its major G7 competitors

Percentage of adults age 15 and older

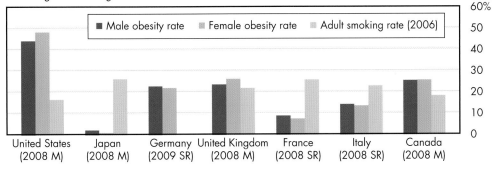

United States (2008 M) Japan (2008 M) Germany (2009 SR) United Kingdom (2008 M) France (2008 SR) Italy (2008 SR) Canada (2008 M)

Note: M = measured obesity rate. SR = self-reported obesity rate.

19.14b States that have the highest percentage of adults age 15 and older who were obese in 2009 are concentrated in the South

Obese
- 18.9–24.0
- 24.5–25.8
- 25.9–27.7
- 28.0–30.1
- 30.2–35.3

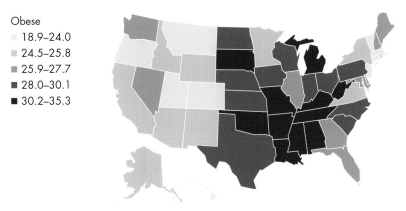

19.14c States that have the highest percentage of adults age 15 and older who were daily smokers in 2007 also are concentrated in the South

Smokers
- 6.4–15.7
- 15.8–17.2
- 17.4–18.5
- 18.6–20.6
- 21.4–25.6

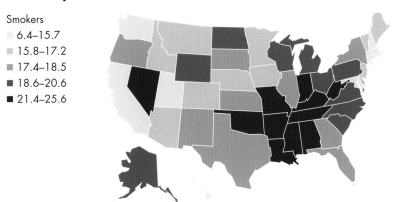

Comparing health system performance across U.S. states poses many of the same challenges as do comparisons across countries.

The variation in health outcomes across states has been an important theme in this section. Some side-by-side comparisons of selected indicators that have been used to rank the performance of states are illustrated in figure 19.15a. Here, the word "performance" recognizes that differences in these indicators might not reflect the quality of medical care delivered in the states. Some indicators such as traffic fatalities better reflect state performance on other dimensions (for example, highway safety) than on health care.

To facilitate comparisons, each indicator has been indexed to the U.S. average for that indicator. This makes it easier to see that the worst performing states on a) years of potential life lost before age 75, b) smoking prevalence, and c) the rate of motor vehicle deaths have rates that are approximately 50 percent higher than the national average. Two conclusions can be drawn from these comparisons.

First, the relative sizes of the differences between states varies widely by indicator. There is only a 75 percent difference between the state that has the highest obesity rate compared with the state that has the lowest. In contrast, there is a 12-fold difference between the states that have the highest and lowest rates of violent crime offenses per 100,000 residents (which include homicides, rapes, robberies, and aggravated assaults).

Second, there is not always much symmetry in how the highest- and lowest-performing states compare with the national average. The state that has the highest obesity rate exceeds the national average by only 25 percent while the best-performing state has an obesity rate 28 percent less than the average. Similarly, the highest state-level smoking rate is 45 percent above the U.S. average, and the state with the lowest rate is 49 percent below that average. The other indicators display more asymmetry. The state with the most years of potential life lost (YPLL) is 69 percent above the national average, but the state with the lowest YPLL is only 25 percent below that average. Rates of violent crimes exhibit the greatest asymmetry.

State rankings (figure 19.15b) therefore depend heavily on what factors are included and the weights given to each factor.

19.15a There are large differences in health system performance across states

Indexes: 100=U.S.

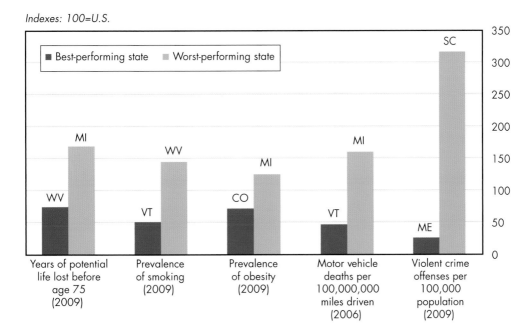

Note: CO = Colorado; ME = Maine; MI = Michigan; SC = South Carolina; WV = West Virginia; VT = Vermont.

19.15b The United Health Foundation 2009 rankings of overall health reveal that most of the states that have the lowest overall health ranking are located in the South

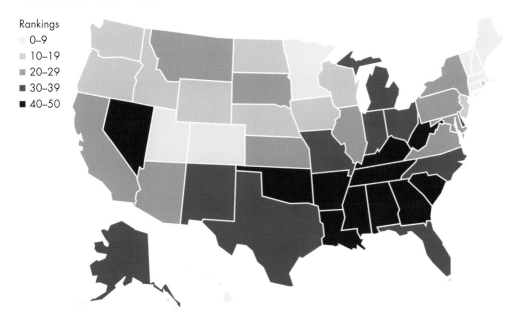

CHAPTER 20

Are Health Spending Trends Sustainable?

Over the next 75 years, health benefits as a share of worker compensation could more than quadruple. Despite this, real cash wages per worker will be 7.5 times as much as the amount in 2008.

If current trends continue, the ratio of health-related fringe benefits to worker wages will more than quadruple. Admittedly, forecasting over a 75-year period is challenging. However, estimates of what wages will be through 2083 use the identical assumptions about growth in real (inflation-adjusted) wages per worker that are embedded in the most recent projections from Social Security trustees. Assuming that changes in these shares mirror what has happened during the past 10 years, the share of total compensation for health benefits and non-health fringe benefits can be projected,.

Using these simple assumptions, the ratio of health-related supplements per dollar of wages would grow over 75 years from 6.4 cents in 2008 to 26.3 cents (figure 20.1). Even after taking into account the growth in non-health fringe benefits as a share of compensation—projected in a parallel fashion—the amount of real cash wages will grow considerably, relative to 2008. That is, in terms of constant purchasing power, workers in 75 years will have nearly eight times as much non-health compensation as they received in 2008.

Succinctly, even though employers will have to devote a growing share of compensation to health care, these costs currently are not growing so rapidly that they will entirely displace the parallel (though slower) growth in real wages. Such a time might come, but not in the foreseeable future.

20.1 At historical growth rates, the amount of health-related benefits per dollar of wages and salaries would quadruple over the next 75 years

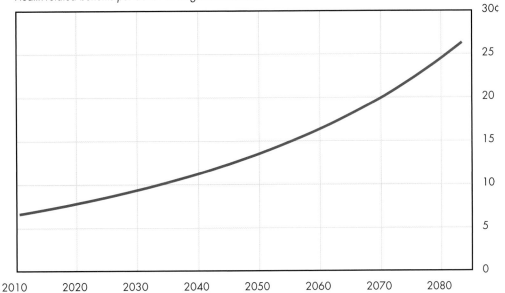

Health-related benefits per dollar of wages and salaries

Technology has been a far more important driver of health spending growth during the past 60 years than has population growth or aging.

Technology and other factors appear to account for approximately half or more of the growth in per capita health spending over the past 60 or more years. As figure 20.2 illustrates, the exact amount depends on the period examined and other methodological assumptions.

The exact contribution of technology is unknown (recall figure 17.3). When analysts have accounted for all the other major factors that contributed to the rise in inflation-adjusted health spending per person (for example, medical price inflation), most of the "residual" that cannot be explained is attributed to technology. Some of it is an income effect, a willingness to purchase medical services (for example, Lasik surgery) if a person has a higher income, but a person who has a lower income was not willing to purchase it. It is difficult to separate out accurately the effect of income from technology. Some would also argue that calculations such as these underestimate the role of insurance in encouraging the development of technology.

However it is defined, this "residual" is what government forecasters use to determine how fast health care expenditures will increase in the future. They can use demographic models to calculate how quickly the population is increasing and how the age-gender mix of the population is changing over time. Relative spending changes over the life cycle, depending on gender (refer to figure 12.5). Thus, if everything were static, it would be a straightforward mathematical exercise to determine how much total spending will rise because of such demographic changes.

However, the big unknown is how much per-person spending for everyone is likely to rise beyond growth in the general economy. To answer this question, forecasters have no choice but to look to the past. They cannot avoid making assumptions about the future. The 2000 Medicare Technical Panel estimated that per capita annual growth in health care spending would be 2.2 percent a year and that long-run real per capita GDP growth would be 1.2 percent. This implies that health spending growth would exceed GDP growth by one percentage point a year. Thus, they recommended using "GDP + 1" (that is, 1.2 percent plus 1 percent) as the basis for projecting health spending over the next 75 years. The Medicare Trustees' reports from the year 2000 forward all have used this assumption in deriving long-term projections (i.e., years 25 through 75 of the projection period).

20.2 The role of technology for health spending growth per person is sizable regardless of the time and assumptions used

■ Technology/all other   ■ Defensive medicine   ▨ Avoidable administrative expense

■ Relative medical price inflation   ▨ Income growth   ■ Insurance   ■ Aging

Components of health expenditure growth (percentage)

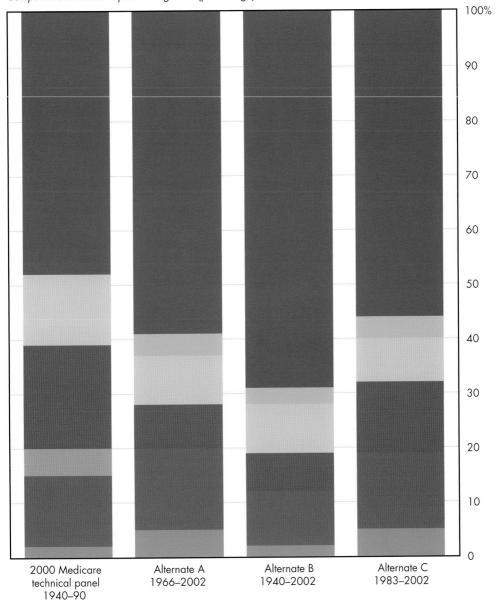

Note: Income growth not accounted for in alternate assumptions A, B, and C because GDP growth is accounted for separately in the projection model.

The excess cost ratio measures how much faster per capita health spending—adjusted for changes in age and gender—increased relative to growth in per capita GDP. Historical variations in the excess cost ratio make predicting future health spending difficult, especially over a long time.

"Excess cost growth" is the name for the residual just described. It is the difference between the U.S. per capita growth rate in age- and gender-adjusted health care costs minus the per capita growth in GDP (both rates are calculated from inflation-adjusted estimates of health spending and GDP). The level of excess cost growth has varied over time. Not surprisingly, this variation has been largest when short (five-year) time intervals are used (figure 20.3a). Over longer periods, there is less variation (but part of the reason is because the observed periods overlap).

Excess cost growth from 1940–1990 was 2.3 percent a year. The data from the longest periods illustrated in figure 20.3a (25 and 32 years) suggest that excess cost growth might have declined to less than 2 percent. However, certainty is impossible to achieve. During this period, many policy changes in Medicare (introduction of a prospective payment system for hospitals in 1983, establishment of the Medicare physician fee schedule in 1992, substantial Medicare cost-containment measures in 1997) might have had the effect of temporarily slowing growth in spending, thereby masking the underlying trend having to do with technology that might continue in the future.

Forecasts of the year in which the Medicare Trust Fund is exhausted have varied substantially over 20 years (figure 20.3b). This is not to suggest that government forecasters are incompetent. First, by their nature, official projections of Medicare spending by Medicare Trustees or of Medicare, Medicaid, and total health spending by the CBO reflect only current policy. Policy can and did change in response to these forecasts. Remember this when using hypothetical forecasts in the following pages to explore whether current trends in health spending are sustainable in the future. Uncertainty is an unavoidable feature of long-term forecasts.

20.3a Measured over long periods of time, annualized growth in health costs in excess of growth in GDP appears to be declining

Annual excess cost growth in per capita health spending, by starting year

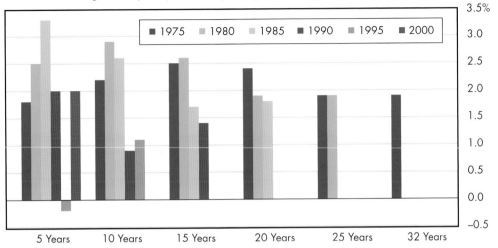

Note: Per capita health spending is adjusted for changes in age and gender. Also, the ending year after 2000 is 2007, not 2005. Thus, five-year excess growth starting in year 2000 is for 2000–2007; 10-year excess growth starting in year 1995 is for 1995–2007, etc.

20.3b Projections of Medicare Trust Fund insolvency have changed considerably over the years

Projected year of Medicare hospital insurance trust fund insolvency

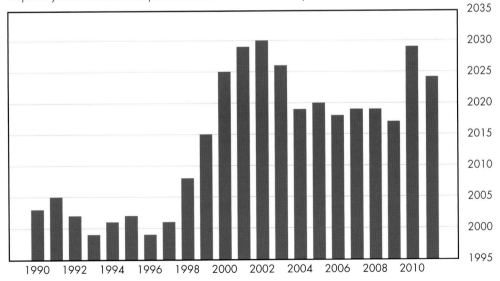

Year of Medicare Trustees' report

> Over the next 50 years, the country can "afford" growth in health spending that exceeds growth in the general economy only if the difference is not too much. Continuing historical rates of excess growth in health spending could result in a decline in real GDP per capita within 30 years.

After deducting amounts for health care, the inflation-adjusted amount of personal consumption spending per American more than tripled in the 80 years since 1929 (figure 20.4a). Despite enormous growth since 1929 in health spending and the size of government—both of which reduced the amount that otherwise would have been available for personal consumption—what Americans had left for everything else still was able to grow. Admittedly, what was left would have been twice as large in a world without any spending on health care or government. No one aspires to live in such a hypothetical world. The purpose of figure 20.4a is to illustrate that the growth in health care (and government) has not been so rapid that it reduced the American standard of living from generation to generation.

However, the United States cannot afford a continuation of historical rates of excess cost growth unless Americans are comfortable with a decline in non-health GDP per capita within the next 75 years. How quickly that occurs will depend on which historical excess cost growth number is used.

Using actual experience from relatively recently (1990–2008), annual excess cost growth was 1.4 percent. Continuing this into the future would produce a downturn in inflation-adjusted non-health spending per capita in the year 2070 (figure 20.4b). However, extrapolating the experience of 1975–2008 (1.9 percent excess cost growth) would result in a decline in real GDP per capita by 2053. This downturn would be so sharp that health care would absorb all of GDP by 2090.

Because people have to have food, clothing, and shelter, 100 percent of GDP logically can never be fully devoted to health care. These projections are not predictions because they lack assumptions about changes in policy or behavior. Their use lies in demonstrating how much of a change in experience is required to "bend the cost curve" enough to avoid an undesirable outcome.

20.4a Despite increasing health spending and taxes, non-health personal spending per capita more than tripled from 1929 to 2009

Inflation-adjusted per capita expenditures (chained 2005 dollars)

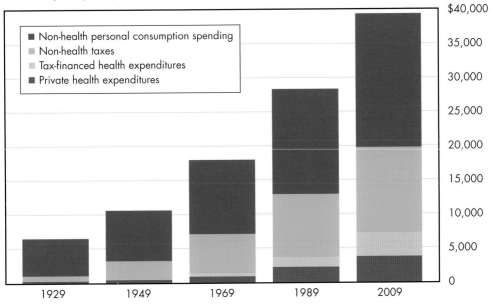

■ Non-health personal consumption spending
▨ Non-health taxes
▨ Tax-financed health expenditures
■ Private health expenditures

1929   1949   1969   1989   2009

20.4b Non-health GDP per person could decline within 50 years if excess cost growth continues at historical levels

Non-health GDP per capita (2010 dollars using adjusted CPI)

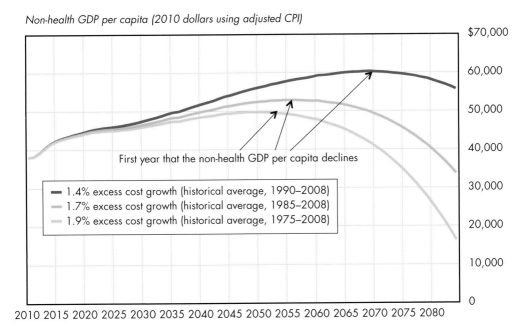

First year that the non-health GDP per capita declines

— 1.4% excess cost growth (historical average, 1990–2008)
— 1.7% excess cost growth (historical average, 1985–2008)
— 1.9% excess cost growth (historical average, 1975–2008)

2010 2015 2020 2025 2030 2035 2040 2045 2050 2055 2060 2065 2070 2075 2080

Much uncertainty exists in 75-year forecasts of health spending; yet if even 1 percent excess cost growth persists, almost 90 percent of annual GDP growth will be devoted to health care by 2085.

Uncertainty is pervasive in long-term forecasts of health spending. An approach called "stochastic modeling" is used by Medicare Trustees and other analysts to try to quantify the extent of that uncertainty.

Because perfect prediction is impossible, the goal of analysts is to identify some boundaries within which the true value of future spending is likely to lie. A 95 percent probability interval (also termed a *confidence interval*) is a typical approach to articulating these boundaries. Given uncertainty in future population, health status, and growth in health-status-adjusted per-beneficiary spending, the actual level of future spending is expected to fall within such an interval 95 percent of the time. There is more than a four-to-one ratio between the estimated Medicare share of GDP at the top of this interval compared with the bottom (figure 20.5a).

Even official forecasts of Medicare spending vary dramatically. In its 2010 annual report, the Medicare Trustees predicted that total Medicare spending in the year 2080 would be 6.4 percent (figure 20.5b). The CBO, using different assumptions about growth in GDP and growth in Medicare spending, concluded that Medicare by 2080 would account for 11 to 12 percent of GDP. Which prediction is "true" is less important than understanding that even highly skilled experts using reasonable variations in assumptions can produce widely disparate estimates of 75-year costs. Even a seemingly small difference in assumptions (for example, GDP will grow 0.1 percent more slowly) accumulates into a vast difference when compounded over decades.

All the official forecasts assume a decline in the excess cost growth rate over the 75-year projection period. After 75 years, the Trustees assume that excess cost growth will be zero, that is, that Medicare will grow at the same pace as the general economy. The CBO, in contrast, assumes that excess cost growth for all other components of health spending (including Medicaid, CHIP, and exchange subsidies) will be zero, but that the excess cost growth for Medicare in 2085 still would be one percentage point. Were excess cost growth of one percentage point to continue for the entire health system, it would imply that by 2085, 90 cents of every extra dollar of GDP would flow into the health system (figure 20.5c).

20.5a There is a huge amount of uncertainty in 75-year forecasts of Medicare or other health spending

Projected Medicare spending as a percentage of GDP

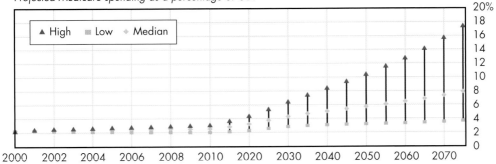

Note: Low and high estimates encompass a 95 percent probability interval. Given uncertainty in future population, future health status, and growth in health-status adjusted per beneficiary spending, the actual level of future spending is expected to fall within this interval 95 percent of the time.

20.5b Official forecasts of Medicare spending differ dramatically due to different assumptions about growth of GDP and health spending

Total Medicare expenditures as a percentage of GDP

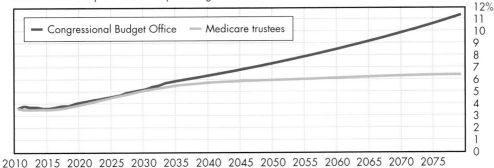

20.5c If 1 percent excess cost growth persists, almost 90 percent of GDP increases will be devoted to health care by 2085

Share of increase in inflation-adjusted GDP per capita devoted to health care

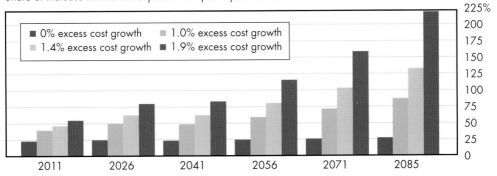

In today's dollars, the long-term unfunded liabilities associated with health entitlements exceed $66 trillion—approximately four times as much as the unfunded liabilities related to Social Security.

The unfunded liabilities for entitlements exceed $80 billion over the long term (figure 20.6a). Only approximately 20 percent has to do with Social Security. The rest ($66 trillion) is due to health entitlements. If it works as planned, the new health plan will reduce unfunded liabilities for Medicare by tens of billions of dollars.

However, both the Medicare actuary and the CBO have raised questions about whether some of the law's underlying premises will be maintained. For example, all the CBO projections used in this section assume that physician fees under Medicare will be cut by approximately 30 percent. With looming physician shortages, few believe such a drastic cut is desirable even though current law technically requires it. As it has for the past eight years, Congress is expected to keep deferring this scheduled cut indefinitely or to change the law to eliminate it. The CBO has developed an alternative fiscal scenario in which this and several other policies designed to limit spending would not continue. Under these alternative assumptions, Medicare spending as a percent of GDP in 2080 (as estimated by the CBO) would be two percentage points higher than illustrated in figure 20.5b.

Calculations for unfunded liabilities assume that current payroll tax levels for Social Security and Medicare Part A remain in effect. Another assumption is that the current level of Medicaid and Medicare Parts B and D spending (as a percentage of GDP) reflect societal willingness-to-pay for these programs. The "unfunded" amount equals the increase in the burden (relative to current levels) required to sustain these programs.

To give some sense of whether these entitlements are "affordable," figure 20.6b expresses the funding shortfall as a percent of payroll. Essentially, the Social Security (FICA) payroll tax of 15.3 percent would have to more than double by the year 2080 simply to bankroll health-related entitlements. In present-value terms, the long-term unfunded liability is five times the U.S. national income (GDP) (figure 20.6c). This is approximately equivalent to assuming a mortgage equal to five times a family income. The unfunded liability is 1.5 times as much as the country's net worth. This is approximately equivalent to borrowing 1.5 times a family's net worth. Countries are not families, but these comparators at least provide a rough sense of just how large the problem of funding future entitlements has become.

20.6a Even assuming that the health reform law works as intended, unfunded liabilities for entitlements will exceed $80 trillion over the long run

Net present value of unfunded liabilities (trillions of 2009 dollars)

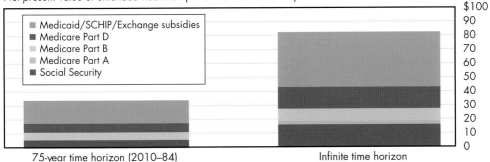

75-year time horizon (2010–84)	Infinite time horizon

Legend:
- Medicaid/SCHIP/Exchange subsidies
- Medicare Part D
- Medicare Part B
- Medicare Part A
- Social Security

Note: For Medicare Part B, Medicare Part D, and Medicaid, unfunded liabilities are calculated assuming that the 2010 share of GDP represents current willingness-to-pay for these programs. Any increase in spending above this share is calculated as an unfunded liability for which higher taxes must be paid eventually.

20.6b The funding shortfall for major entitlements will amount to almost 20 percent of payroll within 70 years

Annual unfunded public sector liability as a percent of payroll

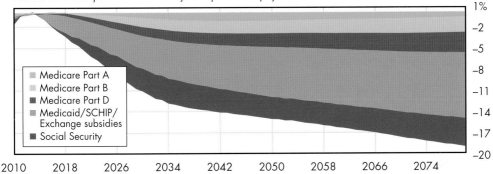

Legend:
- Medicare Part A
- Medicare Part B
- Medicare Part D
- Medicaid/SCHIP/Exchange subsidies
- Social Security

Note: Funding shortfalls for Medicaid, Medicare Part B, and Medicare Part D are calculated assuming the share of GDP devoted to these programs in 2009 represents societal willingness-to-pay for them. Under CBO's alternative fiscal scenario, the 2080 shortfall would be at least 6 percentage points higher than shown.

20.6c Health-related unfunded liabilities alone are at least double the national income; in the end, they exceed current U.S. net worth

Ratio of unfunded liabilities for Medicare and Medicaid relative to measure shown

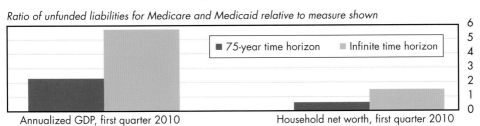

Legend:
- 75-year time horizon
- Infinite time horizon

Annualized GDP, first quarter 2010	Household net worth, first quarter 2010

Note: Unfunded liabilities calculated as of January 1, 2010.

The projected 75-year increase in mandatory federal health spending exceeds current revenues from the three largest sources of federal tax revenue.

The size of the projected increase in mandatory federal health spending dwarfs the amount currently collected through the three largest sources of federal revenue (figure 20.7a). Thus, filling the fiscal gap through higher taxes would imply more than doubling individual income taxes, quintupling the amount collected in corporate income taxes, or tripling current payroll taxes (all approximations). Alternatively, because the long-run increase in mandatory federal health spending amounts to 67 percent of federal tax revenue, this would imply that a minimum 67 percent increase in federal taxes across the board would be needed to tax ourselves out of the health entitlements burden. Of course, given the inevitable behavioral response that would result from increasing taxes by this magnitude, the increase in tax rates would have to be even higher than these multipliers suggest.

Even if taxpayers could find a way to bankroll the enormous increases in health spending reviewed in this section, it is less clear that beneficiaries of public insurance programs such as Medicare can absorb their share of rising health costs. By 2085, the out-of-pocket burden of just Medicare Parts B and D will approximately double for the average Social Security recipient (figure 20.7b). By 2085, premiums and out-of-pocket expenses will absorb more than half of the average Social Security check, assuming that such checks are not trimmed as part of the efforts to save Social Security. This does not even count any cost sharing associated with Medicare Part A. The CMS Office of the Actuary has developed an illustrative alternative scenario that recognizes that some of the Medicare spending reductions contemplated by the health reform law might not occur. For example, the cuts in physician fees required by the sustainable growth rate formula (SGR) now have been overridden by Congress for nine consecutive years. Under this alternative scenario, premiums and out-of-pocket expenses for Medicare Parts B and D would equal four-fifths of the average Social Security check by 2085.

Burdens of this magnitude will amplify pressures for the federal government to subsidize such individuals even more to make their health care affordable. This would then further escalate the amount of federal health spending beyond the levels already described. Finding ways to reduce spending, rather than raising revenues, at least offers the prospect of averting this bind on the elderly who have fixed incomes.

20.7a The projected 75-year increase in mandatory federal health spending exceeds revenues from the three largest sources of federal tax revenue

Percentage of GDP

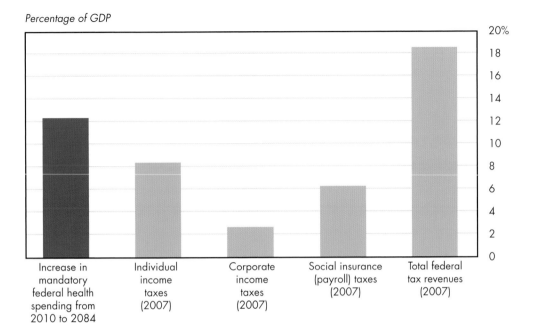

20.7b Typical Medicare premiums and cost sharing for Parts B and D represent an increasing share of the average Social Security check

Monthly premiums and cost sharing as percentage of average monthly Social Security benefit

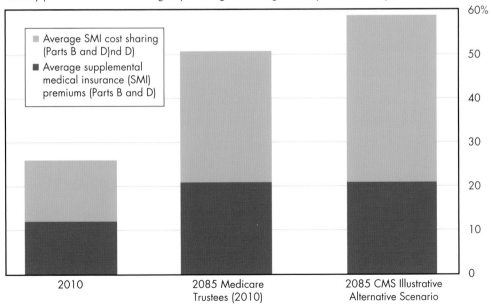

U.S. competitors have already had to confront the challenge of an increasing number of dependents— both children and elderly—per working adult. For the United States, much of this challenge still lies in the future.

The U.S. elderly-dependency ratio is much lower than in any other G7 nation, despite having risen during the past 50 years (figure 20.8a). The elderly-dependency ratio measures the number of people age 65 and older relative to a "working-age" population (those ages 15-64). The U.S. ratio is lower, and in almost all comparisons, it increased less rapidly over the past 25 years (absolutely and relatively) than among the nation's major competitors. Japan's ratio, for example, was less than the U.S. level in 1984, yet by 2007 was almost twice as high.

The OECD projects that this U.S. margin of advantage will persist through 2050, because all these countries will experience sharp rises in their dependency ratios. However, due to the "Baby Boomers," the U.S. ratio is expected to reach almost 45 in the year 2040 before declining to approximately 40 in 2050. Thus, the nation is doing better in relative terms, but it still must face the fiscal challenges posed by the dependency ratio more than doubling over the next few decades. In fact, the number of covered workers per Social Security beneficiary is expected to decline even under the most optimistic assumptions (figure 20.8b).

The U.S. demographic margin of advantage is offset considerably when differences in the relative burden of elderly health spending are taken into account. In the United States, per capita elderly health spending amounts to approximately 45 percent of the average annual compensation for manufacturing workers (figure 20.8c). In the rest of the G7, this fraction is approximately only half as much. Manufacturing compensation is considered a "good" wage in all countries, and standardized cross-national estimates of hourly compensation for such workers are readily available. Because U.S. manufacturing productivity is higher than in these other countries (contributing to its higher wages), this comparison should favor the United States. To observe such a large differential despite a comparison tilted in the nation's favor is quite striking. It implies that relative to a competitor, the United States could face a comparable burden of financing elderly health care even if its elderly-dependency ratio were only half as much.

20.8a Over the past 50 years, the elderly dependency ratio in the United States has increased, but it is lower than ratios in other industrialized nations

Elderly persons (age 65 and older) per 100 persons age 15–64

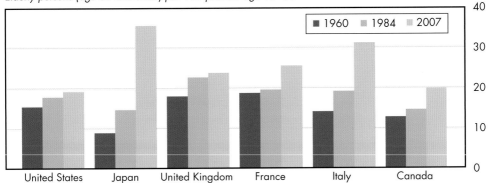

20.8b The number of covered employees per Social Security beneficiary is expected to decline even under the most optimistic assumptions

Number of covered employees per OASDI beneficiary

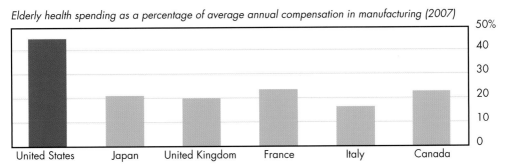

Note: OASDI = Old Age, Survivors, and Disability Insurance.

20.8c Relative to competitors, U.S. health spending per elderly person is a much higher share of average manufacturing compensation

Elderly health spending as a percentage of average annual compensation in manufacturing (2007)

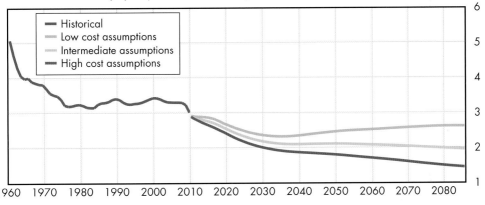

Are Health Spending Trends Sustainable? 285

The United States holds a considerable margin of advantage over its major European rivals in terms of the government share of GDP (figure 20.9a). Compared with countries such as Italy, France, and the UK, that margin of advantage is approximately 10 percent of GDP; in the case of Germany, it exceeds 5 percent of GDP. The size of government (all levels) in Canada and Japan is much more comparable to that of the United States.

Although much of U.S. federal spending has been deficit-financed in recent years, that situation cannot continue indefinitely. Eventually, increased government spending as a percent of GDP translates into relatively higher taxes and the hidden efficiency costs they impose. At the margin, these efficiency losses in the United States amount to more than 40 cents on the dollar. All other things being equal, a country that can minimize such efficiency losses will outperform a nation that has a larger government.

However, absent changes in policy, this margin of advantage could be more than eradicated over the next 50 years simply through increases in mandatory federal health spending for the aging population in the United States (figure 20.9b). Other nations also face a rising tax burden for aging populations. The size of their burden is less, for two reasons. First, many countries are ahead of the United States in terms of the share of their populations that is elderly. Thus, they have comparatively less future aging to address. Second, in nations with universal coverage, government already has been financing their health care in advance of retirement. The incremental increase in tax burdens associated with an already-covered 64-year-old becoming 65 is far less than for a U.S. retiree whose health care for the first time is a federal responsibility.

The United States has been able for decades to enjoy the highest standard of living in the world only by maintaining one of the world's most highly competitive economies. Unless it can address its entitlements crisis without impairing its own competitiveness, the nation might find itself unable to afford either the health care or other goods that its residents desire. Conversely, by addressing entitlements in a responsible fashion, the United States can continue to afford investments in health care that provide good value for the money, with the attendant increases in longevity and years of healthy life that are reasonable to expect from a high-performing health care system.

20.9a The United States has a lower burden of government, compared with its major European competitors

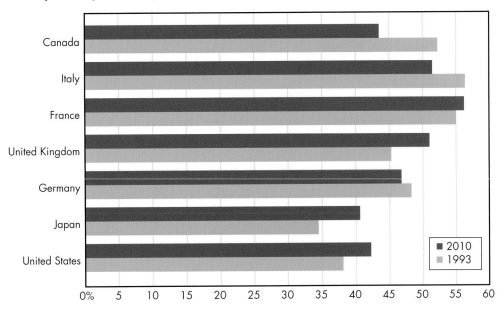

General government spending (all levels) as percentage of GDP

20.9b Rapid growth in government-paid health care threatens to eradicate this margin of advantage

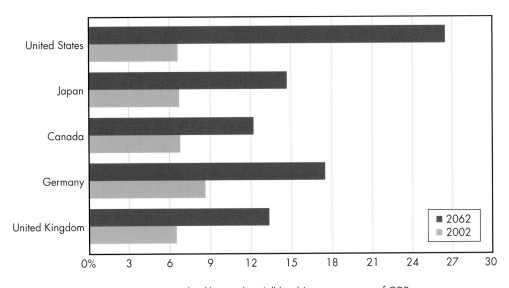

Government health spending (all levels) as percentage of GDP

Note: Data calculated assuming age-adjusted health benefit rates grow at historic rates for 60 years.

Glossary

BEA: Bureau of Economic Analysis in the Department of Commerce

BLS: Bureau of Labor Statistics in the Department of Labor

capital: Tangible and intangible resources that can be used or invested to produce a stream of benefits over time

CBO: Congressional Budget Office

chained-dollar estimate: A measure used to approximate the chained-type index level; it is calculated by taking the current-dollar level of a series in the base period and multiplying it by the change in the chained-type quantity index number for the series since the base period. Chained-dollar estimates correctly show growth rates for a series but are not additive in periods other than the base period.

CHIP (Children's Health Insurance Program): A program similar to Medicaid that provides health insurance for low-income children (also referred to as SCHIP)

civilian employment: Total number of workers, excluding armed forces personnel

civilian non-institutionalized population: Includes everyone except members of the armed forces on active duty and people in penal or mental institutions or in homes for the elderly or infirm

CMS: Centers for Medicare and Medicaid Services, the agency that administers Medicare and Medicaid

compensation: All of the income due to an employee for his or her work during a given period. In addition to wages, salaries, bonuses, and stock options, compensation includes fringe benefits and the employer's share of payroll taxes for social insurance programs, such as Social Security and Medicare.

constant dollar: A measure of spending or revenues in a given year that has been adjusted for differences in prices (such as inflation) between that year and a base year

consumer price index (CPI): An index of the cost of living commonly used to measure inflation. The BLS publishes the CPI-U, an index of consumer prices based on the typical market basket of goods and services consumed by all urban consumers, and the CPI-W, an index of consumer prices based on the typical market basket of goods and services consumed by urban wage earners and clerical workers.

consumption: In principle, the value of goods and services purchased and used up during a given period by households and governments. In practice, the Bureau of Economic Analysis counts purchases of many long-lasting goods (such as cars and clothes) as consumption even though the goods are not used up. Consumption by households alone is also called *personal consumption expenditures* or consumer spending.

corporate profits with inventory valuation and capital consumption adjustments: In NIPA (see below), corporations' domestic profits are adjusted to remove distortions in depreciation allowances caused by tax rules and to exclude the effect of inflation on the value of inventories. Corporate domestic economic profits exclude certain income of U.S.-based multinational corporations that is derived from foreign sources, most of which does not generate corporate income tax receipts in the United States. Domestic economic profits are among the best measures of domestic profits from current production.

current dollar: A measure of spending or revenues in a given year that has not been adjusted for differences in prices (such as inflation) between that year and a base year

disposable personal income: Personal income—the income that people receive, including transfer payments—minus the taxes and fees that people pay to governments

DOD: Department of Defense

entitlement: A legal obligation of the federal government to make payments to a person, group of people, business, unit of government, or similar entity that meet the eligibility criteria set in law and for which the budget authority is not provided in advance in an appropriation act. Spending for entitlement programs is controlled through those programs' eligibility criteria and benefit or payment rules. The best-known entitlements are the government's major benefit programs, such as Social Security and Medicare.

GDP: See *gross domestic product*

GDP price index: A summary measure of the prices of all goods and services that make up gross domestic product. The change in the GDP price index is used as a measure of inflation in the overall economy.

grants-in-aid: Grants from the federal government to state and local governments to help provide for programs of assistance or service to the public

gross domestic product (GDP): Total market value of goods and services produced domestically during a given period. That value is conceptually equal to gross domestic income, but measurement difficulties result in a statistical discrepancy between the two. The components of GDP are consumption (household and government), gross investment (private and government), and net exports.

gross operating surplus (GOS): Value derived as a residual for most industries after subtracting total intermediate inputs, compensation of employees, and taxes on production and imports less subsidies from total industry output. Gross operating surplus includes consumption of fixed capital (CFC), proprietors' income, corporate profits, and business current transfer payments (net).

labor force: Number of people age 16 or older in the civilian non-institutionalized population who have jobs or who are available for work and are actively seeking jobs

labor productivity: Average real output per hour of labor. The growth of labor productivity is defined as the growth of real output that is not explained by the growth of labor input alone.

marginal tax rate: Tax rate that would apply to an additional dollar of a taxpayer's income

national income: Total income earned by U.S. residents from all sources, including employees' compensation (wages, salaries, benefits, and employers' share of payroll taxes for social insurance programs), corporate profits, net interest, rental income, and proprietors' income

national income and product accounts (NIPAs): Official U.S. accounts that track the level and composition of gross domestic product, the prices of its components, and the way in which the costs of production are distributed as income

NHE: National Health Expenditures, the standard measure of total national health spending released annually by CMS. NHE includes health consumption expenditures as well as investment in the medical sector for future consumption. Investment includes non-commercial research as well as purchases of medical structures and equipment. Due to differences in how certain categories of spending are classified or treated, this measure differs somewhat from BEA's estimate of spending for health care goods and services within GDP.

NIPA: See *national income and product accounts*

nominal: A measure based on current-dollar value. Nominal income and spending are measured in current dollars.

OASDI: Old Age, Survivors, and Disability Insurance, what is conventionally known as Social Security

out-of-pocket payments: Includes direct spending by consumers for all health care goods and services, including coinsurance, deductibles, and any amounts not covered by insurance. Premiums paid by individuals for private health insurance are not included because these are counted as part of private health insurance.

output: For purposes of GDP and NHE, output consists of goods and services, generally sold in markets. Thus, unpaid care-giving (informal care) provided by a patient's relatives or friends is not counted as output in either NHE or GDP. Output takes into account both quantity and quality, that is, measured output would increase due to a rise in quality, even if the quantity of services remained constant. *Gross output* consists of sales, or receipts, and other operating income, plus commodity taxes and changes in inventories.

PCE: Personal consumption expenditures (see *consumption*)

PCE price index: A summary measure of the prices of all goods and services that make up personal consumption expenditures. These are more representative of current consumer spending patterns than is the CPI. Also referred to as the *chained price index for personal consumption expenditures*

personal saving: Saving by households. Personal saving equals disposable personal income minus spending for consumption, interest payments, and transfer payments. The personal saving rate is personal saving as a percentage of disposable personal income.

PHCE: Personal health care expenditures

PHCE by location of service: CMS "state of provider" estimates of health spending by the location of health care providers in the 50 states and in the District of Columbia. Care received in Iowa by a Kansas resident would be counted in Iowa's PHCE.

PHCE by state of residence: CMS estimates based on state of provider estimates adjusted for the flow of residents between states to consume health care services. Care received in Iowa by a Kansas resident would be counted in Kansas's PHCE.

physical capital: Also known as *fixed capital* or the *capital stock*—consists of land and the stock of products set aside to support future production and consumption, including business inventories and capital goods (residential and nonresidential structures and producers' durable equipment)

present value: A single number that expresses a flow of current and future income (or payments) in terms of an equivalent lump sum received (or paid) today. The present value depends on the rate of interest (known as the discount rate) that is used to translate future cash flows into current dollars. For example, if $100 is invested on January 1 at an annual interest rate of 5 percent, it will grow to $105 by January 1 of the next year. Hence, at a 5 percent discount rate, the present value of $105 payable a year from today is $100.

private business: All corporate and non-corporate private entities organized for profit and certain other entities that are treated as businesses in the NIPAs, including mutual financial institutions, private non-insured pension funds, cooperatives, non-profit organizations that primarily serve businesses, Federal Reserve banks, federally sponsored credit agencies, and government enterprises

productivity: Average real output per unit of input. Total factor productivity is the average of real output per unit of combined labor and capital services. The growth of total factor productivity is defined as the growth of real output that is not explained by the growth of labor and capital. Labor productivity and total factor productivity differ in that increases in capital per worker raise labor productivity but not total factor productivity.

SCHIP (State Children's Health Insurance Program): A program similar to Medicaid that provides health insurance for low-income children (also referred to as CHIP)

real: Adjusted to remove the effects of inflation. *Real output* represents the quantity, rather than the dollar value, of goods and services produced. *Real income* represents the power to purchase real output. *Real data* at the finest level of disaggregation are constructed by dividing the corresponding nominal data, such as spending or wage rates, by a price index. *Real aggregates*, such as real gross domestic product, are constructed by a procedure that allows the real growth of the aggregate to reflect the real growth of its components, appropriately weighted by the importance of the components.

recovery: A significant, broad-based increase in economic activity that begins just after the economy reaches a trough of activity and ends when the economy reaches the level of its previous peak

sustainable growth rate (SGR): Formula that determines updates to payment rates for physicians under the Medicare program. The SGR sets annual and cumulative spending targets for those payments. If total spending exceeds the targets, an across-the-board reduction is supposed to be made in future fees to bring spending back into line (both annually and cumulatively). Since 2003, however, the Congress and the President have overridden such reductions.

unemployment rate: A measure of the number of jobless people who are available for work and are actively seeking jobs, expressed as a percentage of the labor force.

VA health: Includes health services provided to veterans through VA health facilities as well as care provided to spouses and other dependents of veterans through the Civilian Health and Medical Program of the Veterans Administration (CHAMPVA)

value added: Gross output of an industry or a sector less its intermediate inputs; the contribution of an industry or sector to GDP. Value added by industry can also be measured as the sum of compensation of employees, taxes on production and imports less subsidies, and gross operating surplus.

workers' compensation: Includes expenditures for medical benefits that are paid through federal, state, and local workers' compensation programs

References

1. Alliance for Advancing Nonprofit Health Care. *Basic Facts and Figures: Nonprofit Health Plans.* http://www.nonprofithealthcare.org/resources/BasicFactsAnd Figures-NonprofitHealthPlans9.9.08.pdf (accessed May 31, 2010).

2. American Medical Association. *Competition in Health Insurance, 2010 Update.* Chicago. 2010. Managed Market Survey © 2008, HealthLeaders-InterStudy.

3. Author's calculations.

4. Baicker L and A Chandra. Medicare Spending, the Physician Workforce, and Beneficiaries' Quality of Care. *Health Affairs* April 2004; W4–184. http://content. healthaffairs.org/cgi/reprint/hlthaff.w4.184v1.pdf (accessed July 2010).

5. Berk ML and AC Monheit. The Concentration of Health Care Expenditures, Revisited. *Health Affairs* 2001; 20(2):9–18.

6. Berndt ER and M Aitken. A Different Perspective: The AARP Sponsored Schondelmeyer-Purvis Studies. In *Scaring Seniors: The AARP Drug-Price Reports.* American Enterprise Institute. Washington DC. 2010.

7. Boards of Trustees, Federal Hospital Insurance and Federal Supplementary Medical Insurance Trust Funds, The. 2010 *Annual Report.* US Government Printing Office. August 5, 2010.

8. Brown JD and RM Monaco. *Possible Alternatives to the Medicare Trustees' Long-Term Projections of Health Spending.* US Department of Treasury. Office of Economic Policy. 2004.

9. Burman L, S Khitatrakun and S Goodell. *Tax Subsidies for Private Health Insurance: Who Benefits and at What Cost?* Robert Wood Johnson Foundation. 2009 Update. Princeton. July 2009.

10. Center for Research on Economic and Financial Cycles. *The Beginning and End of the 2007–2009 Recession.* http://sites.google.com/site/crefcus/probabilities-of-recession/The-beginning-and-end-of-the-2007-2009-recession1 (accessed July 29, 2010).

11. Chernew ME, RA Hirth and DM Cutler. Increased Spending on Health Care: How Much Can the United States Afford? *Health Affairs* 2003; 22(4):15–25.

12. Chesson HW, JM Blandford, TL Gift, G Tao and KL Irwin. The Estimated Direct Medical Cost of Sexually Transmitted Diseases Among American Youth, 2000. *Perspectives on Sexual and Reproductive Health* 2004; 36(1):11–19.

13. Chiecka J, T Donley and J Goldman. Work Life Estimates at Millennium's End: Changes over the Last Eighteen Years. *Illinois Labor Market Review* 2000; 6(2). http://lmi.ides.state.il.us/lmr/worklife.htm (accessed June 30, 2010).

14. Cohen JW and NA Krauss. Spending and Service Use among People with the Fifteen Most Costly Medical Conditions, 1997. *Health Affairs* 2003; 22(2):129–38.

15. Cohen SB and W Yu. *The Concentration and Persistence in the Level of Health Expenditures over Time: Estimates for the U.S. Population, 2006–2007.* Agency for Healthcare Research and Quality. Rockville MD. March 2010.

16. Colditz GA. Economic Costs of Obesity and Inactivity. *Medicine and Science in Sports and Exercise* 1999; 31(11):S663–S667.

17. Commonwealth Fund. *Mortality Amenable to Health Care by State.* http://www.commonwealthfund.org/Content/Charts/Report/Aiming-Higher-2009-Results-from-a-State-Scorecard-on-Health-System-Performance/Mortality-Amenable-to-Health-Care-by-State.aspx (accessed June 2010).

18. Congressional Budget Office.

19. Conover CJ with EP Zeitler. *Health Services Regulation Working Paper No. MTS-1.* http://ushealthpolicygateway.files.wordpress.com/2009/06/mts1-medicaltortsystem.doc (accessed August 30, 2010).

20. Cooper BS, NL Worthington and MF McGee. *Compendium of National Health Expenditures Data.* DHEW Pub No (SSA) 73-11903. Office of Research and Statistics. 1973.

21. Corso PS, JA Mercy, TR Simon, EA Finkelstein and TR Miller. Medical Costs and Productivity Losses Due to Interpersonal Violence and Self-Directed Violence. *American Journal of Preventive Medicine* 2007; 32(6):474–82.

22. Cutler DM. *A Health Report Card for the Nation.* ASHE Presentation. June 6, 2006. http://healtheconomics.us/conference/2006/plenaries/powerpoint/cutler-madison.ppt (accessed August 18, 2010).

23. Cutler DM, M McClellan, JP Newhouse and D Remler. *Pricing Heart Attack Treatments. Medical Care Output and Productivity.* National Bureau of Economic Research. http://www.nber.org/chapters/c7634.pdf (accessed August 9, 2010).

24. Cutler DM, A Rosen and S Vijan. The Value of Medical Spending in the United States, 1960-2000. *The New England Journal of Medicine* 2006; 355(9):920–28.

25. Danzon PM and MF Furukawa. International Prices and Availability of Pharmaceuticals in 2005. *Health Affairs* 2008; 27(1):221–33.

26. Dash E. Off to the Races Again, Leaving Many Behind. *New York Times.* Section 3:1 April 9, 2006.

27. Department of Commerce. Bureau of Economic Analysis.

28. Department of Commerce. Bureau of the Census.

29. Department of Health, Education and Welfare. Office of the Surgeon General. *Healthy People: The Surgeon General's Report on Health Promotion and Disease Prevention 1979.*

30. Department of Health and Human Services. Agency for Healthcare Research and Quality.

31. Department of Health and Human Services. Centers for Disease Control and Prevention.

32. Department of Health and Human Services. Centers for Medicare and Medicaid Services.

33. Department of Health and Human Services. Office of Inspector General. *Medication Regimens: Causes of Non-Compliance.* June 1990.

34. Department of Health and Human Services. Office of the Surgeon General.

35. Department of Labor. Bureau of Labor Statistics.

36. Department of Transportation. National Highway Traffic Safety Administration.

37. Econ Data US. *Balance Sheet of Households and Nonprofit Organizations: 1952–2008.* http://www.econdataus.com/worth08.html (accessed July 25, 2010).

38. Ernst FR and AJ Grizzle. Drug-Related Morbidity and Mortality: Updating the Cost-of-Illness Model. *Journal of the American Pharmaceutical Association* 2001; 41:192–99. http://web.whittier.edu/chemistry/newdrug/DrugRelated.pdf (accessed March 28, 2010).

39. Executive Office of the President. Office of National Drug Control Policy.

40. Eyermann C. *Redefining the Health Care Debate—Part Two. Political Calculations.* http://politicalcalculations.blogspot.com/2009/07/redefining-health-care-debate-part-2.html (accessed September 1, 2010).

41. Federal Reserve Bank.

42. Finkelstein EA, IC Fiebelkorn and G Wang. National medical spending attributable to overweight and obesity: How much, and who's paying? *Health Affairs* 2003; W3:219–26.

43. Fisher CR. Differences by Age Groups in Health Care Spending. *Health Care Financing Review* Spring 1980; 65–90.

44. Fisher E, D Goodman, J Skinner and K Bronner. *Health Care Spending, Quality, and Outcomes.* Dartmouth Institute for Health Policy and Clinical Practice. Hanover NH. February 27, 2009.

45. Fortune 500. Our Annual Ranking of America's Largest Corporations. http://money.cnn.com/magazines/fortune/fortune500/2009/performers/industries/profits/index.html (accessed June 9, 2010).

46. Frech HE. The OECD's Study on Health Status Determinant: Roles of Lifestyle, Environment, Health-Care Resources and Spending Efficiency: An Analysis. *American Enterprise Institute Working Paper* #145. February 6, 2009. http://www.aei.org/docLib/20090206-FrechFINAL.pdf (accessed August 31, 2010).

47. Fujisawa R and G Lafortune. The Remuneration of General Practitioners and Specialists in 14 OECD Countries: What are the Factors Influencing Variations Across Countries? *OECD Working Paper Series* No 41. December 18 2008. http://www.oecd.org/dataoecd/51/48/41925333.pdf (accessed July 5, 2010).

48. Gibson RM and CR Fisher. Age Differences in Health Care Spending, Fiscal Year 1977. *Social Security Bulletin* 1979; 42(1):3–16.

49. Glantz SA and WW Parmley. Passive Smoking and Heart Disease: Mechanisms and Risk. *Journal of the American Medical Association* 1995; 273(13):1047–53.

50. Goodman JC, P Villarreal and B Jones. The Social Cost of Adverse Medical Events, and What We Can Do about It. *Health Affairs* 2011; 30:590–95.

51. Graham J. *Index of Health Ownership.* 3rd Edition. Pacific Research Institute. 2009. http://www.pacificresearch.org/docLib/20090720_IHOP_3_2009.pdf (accessed July 2010).

52. Hadley J, J Holahan, T Coughlin and D Miller. *Covering the Uninsured in 2008: A Detailed Examination of Current Costs and Sources of Payment, and Incremental Costs of Expanding Coverage.* Prepared for the Kaiser Commission on Medicaid and the Uninsured. Kaiser Commission on Medicaid and the Uninsured. Washington DC. August 2008.

53. Hagist C and L Kotlikoff. Who's Going Broke? Comparing Healthcare Costs in Ten OECD Countries. *NBER Working Paper* No. 11833. December 2005.

54. Harper MJ, B Khandrika, R Kinoshita and S Rosenthal. Nonmanufacturing industry contributions to multifactor productivity, 1987–2006. *Monthly Labor Review* 2010; June:16–31.

55. Hartman M, A Catlin, D Lassman, J Cylus and S Heffler. US Health Spending By Age, Selected Years Through 2004. *Health Affairs* 2008; 27(1):w1–w12.

56. Harwood H. *Updating Estimates of the Economic Costs of Alcohol Abuse in the United States: Estimates, Update Methods, and Data.* Report prepared by the Lewin Group

for the National Institute on Alcohol Abuse and Alcoholism. December 2000. http://pubs.niaaa.nih.gov/publications/economic-2000/alcoholcost.pdf (accessed March 28, 2010).

57. Harwood H, D Fountain and G Livermore. *The Economic Costs of Alcohol and Drug Abuse in the United States 1992*. Report prepared for the National Institute on Drug Abuse and the National Institute on Alcohol Abuse and Alcoholism. National Institutes of Health. Department of Health and Human Services. NIH Publication No 98-4327. Rockville MD. NIH 1998. http://www.nida.nih.gov/EconomicCosts/ (accessed March 28, 2010).

58. Health Insurance Association of America. *Source Book of Health Insurance Data 1986/1987*. Table 1.1. Washington DC. HIAA 1987.

59. Heston A, R Summers and B Aten. *Penn World Table Version 6.3*. Center for International Comparisons of Production, Income and Prices at the University of Pennsylvania. August 2009. http://pwt.econ.upenn.edu/php_site/pwt_index.php (accessed December 18, 2009).

60. Hodgson TA and L Cai. Medical Care Expenditures for Hypertension, Its Complications and Its Comorbidities. *Medical Care* 2001; 39(6):599–615.

61. Hodgson TA and AJ Cowan. Medical Expenditures for Major Diseases, 1995–Statistical Data Included. *Health Care Financing Review* 1999; 21(2):61–80. http://www3.cms.hhs.gov/HealthCareFinancingReview/Downloads/99winterpg119.pdf (accessed March 23, 2010).

62. Holahan J and S Zedlewski. Who Pays for Health Care in the United States? Implications for Health System Reform. *Inquiry* 1992; 29:231–48.

63. Howard DH, LC Richardson and KE Thorpe. Cancer Screening and Age in the United States and Europe. *Health Affairs* 2009; 28(6):1838–47.

64. Johnson JA and JL Bootman. Drug-Related Morbidity and Mortality and the Economic Impact of Pharmaceutical Care. *American Journal of Health Systems Pharmacy* 1997; 54:554–58.

65. Joumard I, C Andre, C Nicq and O Chantal. Health Status Determinants: Lifestyle, Environment, Health Care Resources and Efficiency. *OECD Economics Department Working Papers* No 627. 2008. doi: 10.1787/240858500130.

66. Kaiser Commission on Medicaid and the Uninsured. *Medicaid: A Primer.* Key Information on Our Nation's Health Coverage Program for Low-Income People. June 2010. http://www.kff.org/medicaid/upload/7334-04.pdf (accessed October 13, 2010).

67. Kaiser Family Foundation, The. *Health Insurance Coverage of the Total Population.* http://www.statehealthfacts.org/comparetable.jsp?ind=125&cat=3 (accessed May 31, 2010).

68. Kaiser Family Foundation, The. statehealthfacts.org.

69. Kaiser Family Foundation, The. Health Research & Educational Trust. *Employer Health Benefits 2010 Annual Survey*. September 2, 2010. http://ehbs.kff.org/?page=abstract&id=1 (accessed November 21, 2010).

70. Krueger KV, GR Skoog and JE Ciecka. Worklife in a Markov Model with Full-time and Part-time Activity. *Journal of Forensic Economics* 2006; 19(1):61–82. http://legaleconometrics.com/P19_JFE8.pdf (accessed June 30, 2010).

71. Lee R and T Miller. An Approach to Forecasting Health Expenditures, with Application to the US Medicare System. *Health Services Research* 2002; 37(5):1365–86.

72. Leigh JP, SB Markowitz, M Fahs, C Shin and PJ Landrigan. Occupational Injury and Illness in the United States. *Archives of Internal Medicine* 1997; 157:1557–68.

73. Levit KR, H Lazenby, DR Waldo and LM Davidoff. National Health Expenditures, 1984. *Health Care Financing Review* 1985; 7(1):1–33.

74. Levit KR, HC Lazenby, CA Cowan and SW Letsch. National Health Expenditures, 1990. *Health Care Financing Review* 1991; 13(1):29–54.

75. MacDorman MS and TJ Mathews. Behind International Rankings of Infant Mortality: How the U.S. Compares with Europe. *National Center for Health Statistics Data Brief* No. 23. Hyattsville MD. National Center for Health Statistics 2009.

76. Machlin S, JW Cohen and K Beauregard. Health Care Expenses for Adults with Chronic Conditions, 2005. *Statistical Brief* #203. May 2008. Agency for Healthcare Research and Quality. Rockville MD. http://www.meps.ahrq.gov/mepsweb/data_files/publications/st203.pdf (accessed November 14, 2010).

77. Mathur A. *Medical Bills and Bankruptcy Filings*. American Enterprise Institute. http://www.aei.org/docLib/20060719_MedicalBillsAndBankruptcy.pdf (accessed July 28, 2010).

78. McGinnis MJ and WH Foege. Actual Causes of Death in the United States. *Journal of the American Medical Association* 1993; 270(18):2207–12.

79. McKinsey Global Institute. *Accounting for the Cost of US Health Care: A New Look at Why Americans Spend More*. November 2008. http://www.mckinsey.com/mgi/publications/US_healthcare/pdf/US_healthcare_Chapter1.pdf (accessed July 8, 2010).

80. Mokdad AH, JS Marks, DF Stroup and JL Gerberding. Actual Causes of Death in the United States, 2000. *Journal of the American Medical Association* 2004; 291(10):1238–45.

81. Mokdad A, J Marks, DF Stroup and J Gerberding. Correction: Actual Causes of Death in the United States, 2000. *Journal of the American Medical Association* 2005; 293(3):293–94 (letter; correction of original study).

82. Murphy KM and RH Topel. The Value of Health and Longevity. *Journal of Political Economy* 2006; 114(5):871–904.

83. National Association of State Budget Officers. *State Expenditure Report Fiscal Year 2008.* http://www.nasbo.org/Publications/StateExpenditureReport/tabid/79/Default.aspx (accessed June 15, 2010).

84. National Science Foundation.

85. *New York Times.* The Wide Divide. April 6, 2006. http://www.nytimes.com/imagepages/2006/04/09/business/businessspecial/20060409_PAY_GRAPHIC.html?ref=executivepay (accessed November 12, 2010).

86. Nolte E and CM McKee. Measuring the Health of Nations: Updating an Earlier Analysis. *Health Affairs* 2008; 27(1):58–71.

87. Office of Management and Budget.

88. Ohsfeldt RL and JE Schneider. How Does the U.S. Health-Care System Compare to Systems in Other Countries? In *The Business of Health: How Does the U.S. Health-Care System Compare to Systems in Other Countries?* American Enterprise Institute. Washington DC. 2006. http://www.aei.org/docLib/20061017_Ohsfeldt SchneiderPresentation.pdf (accessed November 3, 2010).

89. Organisation for Economic Co-operation and Development.

90. Pauly MV. U.S. Health Care Costs: The Untold True Story. *Health Affairs* 1993; 12(3):152–59.

91. Pew Research Center. *Inside the Middle Class: Bad Times Hit the Good Life.* http://pewsocialtrends.org/pubs/?chartid=534 (accessed July 28, 2010).

92. Phelps CE. *Health Economics.* HarperCollins Publishers. 1992.

93. Potetz L and J Cubanski. *A Primer on Medicare Financing.* July 2009. http://www.kff.org/medicare/upload/7731-02.pdf (accessed August 10, 2010).

94. Rice DP. Estimating the Cost of Illness. *American Journal of Public Health* 1967; 57(3):424–40.

95. Rice DP and BS Cooper. National Health Expenditures, 1929–71. *Social Security Bulletin* 1972; 35(1):3–18.

96. Rice DP, TA Hodgson and A Kopstein. The Economic Costs of Illness: A Replication and Update. *Health Care Financing Review* 1985; (1):61–80.

97. Selden TM. *Using Adjusted MEPS Data to Study Incidence of Health Care Finance.* Agency for Healthcare Research and Quality. http://www.ahrq.gov/about/annual conf09/selden/selden.ppt (accessed July 16, 2010).

98. Seldon TM and M Sing. The Distribution of Public Spending for Health Care in the United States, 2002. *Health Affairs* Web Exclusive 2008; 27:5w349–w359. http://content.healthaffairs.org/cgi/reprint/27/5/w349 (accessed June 14, 2010).

99. Sheils J. The Tax Expenditure for Health: Update for 2007. The Lewin Group. April 29, 2008. http://www.newamerica.net/files/SheilsPPT.pdf (accessed November 13, 2010).

100. Shen YC, VY Wu and G Melnick. Trends in Hospital Cost and Revenue, 1994–2005: How Are They Related to HMO Penetration, Concentration, and For-Profit Ownership? *Health Services Research* 2010; 45(1):42–61.

101. Sherlock DB. *Administrative Expenses of Health Plans.* Prepared for the Blue Cross Blue Shield Association. http://www.bcbs.com/issues/uninsured/Sherlock-Report-FINAL.pdf (accessed February 2010).

102. Smith S, JP Newhouse and MS Freeland. Income, Insurance, And Technology: Why Does Health Spending Outpace Economic Growth? *Health Affairs* 2009; 28(5):1276–84.

103. Smith SJ. New Worklife Estimates Reflect Changing Profile of Labor Force. *Monthly Labor Review* March 1982:15–20. http://www.bls.gov/opub/mlr/1982/03/art2full.pdf (accessed June 30, 2010).

104. Social Security Administration.

105. Stein H and M Foss. *The Illustrated Guide to the American Economy.* Third Edition. Washington DC. AEI Press. 1999; page 17.

106. Sutherland JM, ES Fisher and JS Skinner. Getting Past Denial—The High Cost of Health Care in the United States. *New England Journal of Medicine* 2009; 361:1227–30.

107. Steuerle CE and S Rennane. *Social Security and Medicare Taxes and Benefits Over a Lifetime.* Urban Institute. January 2011. http://www.taxpolicycenter.org/UploadedPDF/social-security-medicare-benefits-over-lifetime.pdf (accessed June 10, 2011).

108. Thomas EJ, DM Studdert, JP Newhouse, BI Zbar, KM Howard, EJ Williams and TA Brennan. Costs of Medical Injuries in Utah and Colorado. *Inquiry* 1999; 36(3):255–64.

109. United Health Foundation. *America's Health Rankings 2009: 20th Anniversary Edition.* http://www.americashealthrankings.org/2009%5Creport%5CAHR2009%20Final%20Report.pdf (accessed June 15, 2010).

110. U.S. Health Policy Gateway. Key Questions: How large is the cost-of-illness in the U.S.? http://ushealthpolicygateway.wordpress.com/payer-trade-groups/burden-of-illness/cost-of-illness-coi/cost-of-illness/ (accessed August 11, 2010).

111. Waldo DR, ST Sonnefeld, DR McCusick and RH Arnett III. Health Expenditures by Age Group, 1977 and 1987. *Health Care Financing Review* 1989; 10(4):111–20.

112. Weeks WB, AE Wallace, MM Wallace and HG Welch. A Comparison of the Educational Costs and Incomes of Physicians and Other Professionals. *New England Journal of Medicine* 1994; 330(18):1280–86.

113. Weeks WB and AE Wallace. The More Things Change: Revisiting a Comparison of Educational Costs and Incomes of Physicians and Other Professionals. *Academic Medicine* 2002; 77(4):312–19.

114. Whitman G and R Rand. Bending the Productivity Curve: Why America Leads the World in Medical Innovation. Cato Insitute. *Policy Analysis* No 654. November 18, 2009. http://www.cato.org/pubs/pas/pa654.pdf (accessed August 10, 2010).

115. World Health Organization.

116. Worthington NL. National Health Expenditures, Calendar Years 1929–73. *Research and Statistics Note* No 1. Office of Research and Statistics 1975.

117. Zaloshnja E, TR Miller, BA Lawrence and E Romano. The Costs of Unintentional Home Injuries. *American Journal of Preventive Medicine* 2005; 28(1):88–94.

118. Zuvekas SH and JW Cohen. Prescription Drugs and the Changing Concentration of Health Care Expenditures. *Health Affairs* 2007; 26(1):249–57.

Sources

Figure	Page	Source(s)	Figure	Page	Source(s)
Chapter 1			**Chapter 2**		
1.1a	3	116; 32; 27; 3	2.1a	19	32
1.1b	3	116; 32; 27; 28	2.1b	19	116; 32; 3
1.2a	5	116; 32; 27; 3	2.2	21	116; 32; 27; 28
1.2b	5	116; 32; 27; 28	2.3a	23	101
1.3a	7	116; 32; 27; 3	2.3b	23	101
1.3b	7	116; 32; 27; 3	2.3c	23	101
1.4a	9	89	2.4a	25	116; 32; 3
1.4b	9	89; 3	2.4b	25	116; 32; 3
1.5a	11	116; 32; 27; 28; 3	2.5a	27	76
			2.5b	27	76
1.5b	11	32; 27; 28; 3	2.6	29	31; 42; 117; 38; 36; 56; 57; 16; 39
1.6a	13	89			
1.6b	13	89; 3			
1.7a	15	115; 3			
1.7b	15	115; 3			
1.7c	15	115; 3			

Figure	Page	Source(s)	Figure	Page	Source(s)
Chapter 3			**Chapter 5**		
3.1a	33	116; 32; 3	5.1a	63	116; 32; 27; 3
3.1b	33	32	5.1b	63	116; 32; 27; 3
3.2a	35	32	5.2a	65	32; 27; 3
3.2b	35	28	5.2b	65	116; 32; 27; 3
3.3a	37	116; 32; 27; 3	5.3a	67	89; 3
3.3b	37	116; 32; 3	5.3b	67	89; 3
3.4a	39	87; 99; 3	5.4	69	98
3.4b	39	32; 87; 99; 3	5.5a	71	98
3.5a	41	116; 32; 3	5.5b	71	68
3.5b	41	116; 32; 3	5.6	73	107
3.6a	43	89	5.7a	75	83
3.6b	43	89	5.7b	75	83
3.7a	45	66	5.7c	75	83
3.7b	45	32			
3.8a	47	98	**Chapter 6**		
3.8b	47	93; 101; 7; 3	6.1a	79	27
3.9a	49	52	6.1b	79	27
3.9b	49	52	6.2a	81	32; 3
			6.2b	81	32; 3
Chapter 4			6.3a	83	35
4.1a	53	27	6.3b	83	35
4.1b	53	27	6.4a	85	28
4.2a	55	9	6.4b	85	28
4.2b	55	9	6.5	87	28
4.3a	57	69	6.6	89	58; 28; 3
4.3b	57	69	6.7a	91	52
4.4a	59	69	6.7b	91	52; 3
4.4b	59	69	6.8a	93	35; 3
			6.8b	93	35; 3
			6.9a	95	35; 3
			6.9b	95	89; 3

Figure	Page	Source(s)	Figure	Page	Source(s)
Chapter 7				**Chapter 9** (*continued*)	
7.1	99	28	9.5b	133	84; 3
7.2	101	28	9.6a	135	27; 3
7.3a	103	27	9.6b	135	89; 3
7.3b	103	27	9.7a	137	54
7.4	105	27	9.7b	137	35; 3
Chapter 8			**Chapter 10**		
8.1a	109	27	10.1a	141	27; 3
8.1b	109	27	10.1b	141	35; 3
8.2a	111	27	10.2a	143	89
8.2b	111	27	10.2b	143	89; 3
8.3a	113	27	10.3a	145	89; 90; 3
8.3b	113	27	10.3b	145	89; 90; 3
8.4a	115	27	10.4a	147	35; 3
8.4b	115	27	10.4b	147	35; 3
8.5	117	27	10.5a	149	35; 3
8.6a	119	45	10.5b	149	35; 3
8.6b	119	45	10.6a	151	31; 35; 13; 70; 103
8.6c	119	45			
8.7a	121	45	10.6b	151	31; 35; 13; 70; 103
8.7b	121	45			
8.7c	121	45			
			Chapter 11		
Chapter 9			11.1	155	27
9.1a	125	27; 35; 3	11.2a	157	27; 3
9.1b	125	35; 3	11.2b	157	27; 3
9.2a	127	35; 3	11.3a	159	35;3
9.2b	127	35; 3	11.3b	159	35; 3
9.2c	127	35; 3	11.4a	161	89; 3
9.3a	129	28	11.4b	161	89; 3
9.3b	129	28	11.5a	163	92
9.3c	129	28	11.5b	163	112; 113
9.4a	131	35	11.5c	163	85
9.4b	131	35			
9.5a	133	84; 3			

Figure	Page	Source(s)	Figure	Page	Source(s)
Chapter 12			**Chapter 15**		
12.1a	167	15; 30; 3	15.1a	205	41; 27; 32; 3
12.1b	167	5; 118; 30; 3	15.1b	205	41; 32; 3
12.2a	169	97	15.2	207	41; 32; 3
12.2b	169	97	15.3	209	77
12.3a	171	35; 30			
12.3b	171	35; 30	**Chapter 16**		
12.3c	171	62; 97	16.1	213	27; 32; 3
12.4a	173	30	16.2	215	32; 3
12.4b	173	111; 32; 30	16.3a	217	28; 3
12.5	175	32	16.3b	217	28; 3
12.6a	177	32; 3			
12.6b	177	27; 3	**Chapter 17**		
12.7a	179	32; 27; 3	17.1	221	28; 3; 82
12.7b	179	32; 27; 3	17.2a	223	23
			17.2b	223	6
Chapter 13			17.3	225	102
13.1a	183	28	17.4a	227	110; 96; 27; 28; 31; 3
13.1b	183	28			
13.2a	185	28	17.4b	227	110; 96; 27; 28; 31; 3
13.2b	185	28			
13.3a	187	31			
13.3b	187	31	**Chapter 18**		
13.4	189	28	18.1a	231	114
13.5a	191	28	18.1b	231	114
13.5b	191	28	18.2a	233	89
			18.2b	233	89
Chapter 14			18.3a	235	89
14.1a	195	28; 3	18.3b	235	27; 3
14.1b	195	28; 3			
14.1c	195	28; 3			
14.2a	197	2			
14.2b	197	100			
14.3	199	51			
14.4	201	28; 35			

Figure	Page	Source(s)	Figure	Page	Source(s)
Chapter 19			**Chapter 20**		
19.1a	239	22	20.1	271	27
19.1b	239	24	20.2	273	8
19.2a	241	89	20.3a	275	32
19.2b	241	31; 32; 3	20.3b	275	7
19.3a	243	44	20.4a	277	116; 32; 27; 3
19.3b	243	106	20.4b	277	32; 18; 104;
19.4a	245	89			28; 3
19.4b	245	40	20.5a	279	71
19.5a	247	89	20.5b	279	18; 7
19.5b	247	89	20.5c	279	3
19.5c	247	89	20.6a	281	104; 18; 7; 3
19.6a	249	89	20.6b	281	104; 18; 7; 3
19.6b	249	89	20.6c	281	104; 18; 7; 3; 27
19.7a	251	25	20.7a	283	18; 3
19.7b	251	25	20.7b	283	93; 7
19.8a	253	19	20.8a	285	89
19.8b	253	27	20.8b	285	7
19.9a	255	89	20.8c	285	89
19.9b	255	89	20.9a	287	89
19.10	257	75	20.9b	287	53
19.11a	259	88			
19.11b	259	63			
19.12	261	86			
19.13a	263	29			
19.13b	263	108; 80; 81; 50;			
		49; 33; 31; 3			
19.14a	265	89			
19.14b	265	31			
19.14c	265	31			
19.15a	267	109; 36; 31			
19.15b	267	109			

Index

Access to medical care and premature mortality, 262, 263*f*

Administrative costs, 18, 22–23, 56

Adults, *see* Non-elderly adults

After-tax corporate profits, 114, 115*f*

Age groups
    chronic disease costs, 26, 27*f*
    distribution of health spending and, 172–75
    uninsured status and, 86–87
    See also Children; Elderly; Non-elderly adults

Alcohol use and abuse, cost of, 29*f*, 254, 255*f*, 262, 263*f*

Ambulatory health services
    annual work hours, 148, 149*f*
    employee compensation levels, 156, 157*f*, 158–59
    employment by size of firm, 195*f*
    GOS in, 115*f*
    increase in employment in, 140, 141*f*
    information capital per hour vs. private business, 130–31
    productivity in, 124, 125*f*, 126, 127*f*, 130–31, 136, 137*f*, 158–59

share of national income, 110

women's dominance in employment, 146–47

Amenable mortality rate, 260

Annual work hours per employee, health services, 148–49

Avoidable causes of illness, costs of, 28–29

Avoidable death rate, U.S., 260–63

Balanced Budget Act (1997) (BBA97), 114

Bankruptcies, "medical," 206–9

BEA (Bureau of Economic Analysis), 116, 289

Biological factors in premature mortality, 262, 263*f*

BLS (Bureau of Labor Statistics), 124, 289

"Book profits," 116

Bureau of Economic Analysis (BEA), 116, 289

Bureau of Labor Statistics (BLS), 124, 289

Business cycle
    corporate profits' response to, 114
    health spending and, 10, 104, 212–17

Canada
    obesity rate, 264
    out-of-pocket health spending, 42,
        43f
Cancer screening rates, U.S. vs. Europe, 258,
    259f
Cancer survival rate, U.S. vs. Europe, 258,
    259f
Capital, defined, 289
Capital stock, defined, 293
Centers for Medicare and Medicaid Services
    (CMS), 290
Chained-dollar estimate, 10, 289
Children
    distribution of health spending and,
        172–73
    Medicaid coverage levels, 84,
        188–89
    Medicaid enrollment levels, 44, 45f
    number uninsured, 188, 189f
    public sector coverage for, 35f
    reliance on tax-financed coverage,
        84–85, 188–89
    uninsured access to care, 90, 91f
    uninsured vs. insured out-of-pocket
        spending, 48
Chronic illness, cost of, 26–27
Civilian employment, defined, 289
Civilian non-institutionalized population,
    289
Clinical services, See Physicians
CMS (Centers for Medicare and Medicaid
    Services), 290
Community hospitals, 100, 101f
Compensation, defined, 290
    See also Employee compensation
Concentration in health insurance industry,
    196–97
Confidence interval, 278
Constant dollars, 2, 3f, 290
Consumer Price Index (CPI), 2, 4, 5f,
    290
Consumer spending, See Personal
    consumption on health care
Consumption, defined, 290
    See also Personal consumption on
        health care
Corporate medicine, growth of, 112

Corporate profits
    with inventory valuation and capital
        consumption adjustments, 290
    medical devices, 120–21
    other economic sectors vs., 116–17
    pharmaceuticals, 120–21
    publicly traded vs. other firms in stock
        market, 118–19
    as share of national income, 110, 111f,
        114, 115f
Cost-effectiveness of U.S. health spending
    access to expensive technologies,
        246–47
    avoidable death rate, 260–63
    cancer survival, 258–59
    higher income's contribution to better
        health, 240–41
    life expectancy at birth, 254–55
    malpractice legal system, 252–53
    Medicare regional differences, 242–43
    obesity rate, 264–65
    per capita spending, 244–45
    pharmaceutical costs, 250–51
    pre-term births and infant mortality,
        256–57
    smoking rate, 264–65
    specialists, reliance on, 248–49
    state comparisons, 264–67
    wasted spending, hidden nature of,
        238–39
CPI (Consumer Price Index), 2, 4, 5f, 290
Credentialing factor, 128
"Crowd-out" in Medicaid, 58, 88, 90, 91f, 188
Current dollar, 290

Defensive medicine, 252
Dental services, 24, 25f, 41f, 45f
Department of Defense (DOD), 290
Dependency issue, future, 284–85
Developing countries, health spending data,
    14, 15f
Direct health spending
    premiums, 80, 168, 169f, 170, 171f
    relative burden by income level, 82, 83f
    share of personal income, 80–81
    social burden of illness and, 226, 227f
    tax subsidies vs. Medicaid, 38–39
    See also Out-of-pocket payments

Disabled individuals, Medicaid enrollment, 45*f*

Disposable personal income, defined, 290

Distribution of health spending
elderly vs. other age groups, 172–73
health-related supplements' share of, 108–9
low- vs. high-income families' health cost burden, 168–71
net burden of health care costs, 170–71
population percentage accounting for most health spending, 166–67
regional differences in, 176–79
women vs. men, 174–75

Distribution of national income
corporate profit share of, 114–17
employee compensation vs. proprietor/rental income, 110–11
medical devices profits, 120–21
pharmaceutical product profits, 120–21
proprietor and rental income decline, 110–13
publicly traded health services' profits vs. other stocks, 118–19

DOD (Department of Defense), 290

Drug-related problems, share of PHCE, 29*f*

Drugs, *See* Pharmaceutical drugs

Dual eligibility, Medicaid and Medicare, 46, 84, 190

Durable medical equipment, out-of-pocket payment for, 41*f*

Earnings
health benefit costs vs., 270–71
for health care workers, 111*f*, 128, 129*f*
lifetime earnings and health capital, 220–21
lowering of as indirect cost of ESI, 80
real compensation per hour vs., 154–55

Education level of health care workers, 128–29, 162–63

Elderly
chronic disease cost, 26, 27*f*
in distribution of health spending, 172–73
gender differences in health spending, 174, 175*f*
health care coverage for the poor, 190, 191*f*
hospital use changes, 24
increased health costs for, 92–93
Medicaid for, 44–45, 190, 191*f*
non-health spending growth, 94–95
public sector coverage for, 35*f*, 84–85
rising tax burden of, 286
uninsured, 86, 190, 191*f*
U.S. spending on vs. other countries, 284, 285*f*

Elderly-dependency ratio, U.S. vs. other countries, 284

Employee compensation
ambulatory health services, 156, 157*f*, 158–59
defined, 290
earnings and rising health costs vs., 154–55
earnings for health care workers, 128, 129*f*
general practice vs. specialist physicians, 160–63
health industry vs. other service industries, 156–57
health-related increase, 52, 53*f*
health-related supplements to wages, 108–9, 154–55, 270–71
increases in all types of, 53*f*
proprietor and rental income vs., 110–11
as share of national income, 108, 109*f*
See also Employer-sponsored insurance (ESI); Income; Workers' compensation

Employer-sponsored insurance (ESI)
actual cost for employer, 80, 81*f*
effect on uninsured numbers, 88
erosion of, 58, 59*f*
indirect consequences for workers, 54, 80
monetary contribution to premium, 154–55

Employer-sponsored insurance (ESI) (*continued*)
poor children's rates of, 189*f*
as primary cost assistance, 34, 35*f*
as primary resource for non-elderly
adults, 84, 85*f*
tax subsidies
cost of, 38, 39*f*
income level and, 52–53, 54,
55*f*, 70
variation in access to, 56–57
Employment in health sector
annual work hours per employee,
148–49
historical increase in, 140–41
opportunity cost for U.S. vs. other
countries, 144–45
retirement period changes for men vs.
women, 150–51
services area trends, 156–59
share of total employment, U.S. vs.
other countries, 142–43
by size of firm, 194–95
women's dominance in, 146–47
End-of-life health costs, 174
Entitlements
defined, 291
unfunded liabilities associated with,
280–81
Environmental factors in premature mortality, 262, 263*f*
ESI, *See* Employer-sponsored insurance
Ethnicity and health, *See* Race and ethnicity
Excess cost growth and health spending prediction, 274–79

Far West region
health spending, 176–77, 178, 179*f*
regulation of health sector, 198
Federal Employee Health Benefits Plan
(FEHBP), 32
Federal government
health spending increases, 6, 7*f*, 32,
33*f*, 62–63
Medicaid responsibility, 6, 34, 74, 75*f*
Medicare expenditure share, 6, 32, 33*f*
tax revenues necessary to fund health
spending, 282–83
tax subsidies for health, 38–39

Federal Trade Commission (FTC), 196
FEHBP (Federal Employee Health Benefits
Plan), 32
Final purchases in service economy, health
care share of, 102–3
Fixed capital, defined, 293
For-profit organizations, *See* Private business
Fringe benefits
erosion of as health care cost grows, 80
fluctuations in non-health, 108, 109*f*
health-related supplements, 108–9,
154–55, 270–71
See also Employer-sponsored insurance
(ESI); Medicare
FTC (Federal Trade Commission), 196

G7 countries vs. U.S., *See* Global comparison
GDP (gross domestic product)
defined, 291
health output share, 6–7, 104–5
health spending impact on future,
274–79
health spending share of, 3*f*, 6–7,
10–13, 102, 103*f*
net worth, growth vs., 204, 205*f*
physicians and nurses, spending on,
145*f*
PPP method for cross-country comparison, 8
publicly financed health spending
share of, 62
R&D capital ratio, 133*f*
social burden of illness as percent of,
227*f*
tax-financed health care share, 62–63,
66–67, 286–87
GDP deflator, 2, 10
GDP price index, 291
Gender
distribution of health spending and,
174–75
earnings of health care workers, 129*f*
retirement period changes in health
services, 150–51
women's dominance in health services
employment, 146–47
General practice health professionals, 160–
63, 248

Generic drugs, 232, 250, 251*f*

Global comparison (U.S. vs. other industrialized countries)
    elderly, health spending on, 284, 285*f*
    employment in health sector, 142–45
    health professional incomes, 160–61
    health spending, 8–9, 12, 13*f*, 14–15, 244–45
    innovation, 230–31
    out-of-pocket expenses, 42–43
    personal savings rate, 134, 135*f*
    R&D investment, 232–33
    tax-financed health care, 42, 66–67
    See also Cost-effectiveness of U.S. health spending

GNI (gross national income), U.S. share of worldwide, 14

Goods-producing portion of health sector
    annual work hours, 148, 149*f*
    employment by size of firm, 194, 195*f*
    gender differences in employment, 146–47
    pricing in, 222–25
    productivity in, 126
    See also Medical device industry; Pharmaceutical drugs

GOS (gross operating surplus), 114, 115*f*, 291

Government
    direct health care output share, 100–101
    health services compensation in private sector vs., 157*f*
    health spending by
        beneficiaries' costs for Medicare vs., 46–47, 70–71
        highest-income families, outlay for, 72–73, 190
        increase in, 6, 7*f*, 32–33, 62–63
        pace of increase vs. non-health spending, 64–65
        for people in poor health, 68–69
        public health activities, 18
        share of GDP, 62–63, 66–67, 286–87
        sustainability question, 286–87
    insurance provision for the poor, 184–85
    See also Federal government; States and localities; Tax-financed health care

Grants-in-aid, 291

Great Lakes region, health spending, 179*f*

Gross domestic product, *See* GDP

Gross national income (GNI), U.S. share of worldwide, 14

Gross operating surplus (GOS), 114, 115*f*, 291

Gross output, defined, 292

Gross state product, health spending as share of, 178

Group health insurance, 22, 23*f*, 46, 58
    See also Employer-sponsored insurance (ESI)

Hatch-Waxman Act (1984), 232

Health capital, 220–21

Health care in U.S., priority for consumers of, 10
    See also Health output; Health spending

Health care practitioners
    cost of, 24, 160–61, 246
    nurses, 160, 161*f*, 248, 249*f*
    physicians (*See* Physicians)
    primary care providers, 160–63, 248
    unionization levels, 200, 201*f*
    See also Employee compensation; Employment in health sector

Health facilities
    employment increase, 140, 141*f*
    GOS in, 115*f*
    productivity in, 125*f*, 126, 127*f*, 136, 137*f*
    profitability of, 119*f*
    See also Hospitals; Nursing and residential care facilities

Health insurance, *See* Medicare; Private health insurance

Health output
    defined, 292
    vs. factors of production, 136–37
    by government, 100–101
    per capita increase, 4–5
    public sector as primary provider, 98–99
    R&D as share of, 132
    relationship to spending, 10
    share of GDP, 6–7, 104–5
    See also Goods-producing portion of health sector; Health services; Productivity

Health reform plan
    bankruptcy risk reduction potential, 208
    effect on health spending, 104, 172
    employer-sponsored insurance inequi-
      ties, 54, 55*f*
    employment impact for health services
      industry, 156
    lack of universal coverage from, 88
    Medicaid eligibility changes, 184
    Medicare benefits for high-income
      families and, 72
    out-of-pocket expense changes, 40
    primary care provider incentives, 248
    public insurance increase, 34, 38
    regulatory consequences for, 198
    unfunded entitlement liabilities issue,
      280, 281*f*
    uninsured numbers, effect on, 86
Health-related social insurance, 109*f*
    See also Medicare; Workers'
      compensation
Health-related supplements to wages, 108–9,
    154–55, 270–71
    See also Employer-sponsored insurance
      (ESI); Medicare
Health sector
    cost vs. real output of, 2
    employment in (*See* Employment in
      health sector)
    lack of employer-sponsored insurance,
      56–57
    productivity in, 128–29
    structure of, 194–201
    unionization in, 110, 200–201
    See also Health output; Productivity
Health services
    ambulatory (*See* Ambulatory health
      services)
    dental, 24, 25*f*, 41*f*, 45*f*
    employee compensation, 156–57
    employment by size of firm, 194, 195*f*
    employment increase, 140–41
    employment trends, 156–59
    factors in demand for, 225*f*
    gender differences in employment,
      146, 147*f*
    growth vs. private business overall,
      126–27

home health
    Medicaid spending for, 44, 45*f*
    public vs. privately owned/
      managed, 101*f*
    tax-exempt providers for, 98, 99*f*
    women's dominance in employ-
      ment, 146, 147*f*
hospital care (*See* Hospitals)
nursing home care (*See* Nursing and
    residential care facilities)
owner income in, 112, 113*f*
personal share of health spending,
    18–21
pricing of, 222–25
publicly traded profits vs. other stocks,
    118–19
quality of life and, 220–27
retirement period changes, 150–51
share of final purchases, 102–3
share of GDP, 104–5
unionization levels, 200
use levels vs. access, global compari-
    son, 246, 247*f*
See also Distribution of health spending
Health spending
    age group comparison, 172–73
    business cycle and, 10, 104, 212–17
    categories of
      administrative costs of insurers,
        22–23
      avoidable causes of illness,
        28–29
      chronic illness share, 26–27
      hospitals, 24–25
      nursing and residential care,
        24–25
      personal health services share,
        18–21
    cost-effectiveness of (*See* Cost-effective-
      ness of U.S. health spending)
    direct (*See* Direct health spending)
    excess cost growth, 274–79
    global comparison, 8–9, 12, 13*f*,
      14–15, 244–45
    by government (*See* Government)
    growth of per capita, 10–11
    health reform plan's effect on, 104, 172
    health status and, 26–27, 68–69, 186–87

Health spending (*continued*)
    net worth and, 204–9
    NHE (*See* NHE)
    out-of-pocket (*See* Out-of-pocket
        payments)
    per person increase, 2–3
    personal savings vs., 134–35
    PHCE, 18, 20, 21*f*, 24–29, 293
    poverty definition and, 182–83
    private health insurance share, 34–37,
        40, 41*f*, 42
    productivity as driver of, 224, 225*f*
    public sector share, 6, 7*f*, 10, 32–37,
        40, 41*f*, 62
    regional differences, 176–79
    share of GDP, 3*f*, 6–7, 10–13, 102,
        103*f*
    standard of living in U.S. and, 10, 276,
        286
    technology as driver of, 224–25,
        272–73
    for uninsured, 90–91
    See also Distribution of health spend-
        ing; Sustainability of health
        spending
Health status and health spending, 26–27,
    68–69, 186–87
Health support occupations, unionization
    levels, 200, 201*f*
Herfindahl-Hirschman Index (HHI), 196
High-income workers/households
    contribution to better health, measur-
        ing, 240–41
    factors in demand for health services,
        225*f*
    government expenditure for health,
        72–73, 190
    health cost burden, 82, 83*f*, 168–71
    Medicare support, 72–73, 190
    tax subsidy level for health care,
        52–53, 54, 55*f*, 70
Home health services
    Medicaid spending for, 44, 45*f*
    public vs. privately owned/managed,
        101*f*
    tax-exempt providers for, 98, 99*f*
    women's dominance in employment,
        146, 147*f*

Hospitals
    annual work hours, 148, 149*f*
    community, 100, 101*f*
    concentration in industry, 197*f*
    cost of, 24–25
    employee compensation levels, 156,
        157*f*
    employment by size of firm, 194, 195*f*
    employment increase, 140, 141*f*
    health care revenue share, 98, 99*f*
    Medicaid spending for, 45*f*
    personal consumption share, 78
    reduction in out-of-pocket payment
        for, 41*f*
    unemployment levels for workers in,
        216, 217
    women's dominance in employment,
        146, 147*f*
Hourly earnings vs. real compensation per
    hour, 154–55
Households, share of Medicare expenditure,
    33*f*
    See also High-income workers/
        households; Low-income workers/
        households
Hypertension, share of PHCE, 29*f*

IGTs (intergovernmental transfers), 64, 65*f*
Illicit substance abuse, share of PHCE, 29*f*
Implicitly subsidized care, 48–49
Income
    ambulatory health services increase,
        156, 157*f*, 158–59
    direct health spending share, 80–81
    earnings and wages (*See* Earnings)
    health industry vs. other service indus-
        tries, 156–57
    health professionals, U.S. vs. other
        countries, 160–61
    owner income in health services, 112,
        113*f*
    physician rate of return for education,
        160–61
    regional differences, 176–77
    U.S. share of worldwide GNI, 14
    See also High-income workers/
        households; Low-income workers/
        households; National income

Industrialized countries vs. U.S., *See* Global comparison

Infant mortality, 256–57

Information capital per hour, ambulatory health vs. private business, 130–31

Innovation, 120–21, 222–23, 230–31

Insurance industry, employment by size of firm, 194, 195*f*
    See also Private health insurance

Intangible value of human life factor, 220–21, 226, 227*f*, 238

Intergovernmental transfers (IGTs), 64, 65*f*

International context, *See* Global comparison

Labor force, defined, 291
    See also Employment in health sector

Labor productivity, defined, 291
    See also Productivity

Large firms
    employer-sponsored insurance vs. small firms, 58–59
    as share of health sector employers, 194–95

Life expectancy, 72, 150, 151*f*, 254–55

Lifetime earnings and health capital, 220–21

Local governments, *See* States and localities

Long-term care services, 44, 45, 190
    See also Nursing and residential care facilities

Low-income workers/households
    factors in demand for health care services, 225*f*
    financial risk from health spending, 206, 207*f*
    health cost burden, 72–73, 168–71
    Medicare support, 72–73, 190
    near-poor, 184, 186
    tax subsidy for health care, 52–53, 54, 55*f*, 70
    See also Poverty

Malpractice legal system in U.S., 252–53

Marginal tax rate, 291

Medicaid
    adult coverage by, 190, 191*f*
    children and, 44, 45*f*, 84, 188–89
    countercyclical levels of spending, 214–15

as coverage for the poor, 70, 184–85, 190, 191*f*

crowd-out of private insurance by, 58, 88, 90, 91*f*, 188

demand for health care and, 104

dual eligibility, 46, 84, 190

elderly and disabled share of spending, 44–45, 190, 191*f*

eligibility restrictions of, 184

federal vs. state responsibility for, 6, 34, 74, 75*f*

growth in, 36, 37*f*, 40

reduction in uninsured risk and, 86

share of coverage, 34, 35*f*

state variations in spending, 70, 71*f*, 74, 75*f*

tax subsidies vs. direct spending, 38–39

"Medical" bankruptcies, 206–9

Medical device industry
    employment by size of firm, 195*f*
    growth of, 130
    productivity of, 126, 127*f*, 136, 137*f*
    profits in, 120–21
    regulation of, 198
    U.S. as early adopter for new devices, 246

Medical facilities, *See* Health facilities

Medical liability, 198, 252–53

Medical tourism, 234

Medicare
    administrative costs, 22, 23*f*
    beneficiaries' vs. government's contribution, 46–47, 70–71
    contribution to health care demand, 104
    cost forecasts, 278, 279*f*, 282, 283*f*
    as coverage for most elderly, 84
    crowd-out of private insurance by, 88
    drug plan (Part D) cost, 92
    dual eligibility, 46, 84, 190
    employee benefit vs. social contract issue, 154, 155*f*
    federal vs. state financing of, 6, 32, 33*f*
    growth in, 36, 37*f*
    high- vs. low-income families, 72–73, 190
    hospital short-stay incentive, 24

Medicare (*continued*)
    increased public health spending role,
      40
    insolvency projections, 275*f*
    payroll deduction for, 53*f*, 80, 108
    regional differences in spending,
      242–43
    share of coverage, 34, 35*f*
    sources of funding, 46, 47*f*
    taking care of those in poorest health
      and, 68
    uninsured, spending vs., 91*f*
Medicare PPS, 21, 114
Medigap policies, 46
Men vs. women, *See* Gender
Mideast region (U.S.), health spending, 179*f*
Morbidity losses, 226, 227*f*
Mortality
    due to health conditions, 260–61
    infant, 256–57
    premature, 226, 227*f*, 240–41,
      262–63
    reductions due to health care, 238
Motor vehicle accidents, share of PHCE, 29*f*
Multifactor productivity, 136, 137*f*

National Health Expenditures, *See* NHE
National income
    defined, 291–92
    distribution of
      compensation vs. proprietor/
        rental income, 110–11
      corporate profit share of, 114–17
      medical devices profits, 120–21
      pharmaceutical product profits,
        120–21
      proprietor and rental income
        decline, 110–13
      publicly traded health services'
        profits, 118–19
    employee compensation share, 108,
      109*f*
National income and product accounts
    (NIPAs), 108, 290, 292
National Institutes of Health (NIH), 230
Near-poor
    health status of, 186
    Medicaid eligibility, 184

Netherlands, out-of-pocket health spending,
    42, 43*f*
Net national product (NNP), 108
Net worth and health spending, 204–9
New England region, health spending,
    176–77, 178, 179*f*
NHE (National Health Expenditures)
    components of, 18
    costs included in, 7n
    defined, 2, 292
    government vs. business spending,
      38, 39*f*
    growth vs. GDP, 3*f*, 10–11
    health output per capita, 4–5
    personal savings vs., 134, 135*f*
    PHCE share of, 18, 19*f*
    share of GDP, 7*f*
    social burden of illness, 226
NIH (National Institutes of Health), 230
NIPAs (national income and product
    accounts), 108, 290, 292
NNP (net national product), 108
Nominal monetary measurement, 292
Non-durable medical products, sales of,
    24, 25*f*
Non-elderly adults
    distribution of health spending,
      172–73
    employer-sponsored insurance as
      primary support, 84, 85*f*
    gender differences in health spending,
      reproductive years, 174–75
    health spending growth vs. elderly,
      92–93
    lack of health care coverage for poor,
      190–91
    Medicaid enrollment, 45*f*
    non-health spending growth,
      94–95
    uninsured, 84, 190, 191*f*
Non-profit organizations as health care
    providers, 49*f*, 98–99, 100
Northeast region, regulation of health sector,
    198
Nurses, 160, 161*f*, 248, 249*f*
Nursing and residential care facilities
    annual work hours, 148, 149*f*
    cost of, 24–25

Nursing and residential care facilities
  (*continued*)
    employee compensation levels, 156,
      157*f*
    employment by size of firm, 195*f*
    employment increase, 140, 141*f*
    Medicaid spending for, 44, 45*f*, 70
    out-of-pocket payment for, 41*f*
    personal consumption share, 78
    public vs. privately owned/managed,
      101*f*
    tax-exempt providers for, 98, 99*f*
    women's dominance in employment,
      146, 147*f*

OASDI (Old Age, Survivors, and Disability
  Insurance) (Social Security), 280, 284,
  285*f*, 292
Obesity, 29*f*, 264–65, 266, 267*f*
Occupational breakdown by gender in health
  services, 146, 147*f*
OECD (Organisation for Economic
  Co-operation and Development)
    health professionals' income,
      160–61
    health spending per capita, 8, 9*f*,
      244–45
    mortality rate due to health
      conditions, 260–61
    out-of-pocket share of health
      spending, 42, 43*f*
    pharmaceutical exports, 235*f*
Offer rates, health insurance, 58
Opportunity cost of health care, 2, 8–9,
  144–45
Organisation for Economic Co-operation
  and Development, *See* OECD
Out-of-pocket payments
    defined, 292
    dental vs. other medical services,
      24, 25*f*
    global comparison, 42–43
    health spending share, 34, 35*f*,
      40–41, 80
    historical decline in, 37*f*
    net health cost burden and income
      level, 168, 169*f*, 170, 171*f*
    for uninsured vs. insured, 40, 48

Outpatient care, shift to, 24
    See also Ambulatory health services
Output, health, *See* Health output
Over-the-counter drugs, 250, 251*f*
Overweight, share of PHCE, 29*f*
Owner income in health services, 112,
  113*f*

Part A, Medicare, 46, 47*f*, 84
Part B, Medicare, 46, 47*f*, 84
Part D, Medicare, 46, 47*f*, 84, 92
Patents and profitability, 120
Payers for health services, *See* Private health
  insurance; Public sector
Payroll deductions, Medicare and workers'
  compensation, 53*f*, 80, 108
PCE (personal consumption expenditures),
  6, 18–21
PCE price deflator, 4, 5*f*, 154
PCE price index, 292–93
Personal consumption on health care
    as basis for net health cost burden,
      170, 171*f*
    for children, 84–85
    direct vs. indirect percentage,
      80–81
    for elderly, 84–85, 92–95
    general increase in, 276, 277*f*
    health care's share of, 7*f*, 78–79
    for non-elderly adults, 92–95
    PCE, 6, 18–21
    personal savings vs. health spending,
      134–35
    PHCE, 18, 20, 21*f*, 24–29, 293
    relative burden for highest income
      earners, 82, 83*f*
    uninsured status, 86–91
Personal health care expenditures (PHCE),
  18, 21*f*, 24–29, 293
Personal saving, 134–35, 293
Pharmaceutical drugs
    costs of
      global comparison, 250–51
      innovation risk and, 222, 223*f*
      Medicaid spending for, 44, 45*f*
      out-of-pocket payment for, 24,
        25*f*, 41*f*
    global comparison of use, 246, 247*f*

Pharmaceutical drugs (*continued*)
manufacturers
employment by size of firm, 194, 195*f*
innovation in U.S., 230, 231*f*
national income share, 120–21
productivity of, 126, 136, 137*f*
R&D, 120, 230, 231*f*, 232–35
regulation of, 198
Part D, Medicare, 46, 47*f*, 84, 92
retail profitability, 119*f*
U.S. access to, 258
PHCE (personal health care expenditures), 18, 20, 21*f*, 24–29, 293
Physical capital, defined, 293
Physical inactivity, share of PHCE, 29*f*
Physicians
compensation comparison, global, 160, 161*f*
fee cuts in health reform plan, 280
Medicaid spending for, 44, 45*f*
reduction in out-of-pocket payment for, 41*f*
return rate on medical education, 162–63
on salary vs. as proprietors, 110, 111*f*, 112–13
share of health output, 99*f*
share of health spending, 24, 145*f*
specialist vs. general practice, 160, 161*f*, 162, 163*f*, 248–49
Plains region, health spending, 179*f*
Poor diet and inactivity, mortality effect of, 262, 263*f*
Poor health, cost of caring for those in, 26–27, 68–69, 186–87
Population growth vs. health spending growth, 2
Population percentage accounting for most health spending, 166–67
Poverty
children, public sector coverage for, 188–89
definitional issues for poverty, 182
elderly's coverage, 190, 191*f*
medical expense support and, 182–83
non-elderly adults' coverage, 190, 191*f*
poor health and, 68, 186–87

proportion of spending on health care, 82, 83*f*
target efficiency for public sector coverage, 70, 71*f*
uninsured status, 184–85, 190–91
PPP (purchasing power parity), 8, 9*f*, 14
PPS (prospective payment system), Medicare, 24, 114
Practice style and Medicare regional spending differences, 242
Premature mortality, 226, 227*f*, 240–41, 262–63
Premiums, health insurance, 80, 168, 169*f*, 170, 171*f*
Present value, defined, 293
Pre-tax corporate profits, 110, 111*f*, 114, 115*f*
Pre-term births and infant mortality, 256–57
Preventive health spending, 18, 226
Prices of medical goods and services, 222–25
Primary care providers, 160–63, 248
Private business
annual hours per worker, 149*f*
compensation in, 158–59
defined, 293
employment by size of firm, 194, 195*f*
employment increases, 141*f*
health services compensation vs., 157*f*
increased role in health services, 114
information capital per hour, 130–31
Medicare expenditure share, 33*f*
productivity of, 126–27
R&D, 132, 133*f*
share of health spending and tax exclusion, 38, 39*f*
subsidies from for uninsured, 48, 49*f*
See also Corporate profits; Medical device industry; Pharmaceutical drugs
Private health insurance
administrative costs, 22, 23*f*
concentration in industry, 196–97
cost of health care as justification for, 166
as disincentive to economize, 78, 224, 225*f*
elderly poor, 190, 191*f*
as fringe benefit, 52–53

Private health insurance (*continued*)
    group, 22, 23*f*, 46, 58
    health spending share, 34–37, 40, 41*f*, 42
    Medicare costs and, 46
    non-profit sector as provider, 100
    per capita spending vs. uninsured, 90, 91*f*
    profitability, 119*f*
    regulation of, 198
    socioeconomic status and, 184–85, 188
    See also Employer-sponsored insurance (ESI)
Producers/providers of health output, regulation level for, 198
    See also Health output
Productivity
    defined, 293–94
    as driver of health spending, 224, 225*f*
    education level and, 128–29
    growth rate, 126–27, 136–37
    increase in, 124–25
    information capital per hour, 130–31
    morbidity losses, 226
    personal savings vs. health spending, 134–35
    R&D contribution to, 132–33
    real compensation per hour for ambulatory services, 158–59
Profit margin (ROR), 118, 119*f*, 121*f*
Profits, *See* Corporate profits
Proprietor and rental income decline, 110, 111*f*, 112–13
Prospective payment system (PPS), Medicare, 24, 114
Publicly traded health services' profits vs. other stocks, 118–19
Public sector
    global comparison, 66–67
    as health care provider, 98–99
    health spending share, 6, 7*f*, 10, 32–37, 40, 41*f*, 62
    non-profit organizations, 49*f*, 98–99, 100
    population groups covered by, 34, 35*f*, 84–85, 188–89

    tax subsidies for care, 48, 49*f*
    See also Government; Tax-financed health care
Purchasing power parity (PPP), 8, 9*f*, 14

Quality-adjusted life-year (QALY), 238, 239*f*
Quality of life and health services, 220–27

Race and ethnicity
    amenable mortality rate, 260
    cancer survival rate and, 258, 259*f*
    health status and, 186, 187*f*
    Medicare spending and, 243
"Real" designation, 10, 294
Recovery, defined, 294
Regional differences
    in financial burden, 178–79
    Medicare, 242–43
    in provision of care, 176–77
    regulation of health sector, 198
Regulatory level for health sector, 198–99
Rental income decline, 110, 111*f*, 112–13
Reproductive years, women's vs. men's health spending, 174–75
Research and development (R&D) investment
    pharmaceutical, 120, 230, 231*f*, 232–35
    productivity contribution of, 132–33
Residential care facilities, *See* Nursing and residential care facilities
Retail pharmacy, profitability, 119*f*
Retail trade, lack of employer-sponsored insurance, 56–57
Return on assets (ROA), 118, 119*f*, 121*f*
Return on equity (ROE), 118, 119*f*, 121*f*
Return on revenue (ROR), 118, 119*f*, 121*f*
Risk premium for insurance coverage for small firms, 56
Rocky Mountain region
    health spending, 176–77, 179*f*
    regulation of health sector, 198

Saving, personal, 134–35, 293
SCHIP, *See* State Children's Health Insurance Plan

Service economy, health sector role in, 102–3, 104, 156–57
    See also Health services
Sexually transmitted diseases, share of PHCE, 29*f*
SGR (sustainable growth rate), 294
Small firms
    lack of employer-provided health coverage, 56–59
    as majority of health sector employers, 194–95
Smoking
    life expectancy and, 254, 255*f*
    mortality rate and, 262, 263*f*
    share of PHCE, 29*f*
    state-to-state variation in, 266, 267*f*
    U.S. rate of, 264–65
Social burden of illness, 226–27
Social discount rate, 220
Social insurance, health-related, 109*f*
    See also Medicare; Workers' compensation
Social Security program (OASDI), 280, 284, 285*f*, 292
Socioeconomic status, 186–87, 243
    See also High-income workers/households; Low-income workers/households
Southeast region
    health spending, 176–77, 178, 179*f*
    regulation of health sector, 198
Southwest region, health spending, 179*f*
Specialist physicians, 160, 161*f*, 162, 163*f*, 248–49
Spending on health care, *See* Health spending
Sponsor view of health spending, 32, 33*f*
Standard of living, U.S., and health spending, 10, 276, 286
State Children's Health Insurance Plan (SCHIP)
    contribution to erosion of employer-based coverage, 58
    enactment during economic growth period, 214
    expansion of, 188
    reduction in uninsured risk and, 86
    state-to-state variations in spending, 70, 71*f*, 74, 75*f*

States and localities
    health outcome comparisons, 264–67
    health spending burden, 178, 179*f*
    health spending increases, 6, 7*f*, 32, 33*f*, 64, 65*f*
    Medicaid role
        eligibility, 184
        health spending share, 34
        physician fees, 44
        variation in spending, 70, 71*f*, 74, 75*f*
    Medicare role, 6, 32, 33*f*
    regulatory variation for health sector, 198–99
    shift in health care financing to federal level, 62
Statistical life, 220
Stock of health for typical American, 220–21
Supplemental employee payments, *See* Employee compensation
Supplemental policies to Medicare, 46
Sustainability of health spending
    burden on government and, 286–87
    dependent increase, facing, 284–85
    excess cost ratio, 274–75
    impact of growth on future GDP, 276–79
    lack of, 282–83
    technology as driver of health spending and, 272–73
    unfunded liabilities and entitlements, 280–81
    wages vs. health benefit costs, 270–71
Sustainable growth rate (SGR), 294
Switzerland, out-of-pocket health spending, 42, 43*f*

Tax-exempt institutions, 98, 100–101
Tax-financed health care
    children's reliance on, 84–85, 188–89
    elderly's reliance on, 84–85, 286
    expansion vs. private insurance, 37*f*
    global comparison, 42, 66–67
    increase in, 62–65
    net burden by income, 168–69
    share of GDP, 62–63, 66–67, 286–87
    for those in poorest health, 68–69
    See also Medicaid; Medicare

Tax revenue
    future needs for health care, 282–83
    health spending percentage of, 6, 7f
Tax subsidies for health care
    cost of, 38, 39f
    income level and, 52–53, 54, 55f, 70
    for uninsured, 48, 49f, 90–91
Technical occupations in health sector,
    unionization levels, 200, 201f
Technology, health care role of, 224–25, 246,
    247f, 272–73
Trade imbalance, pharmaceutical role in,
    234

Unemployment rate, 216–17, 294
Unfunded liabilities and health entitlements,
    280–81
Uninsured status
    children, 188, 189f
    elderly, 86, 190, 191f
    non-elderly adults as majority in, 84,
        190, 191f
    out-of-pocket spending vs. those
        insured, 40, 48
    poverty and, 184–85, 190–91
    risk changes over time, 86–89
    taxpayer and private payer subsidy for,
        48–49, 90–91
Unintentional home injuries, share of PHCE,
    29f
Unionization in health sector, 110, 200–201
United States vs. other industrialized
    countries on health care, See Global
    comparison

VA health, defined, 294
Value added concept, defined, 294
Value added data for health services, 102,
    103f
Value for the money of U.S. health care, See
    Cost-effectiveness of U.S. health spending
Violence
    share of PHCE, 29f
    state-to-state variation in, 266, 267f
    U.S. deaths due to, 254, 255f
Voluntary health insurance, disincentive for
    healthy individuals, 166

Wages, See Earnings
Wasted spending, hidden nature of, 238–39
Wealth and debt, 204–9
Wholesalers, health care, profitability, 119f
Willingness-to-pay value of a life, 220, 221f,
    226, 227f, 238
Women vs. men, See Gender
Workers' compensation
    defined, 294
    effect on earnings over time, 154, 155f
    as health-related supplement, 108
    payroll deduction for, 53f, 108
    social insurance share of, 54–55
Workers per Social Security beneficiary, 284,
    285f
Working-life expectancy, 150, 151f
Work-related illnesses, share of PHCE, 29f
Work-related injuries, share of PHCE, 29f

Years of potential life lost (YPLL), state-to-
    state variation in, 266, 267f

About the Author

Christopher J. Conover is a Research Scholar in the Center for Health Policy and Inequalities Research at the Global Health Institute at Duke University. He also is an adjunct scholar at AEI. He received a PhD in policy analysis from the Pardee RAND Graduate School.

His research interests are in the area of health regulation and state health policy, with a focus on issues related to health care for the medically indigent (including the uninsured), and on estimating the magnitude of the social burden of illness. Over two decades, he has provided policy advice on access and cost issues to governors and legislative groups from several states across the United States. He also served as a consultant to the North Carolina Department of Insurance on the impact of conversion of Blue Cross and Blue Shield of North Carolina to for-profit status. Most recently, Dr. Conover has developed estimates of the cost of health services regulation for the Agency for Healthcare Research and Quality (AHRQ) and has testified before Congress on this issue. He currently is engaged in updating these estimates for dissemination in a series of working papers and a monograph.

Dr. Conover is the editor of News and Notes for the *Journal of Health Politics, Policy and Law* and the U.S. Health Policy Gateway, a portal site for American health policy.